A History of the
PERKINS
SCHOOL
of
Theology

Lewis Howard Grimes
Edited by Roger Loyd

Southern Methodist University Press
Dallas

Copyright © 1993 by Southern Methodist University Press
All rights reserved
Printed in the United States of America

FIRST EDITION, 1993

Requests for permission to reproduce material from this
work should be sent to:
Permissions
Southern Methodist University Press
Box 415
Dallas, Texas 75275

Unless otherwise credited, photographs are from
the archives of the Perkins School of Theology.

Library of Congress Cataloging-in-Publication Data

Grimes, Lewis Howard, 1915–1989.
A history of the Perkins School of Theology / Lewis Howard Grimes,
—1st ed.
p.   cm.
Includes bibliographical references and index.
ISBN 0-87074-346-5
1. Perkins School of Theology—History.   2. Theological
seminaries, Methodist—Texas—Dallas—History.   3. Dallas (Tex.)—
Church history.   I. Loyd, Roger.   II. Title.
BV4070.P47G75   1993
207'.7642812—dc20   92-39891

A History of the Perkins School of Theology

Contents

Preface

For several years before his death, Howard Grimes and I had discussed his work on this project. As time was available, he worked in the archival collections of the School of Theology, housed in the Bridwell Library, with some assistance from me in my role as Associate Librarian and Curator of the Methodist Historical Collections. He invited me to edit his work on the school's history, and to complete any chapters he was unable to finish. As a graduate of Perkins School of Theology (1971) and a current staff member, I have found this work highly rewarding.

Within quotations, and as appropriate within the body of the essay itself, the original forms of reference to gender, race, religious bodies, and theological positions have been left unchanged, without the interruptions of the notation [sic.], though current usage would often require changing these terms to a more inclusive or currently accepted term.

Readers will find that the end notes are in abbreviated form, with the explanation of the·abbreviations in the Bibliography following the Notes. Unless otherwise noted, all manuscript and archival collections cited are in the Bridwell Library, Perkins School of Theology, Southern Methodist University.

For their valuable help to me as I prepared this manuscript for publication, I should like to thank Johnnie Marie Grimes, James E. Kirby, Merrimon Cuninggim, Joseph D. Quillian, W. Richey Hogg, Richard P. Heitzenrater, Decherd Turner, Joseph L. Allen, Charles M. Wood, and H. Neill McFarland.

In the final stages of preparing the text, the sad news arrived of the death of Dean Joseph D. Quillian, Jr., on the third day of April, 1992, in Chewelah, Washington. May he rest in peace!

Roger Loyd
April 1992

Introduction

How did this history of Southern Methodist University's Perkins School of Theology in Dallas, Texas, come to be written? That question arises for one reason: before his death, Howard Grimes had not yet drafted its preface. Had he done so, he probably would have included in it the book's origins.

To uncover its beginnings, I talked with several knowledgeable people in Dallas who made it plain that Dean Emeritus (1982) Joseph D. Quillian, Jr., had been significantly involved in launching the history, but only he could provide an accurate account. A phone call to the retirement household of the Quillians at Chewelah, Washington, brought the Dean's familiar and friendly voice.

Quillian readily recalled the occasion. "It was in 1978 or 1979," he said, "and I don't know whether Howard or I first mentioned the project. Perhaps it just came up in the course of the conversation." The Dean knew then that he would be retiring within two or three years and had suggested specific writing projects to several faculty members who were especially fitted for those jobs.

He hastened to add, "For a history of Perkins School of Theology, Howard was clearly the right person for the task. His whole background and experience prepared him for it. He had been graduated from SMU's School of Theology in the late 1930s, came on the faculty of Perkins in 1949, and was at Perkins from the beginning of Merrimon Cuninggim's deanship." I asked whether the idea for the history perhaps had first germinated in Howard's own thinking. "I don't know or recall," said Quillian, "but he was very positively willing to undertake it and responded to it as a gladsome duty."

Dean Quillian retired officially in May 1982, but by taking a well-deserved faculty leave in 1981–82, he facilitated James E. Kirby's assuming the deanship in 1981. Also retired from Perkins in 1982, Howard Grimes almost immediately began at First United Methodist Church, Dallas, a full-time ministerial post in communications. In that role he established a well-equipped Media Department and its ministry there. As a result he devoted much less time in the next four years to his history project than he had anticipated, but he kept searching through and reading the University and School of Theology files whenever he could. Then, for reasons of health, Howard Grimes had to relinquish his post in 1987.

When his colon cancer was discovered in 1987, it had already spread considerably. The surgeon did his utmost to excise all the malignant growth, but feared that it had spread beyond effective reach. Howard's illness and the ensuing medication took their toll. Yet the disease that would take his life spurred a rare determination. As increasing weakness made life daily more complicated and difficult, Howard prayed that he might be given strength sufficient to complete the task. The disease steadily undermined his weakening body. Yet many who knew him well believed that his driving commitment to finish the history kept him alive until he had almost done so. He produced most of this book after the illness assailed him, and to some degree that had to affect his writing. He died on 11 December 1989.

Uncompleted at his death were his own editing of the entire manuscript, a preface, and a brief chapter covering the years 1981 to the present. Thus Roger Loyd, Associate Director of the Bridwell Library, has edited the manuscript, has written the chapter concerning the years 1981 to the present, and has prepared the entire volume for publication. Dean James E. Kirby has provided a perspective on the seminary's future. William Richey Hogg, Professor of World Christianity Emeritus, has written this introduction. Each has benefited from the gracious help and suggestions of Mrs. Johnnie Marie Grimes, who was Howard's wife and able colleague for nearly 43 years.

Generations of students studied under Howard Grimes at Perkins School of Theology, and in seminars across the country. Yet how many knew the background of and shaping forces in the life and career of this able but unassuming man?

His parents, Lewis Frederick and Julia Ophelia McClenny Grimes, lived in Breckenridge, Texas, about 95 miles west of Fort Worth, when Lewis Howard Grimes was born on 10 July 1915. They were "Poor . . . and humble, but [they held] high standards," Howard said of them in the 1980s. "Small ranchers or farmers," they labored diligently to succeed and to educate their four children. "Church oriented," both were loyal and active Methodists, reared their children in that tradition, and Mrs. Grimes taught a Sunday School class for years. Fearing that an oil boom might develop in the area and be a disruptive force in family life, Mr. Grimes moved the family, when Howard was four, to Weatherford, some 20 miles west of Fort Worth. Yet he was wise and venturesome enough to keep the farm and its parcel of oil land which provided a supplement to income across the years.

Completing his primary and secondary education in Weatherford, Howard continued from 1932 to 1934 in Weatherford Junior College. He then entered the University of Texas at Austin, majored in English, won his Phi Beta Kappa key, and gained his B.A. there in 1936 with Highest Honors. In 1936–37 in Cookville, a few miles east of Mt. Pleasant, he taught English and government in the high school, and in the summers of 1936 and 1937 he taught in Weatherford Junior College.

He spent the years 1937–40 at Southern Methodist University's School of Theology and gained his B.D. There, among others, he studied under Professors Seehorn Seneker (Christian Education), John Hicks (Old Testament), and Robert Goodloe (Church History), and was helped by Librarian Kate Warnick and Registrar Nell Anders—all appointees from the 1921–25 period. Eugene B. Hawk had been Dean from 1933, and Wesley Davis (New Testament), J. T. Carlyon (Theology), and Paul Root (Sociology of Religion), an able man whom Howard assisted, had come in 1934 and 1935. Fred Gealy (New Testament, Missions, and the Seminary Singers) arrived in 1938. Umphrey Lee became President of SMU in November 1938. In this book Grimes "attests" that those faculty members were "competent *teachers*," but that their heavy work load in the seminary and the work expected of them in the churches precluded adequate study and left virtually no time for research or writing.

From SMU he went directly to Union Theological Seminary in New York City in 1940 and there gained his S.T.M. in May 1941. His thesis dealt with the sociology of conversion and reflected Root's influence. Except for Root, the same group was in place to welcome Howard to the SMU Theology faculty in 1949.

Pursuing his ministerial path, Grimes in 1941 in Daingerfield, Texas, received his license to preach, served the First Methodist Church in Duncan, Oklahoma, during the summer and fall in 1941, and became an associate pastor of the First Methodist Church in Houston, under the Rev. Dr. Paul W. Quillian, from late 1941 to July 1942. Ordained deacon and elder in the Texas Conference of the Methodist Church in 1942, he entered the U. S. Army Chaplaincy in July 1942 and served until November 1945. His fields of service included England, North Africa, Sicily, and Italy, and he received the Purple Heart, the Legion of Merit, and the Italian Medal of Valor. After the end of World War II, he returned late in 1945 to Houston and resumed the post he had held there earlier.

Grimes quickly determined to enter Columbia University in New York City for a Ph.D. and to live in McGiffert Hall across from the Union Seminary apartments. Meanwhile Paul Root had been elected Dean of the Duke Divinity School, and he asked Howard to accompany him there as his assistant. Root's untimely death in May 1947 resolved a difficult decision for Howard. He went on to Columbia in June 1947, gained his doctorate in 1949, and joined the Perkins School of Theology faculty in the fall of 1949.

Yet a most important segment of Grimes's story remains to be mentioned. At First Methodist Church in Houston in 1941–42 he had met Johnnie Marie Brooks, Director of Religious Education there. On his entering the chaplaincy, he and Johnnie Marie agreed that as good friends they would correspond regularly. They did.

Johnnie Marie's background deserves noting. Her great-great-grandfather had fought at San Jacinto in April 1836, and from that battle soon emerged the Republic of Texas. She herself was born at Bellville, some 55 miles northwest of Houston, on 16 October 1905 to John Williamson Brooks and Mary Eunice Styers Brooks. Her mother, a home-maker, taught a Sunday School class and worked in the Methodist Woman's Missionary Society in Bellville's Methodist Church where the whole family grew up and was shaped religiously. This young Daughter of the Republic of Texas earned her B.A. at Southwestern in Georgetown in 1927.

From her second year there, she had become an active member in the Campus YWCA and developed into a creative leader at the regional level. The personnel officer in the National YWCA soon noticed her, indicated the YW's interest in her, and urged that after graduation she gain more experience.

To do so, she taught history for a year, served two years as a church youth director, and was soon selected by the YWCA's National Personnel Office to serve in the Beaumont YWCA as Director of Business and Industrial Girls' Work. Six years later the New York office promoted her to the YWCA in Oklahoma City and there she joined St. Luke's Methodist Church where Dr. Paul Quillian was pastor. Quickly recognizing her remarkable capabilities, and knowing that he was shortly to go to First Methodist Church of Houston, he asked her to become Director of Christian Education there. Countering her protests of inadequate preparation for that post, he added, "I'll teach you everything you need to know about the work."

The Quillians were in Houston from 1937 to 1947, and so was Johnnie Marie, except for her stint with the United Nations Relief and Rehabilitation Agency (UNRRA), 1943–46. After her work in England, Scotland, France, and Germany, she returned to First Methodist in Houston. Not surprisingly, she and Howard, already there, were married in that church on 7 February 1947.

The Grimeses went to Columbia University in 1947, where Johnnie Marie took her M.A. in 1948 through the joint Union-Columbia program. When Howard had completed his Ph.D. at Columbia in 1949, they returned to Dallas, Texas, and he joined the faculty of Perkins School of Theology (the SMU Board of Trustees had voted the change of name on 6 February 1945) as Assistant Professor of Christian Education. In fall 1950, Dean Hawk invited the Grimeses to occupy an apartment in Perkins Hall, where they lived for several years.

Meanwhile Willis Tate had entered SMU's administrative ranks as Dean of Students and in 1950 became Vice-President of Development and Public Relations. In May 1954, when on medical advice President Umphrey Lee resigned from his office, Willis M. Tate became President of Southern Methodist University.

Tate had known the Grimeses in Houston, and during a 1952 visit to their campus apartment, he asked Johnnie Marie Grimes to come and work for him. She accepted and began as Director of SMU's annual Sustentation Campaign. Upon Tate's election as President of SMU, she became his Assistant for Research and Planning, a post she held until his retirement. This position came to involve much writing, including major memoranda and drafts of position papers. In 1977 she compiled and edited *Willis M. Tate: Views and Interviews* (Dallas: SMU Press, 1978). All the while as a volunteer, she served the YWCA on its boards local and national, on state education committees, as a founding member of the Women's Center of Dallas, and the list goes on. She became a key leader in the First United Methodist Church of Dallas and also in the broader work of the church at district, conference, national, and world levels.

Howard and Johnnie Marie supported and encouraged each other in their multiform activities. From the broad background of their diverse endeavors the Grimeses observed, participated in, and assessed much of SMU's history from 1949 through 1989. Among SMU's several faculty and staff couples, they had a unique vantage point. All this forms part of the background Howard brought to the writing of this book.

Asked which people had most influenced him, Howard responded that no one person had been most influential, but that four or five in that category would be his parents, his wife Johnnie Marie, Paul Root, and Paul W. Quillian (who also had a major impact on Johnnie Marie).

Yet another question may afford greater insight. What theologies, educational theories, and the like had shaped Howard Grimes's growing understanding of his own theology and the meaning of Christian education? Happily, he had written a detailed yet compact twenty-five-page summation of these matters, which some judge to be his best writing. In 1982–83, for *Modern Masters of Religious Education*, edited by Marlene Mayr (Birmingham, Ala.: Religious Education Press, 1983), he wrote a chapter entitled "How I Became What I Am as a Christian Religious Educator." It belongs to the "How My Mind Has Developed During 35 Years of Teaching" genre. For former students or others who want a thoughtfully drawn, honest, and open statement of Grimes's intellectual, theological, and Christian pilgrimage, this presents his personal answer.

It would be impossible to provide here an adequate summary of Howard's essay, but a few points drawn from it may be instructive. At Union Seminary and then Columbia Howard encountered Reinhold Niebuhr, Paul Tillich, and the "New Theology" of the 1940s. Much of the Neo-orthodoxy of Barth, Brunner, Niebuhr and others he found helpful. Yet he insisted that he was never a Barthian because of his strong Wesleyan heritage and convictions. He rebelled against the then current Protestant liberalism (human nature as essentially neutral or good and needing only education) that in his judgment suffused much of that day's Christian education. Reinhold Niebuhr struck the right note for Grimes who paraphrased it: "There is enough good in persons to make Christian nurture possible, and enough evil to make it necessary."

Harrison S. Elliott, "an unreconstructed liberal in religious education," directed Howard's dissertation but allowed Howard to hold to his own theology. Grimes admired Elliott's clear mind and adopted his "issue-centered" approach. The dissertation dealt with "the place and training of the laity in the Methodist tradition." Later Dean Merrimon Cuninggim urged Howard and Johnnie Marie to take a sabbatical at Yale and rework it for publication. In that process, he was strongly influenced by F. W. Dillistone's *The Structure of the Divine Society*, which he regarded as a "seminal" work (as did many in the 1950s concerned with the mission of the church). Howard published his revised dissertation as *The Church Redemptive* (New York: Abingdon Press, 1958). Within the context of Christian education, it expressed his theology of the church, and many view it as his most significant book. A year later, when Dean Cuninggim sat for the portrait that now hangs in Kirby Parlor, it was no accident that he held Howard's book in his hand.

The above may suggest some of the theological undergirding for Howard's deep interest in "practical theology" as Schleiermacher used the term in the nineteenth century. For Grimes it meant "critical reflection on the life of the church as it relates to the world in the light of . . . the Christian witness of faith," the latter five words being Schubert Ogden's phrase. Significantly, he adds that he regarded Christian religious education as "a branch of practical theology rather than of general education."

Turning again to Grimes's *History of Perkins*, I observe two elements, among others, that stand out. The first consists of a major motif that sets forth the close relationship between SMU's seminary and the church and the need of each for the other. The church brought SMU and its seminary into being, and the seminary quite early defined its two aims as (1) training ministers and (2) aiding the church. Admittedly, in ministerial training some tension always is potentially present between academy and church, particularly for a seminary that is an integral part of a university. Points of conflict involve freedom of speech and action, theological positions taken, affirmed, or denied, and moral and social

stands. Yet despite occasional misunderstandings concerning matters of orthodoxy or propriety, the seminary from its beginning maintained a close bond
with the church, and wisely also required courses that would relate "students
to the world" in which they lived and worked.

The seminary sought to meet the second aim through various means. In the
early days, faculty members were expected to work in churches by preaching,
teaching church school classes, aiding in special events, and other ways. The
slogan "Take the School of Theology to the Church" made its impact. Dean
Eugene Hawk introduced Ministers' Week in 1936, and began his Theological
Circulating Library for pastors in 1938.

Furthering that thrust, the *Perkins School of Theology Journal* (1947–91)
sought to serve clergy in the South Central Jurisdiction. Some professors taught
church school adult classes, for one, three, ten years or longer, and indeed
Howard and Johnnie Marie Grimes probably held the record. They began
teaching the Aldersgate Class of then-young couples at First Methodist in
Dallas in January 1950, and were still carrying on in 1989. Efforts to help rural
churches, emergence of the Cooperative Parish, special links with the Rio
Grande Conference, recruiting of African-American students, and much more
were part of this two-way street.

International students, carefully selected, have returned to their homelands,
and many as bishops, pastors, college presidents, seminary deans, and professors have created special links overseas. The post of Bishop in Residence,
created by Dean Quillian, has proved most useful and has been adopted
elsewhere. The Internship Program, developed by Claus Rohlfs, over the past
twenty years in remarkable and reciprocal fashion has involved people in many
congregations in working with and helping seminary interns learn what it
means to be a pastor. Special curricular offerings such as the Master of Sacred
Music and the Master of Religious Education Programs, the Master of Theological Studies (for those wanting theological study, e.g., for classroom
teaching, but not seeking ordination), and the Doctor of Ministry Program are
all designed to aid students and churches. Except for the M.T.S., they all require
some church members to be engaged with the students.

Yet the greatest reciprocal involvement of Perkins with the churches,
especially in the South Central Jurisdiction, springs from the great and growing
number of Perkins graduates since 1945, who have supplied Methodist, then
United Methodist, pulpits in this Jurisdiction. Representatively through the
Alumni Association, they work with the seminary in projecting needs, offering
counsel, and considering policy. Each dean also plays an indispensable role in
varied ways with bishops, district superintendents, ministers, and congregations.

Walter Vernon, with his broad knowledge of Methodism and as a respected church historian, put the situation succinctly and accurately in *Methodism Moves Across North Texas* in 1967. Grimes cites it in Chapter 6, but it seems highly appropriate to repeat it here:

> Perkins School of Theology is more deeply involved in the life of the churches than any other of the seminaries of the country, in the judgment of some who know this relationship at first hand. This situation augurs well for the future of both church and seminary, for they are dependent each on the other for strength and direction.

The second notable element traces the story of one continuum: Southern Methodist University's special provision from 1915 to the present for the graduate professional training of Christian ministers. Thus far that continuum incorporates two distinct periods. The initial one began with the SMU School of Theology—underfunded, relatively small, but with a dedicated faculty. It opened in 1915 and continued—first on the third floor of Dallas Hall, and then from September 1924 in the old Kirby Hall—at the north end of the SMU campus through the fall of 1950.

The second period began visibly in the fall of 1950 when SMU's Perkins School of Theology at the south end of the campus—made possible by the gifts of Mr. Joe J. Perkins and his wife Lois Parker Perkins, of Wichita Falls, Texas—enrolled its first students to study in the Theology Quadrangle. Yet the process had required a six-year transition, 1944–50. The gift from the Perkins family was confirmed in June 1944, but the Board of Trustees formally announced it on 6 February 1945 at its meeting and also changed the School's name to Perkins School of Theology. The Board settled on the new and present location on 31 October 1947, construction began several months later, students first entered the new dorms and classrooms in January 1951, and the new buildings were dedicated in February 1951.

When Merrimon Cuninggim, with earned degrees from Vanderbilt, Duke, Oxford, and Yale (B.D. and Ph.D.) and also a Navy chaplain, became dean-designate early in 1951, he made a bold and decisive move. He persuaded Albert C. Outler to leave his prestigious Timothy Dwight Professorship of Theology at Yale Divinity School and to share in the great adventure of building in Texas a "new" Methodist seminary with a national purview. The two old friends began together at Perkins in September 1951, and share they did on matters of policy and new faculty.

Indeed when Willis Tate became President of SMU, they shared with him on numerous occasions their wisdom and counsel on strengthening the university. Perkins was and remains an integral part of SMU, and their suggestions to move

SMU further toward academic excellence sprang from their loyal concern for the university's larger enterprise. To this then-young observer, watching Tate, Cuninggim, and Outler (and from time to time others as well) quietly advancing ideas to enhance the whole university provided some thrilling and grateful reflection. A somewhat similar pattern continued for some years after Cuninggim's departure.

By 1959, except for Marsh and Grimes, the pre-1951 faculty had retired. Dean Cuninggim thus had the rare task of building virtually an entirely new faculty and enlarging it during the decade of the 1950s.

Designed by architect Mark Lemmon, the new Georgian-style Theology Quadrangle graced the campus. Yet designing and crafting the academic infrastructure essential for the new Perkins School of Theology required a different kind of architect, and one uniquely qualified. President Umphrey Lee found and brought to SMU for that purpose the remarkably talented Merrimon Cuninggim. Enlarging SMU's commitment to ministerial theological training, and with its new resources, he brought about a sea change—a first-class seminary and a national reputation of excellence for Perkins.

Part of that perceived excellence relates to the Bridwell Library, made possible by J. S. Bridwell and his daughter Margaret Bridwell Bowdle of Wichita Falls, with its remarkable and magnificent collections begun by librarian Decherd Turner. Significant, too, was the way in which the great majority of those appointed to and gaining tenure on the Perkins faculty remained at Perkins and provided a strong teaching core, a fact observed especially by some visiting professors, including those from overseas.

Also important to note was the arrival in 1954 of a Cuninggim appointee, Joseph D. Quillian, Jr., as Professor of Homiletics and Worship. With his Vanderbilt B.D. and Yale Ph.D., and also a Navy chaplain, he had come from the presidency of Martin College in Pulaski, Tennessee. When in mid-1960 Cuninggim accepted the Danforth Foundation's invitation, Quillian succeeded him as Dean. He continued to build on the foundation laid by his predecessor and greatly to enhance the growth and strength of Perkins during his twenty-one-year active tenure.

James E. Kirby, a Perkins student during Cuninggim's near-decade with a B.D. (1957) and an S.T.M. (1959), had gone to Cambridge (1957–58), and gained his Ph.D. from Drew in 1963. After teaching at Sweet Briar (1963–67), he went to Oklahoma State University (1967–76) as Professor of Religion and Chair of the Department of Religion (1967–70) and then as Director of the School of Humanistic Studies. Dean of Drew Theological Seminary (1976–81), he succeeded Quillian at Perkins in 1981, and continues as Dean today.

Howard Grimes, late Professor of Christian Education Emeritus, having known and studied under the SMU School of Theology faculty in place from the early 1920s and those added in the 1930s, and having been on the Perkins faculty from 1949 to 1982, had experienced both sides of the sea change. He was unusually qualified to write this history of the seminary. He loved Southern Methodist University, Perkins School of Theology, and the United Methodist Church. He produced this book as a labor of love and commitment and, despite the massive physical odds arrayed against him, virtually completed it. On behalf of the Perkins faculty, I express our deep gratitude for our beloved and departed colleague and author of this book, Howard Grimes.

William Richey Hogg
October 1990

1

The Birth of a University

On a rainy Wednesday, 22 September 1915, 436 students completed registration, and thirty more completed the process the next day. Before the academic year ended, 706 individuals had registered in a university prepared to receive 500.[1] Fourteen of these students in the newly created Southern Methodist University were graduate theological students enrolled in the Bachelor of Divinity program. Other theological students included undergraduates, who for some years were counted in the theological total, and students enrolled in special programs to make a total of ninety. Those who had seen the need for a theological school, as well as those who had pushed for a university in Dallas, were thus vindicated through the largest enrollment, President Hyer believed, any university had ever had on its opening day.

On that opening day, SMU was scarcely a university—it consisted of a College of Arts and Science with theological and music faculties attached. The campus contained two permanent buildings, Dallas Hall and a dormitory originally intended for men but used for women, and three brick veneer dormitories, not in the permanent plans, for men. Fortunately the Waxahachie District of the Methodist Episcopal Church, South, had provided the money to build a wide boulevard extending from Mockingbird Lane to the steps of Dallas Hall. This boulevard, named for Dr. Horace Bishop, the presiding elder of the Waxahachie District, provided ready access to the main building, but what sidewalks there were were wooden. The black, sticky mud of the prairie campus must have horrified President Hyer as he saw it tracked into the rotunda of a building which he classed with the great buildings of the world. And this Dallas Hall was the one building to house all classrooms, offices, library, and chapel.[2]

The Urge to Build a Methodist University in Texas

This opening day of Southern Methodist University, including its department or school of theology,[3] culminated four years of intense planning and preparation and at least fifteen years of discussion concerning a Methodist university in Dallas. The central actor in this process from the very beginning was Robert Stewart Hyer, scientist, church leader, and educator extraordinaire.

1

Exactly when the process began and all the people involved will probably never be known with certainty. Walter Vernon, the historian of Texas Methodism, says that the earliest record he has found in reference to such a school was in the *Texas Christian Advocate* of 25 September 1902. A letter from A. P. Smith of Valley Mills, Texas, contains these words: "Was it not a sad mistake for Methodism that Southwestern University was . . . located in Georgetown? . . . Dallas would be a fine place for the location of our university."[4] Hyer, in a handwritten copy of his account of the founding of Southern Methodist University, written in 1915 but made public in Mrs. Hyer's handwriting after Dr. Hyer's death in 1929, asks the question: "Who first thought of founding a Methodist University in Dallas?" He then recounts the advice of Dr. Wallace Buttrick of the General Board of Education, a Rockefeller-funded foundation for aid to southern education. Buttrick came to Georgetown around 1905 to look over Southwestern as a possible place for the Board to do some of its work. "You must move to a city where you can get the support and patronage of the city," he said, "before the General Board will agree to help you." Hyer then asked about Dallas, and according to the manuscript, Buttrick replied: "It is the best unoccupied territory in the south."[5]

In 1906 the Southern Methodist conferences in Texas called a meeting in Dallas which about 1,200 representatives attended. It followed an earlier such convention held in 1870 and 1871, and out of which Southwestern University was established as a central Methodist university for Texas.[6] In the addresses of the 1907 convention it is taken for granted that Vanderbilt is the principal university for Southern Methodism.[7] Never is the possibility of moving Southwestern or establishing another university mentioned. It is significant, however, that out of this convention came the appointment of a Texas Methodist Education Commission whose purpose was to "devise and direct such educational movements as shall be for the good of all our schools in the State."[8]

Also during 1906, at the meeting of the General Conference of the M. E. Church, South, in Birmingham, Alabama, Mr. R. S. Munger promised to give $25,000 for a university in Dallas. The promise was made to Hyer in a conversation that also included Dr. John R. Nelson.[9]

A few years later, Bishop Seth Ward, shortly before his death, proposed to Dr. Hyer that a theological school apart from a university be established in Dallas. One of his reasons for wanting this was the uneasy feeling he had about Vanderbilt University (soon, it turned out, to be detached from the Methodist Episcopal Church, South). Bishop Ward added, " . . . if I were satisfied [with Vanderbilt], I think that our church needs another school and I am sure that it should be located in Dallas."[10] He proposed to begin at once in the raising of $100,000.

Hyer stoutly opposed a school of theology separate from a total university, but the two agreed that Ward would begin his campaign but not mention a location.[11] Unfortunately Bishop Ward died in Kobe, Japan, in 1909 a short time after the conversation, and no one else had been prepared to take up the cause.[12]

Why a University in Texas?

In the meantime Southwestern University had not stood still. It was declared as the successor to earlier colleges in Texas, such as Rutersville, and therefore its beginning has consistently been traced back to the 1840s. Dr. F. A. Mood had founded Southwestern in 1873 as a college for men. In 1878 it became co-educational, with a parallel college for women. In 1891 Dr. John H. McLean became its regent (president), followed by Robert D. Hyer in 1897.[13] Hyer had taught science there since 1882. The school had a good beginning under Mood and McLean and it grew and prospered under Hyer's leadership. Southwestern was considered the only Class A college the Methodist church had in Texas.[14]

During Hyer's presidency, in 1903, Southwestern established a medical school in Dallas, and by 1905 the school had a new $50,000 building at Hall and Bryan, largely through the efforts of the Rev. John R. Nelson, a minister in the North Texas Conference.[15] The school was located across the street from St. Paul Hospital and boasted first-rate medical doctors on its teaching staff.

During 1907 a vigorous campaign was waged to increase support for Southwestern. Numerous articles are included in the *Texas Christian Advocate* during the year. The school still maintained a preparatory department (called picturesquely a "fitting school"), with 133 of its total student body of 510 being in that department in 1907.[16] This was deemed necessary since many Texas students at that time did not have access to college preparatory education.

Then in 1908 a theological department was established at Southwestern to meet the needs of the large number of pre-ministerial students on campus, with E. D. Mouzon as head of the department.[17] According to the *Texas Christian Advocate*, Southwestern had had 550 ministerial students since its opening.[18] Frank Seay was brought to the department for Greek and biblical studies a year later.[19] But the question that many people raised, as we have already seen, was this: Could a major university receive the support it needed if that school were located in a small town? Many people had decided that it could not.

As church leaders, and later the church officially through its Educational Commission, began to think seriously about this question, other facts also entered into their deliberations. One must have been the growth of the state schools. Until the 1870s, higher education was provided by the church schools: the older Baylor in 1845 and the combined Waco and Baylor, at Waco, in 1886, for example. The Presbyterian entry was Trinity University at Tehuacana in 1869, with a move to Waxahachie in 1902 (and now in San Antonio). Texas Christian University was established in 1910 but grew out of a small college at Tharp Springs much earlier.[20] Rice Institute, a private school, began in 1912, and awarded its first Ph.D. degree in 1918.[21]

The first state college was Texas A & M, founded in 1876 at College Station. The first teacher training school came into being at Huntsville in 1879, Sam Houston Normal Institute. And the University of Texas at Austin was a relative latecomer, in 1883.[22]

Always present in the thinking of those interested in Methodist education in Texas was the threat of losing Vanderbilt by the M. E. Church, South. Founded early in 1873 and opened for classes in 1875, Vanderbilt early came under the influence of outside forces because of the gifts of Cornelius Vanderbilt.[23] With a self-perpetuating Board of Trustees and no clear statement in its charter of its Methodist ties, it was decided by the Supreme Court of Tennessee in 1914 "that the church no longer held any rights in Vanderbilt University."[24] Because of this experience, the control of SMU was carefully placed in the hands of the Methodist Episcopal Church, South,[25] and after unification, ownership was given to the South Central Jurisdiction of The Methodist Church.

Another motive in the establishing of a university in Dallas was so that both the lay and clerical leadership of Southern Methodism would have a first-class university in the state. The documents from about 1911 to 1920 make this quite clear.[26] Included in this desire was also the need felt by many for a school of theology near enough that more candidates for ministry would attend. As early as 1907 material began to appear in the *Texas Christian Advocate* concerning the shortage of Methodist preachers.[27] A subsequent article noted that many preachers were not serving full time.[28] An editorial a short time later surmised that not many students would go to Vanderbilt or Drew, and that the new theological department at Southwestern was the place for them to receive their training.[29] There was, to be sure, still a suspicious attitude toward theological schools by many Methodists in Texas, but the leadership at least recognized the increasing need in education beyond the basic degree and the establishing of a university made it possible to have a theological school for advanced training. It is difficult to tell from the extant evidence, however, just how much of a factor this was in the establishing of Southern Methodist University.

Hyer's Planning Work

Hyer, of course, was president of Southwestern University until 1911. This did not prevent him from investigating Dallas as a possible site for a university. Naturally, not everyone approved of this thinking (since it could not be kept secret), and many citizens of Georgetown, who feared the loss of Southwestern, were open in their criticism of him.[30] Among other advocates of a university in Dallas was David F. Houston, President of Washington University in St. Louis and a trustee of the General Board of Education. Houston had been president of both Texas A & M and the University of Texas according to Hyer, and was later Secretary of Agriculture. In 1910 John M. Moore and Hyer visited Houston in St. Louis, and Houston asserted his conviction that Dallas would be a great place for a university and encouraged Hyer in Hyer's hope for a grant from the General Board of Education to accomplish this purpose. Both Houston and Moore agreed to come to Dallas to make an appeal to the citizens of Dallas for support of such a university.[31]

Although it was not possible to keep all this a complete secret, it had not been made public in a general sense. All of this changed when H. A. Boaz, then president of Polytechnic College in Fort Worth, wrote to Hyer on 7 March 1910, advocating that Southwestern be moved to the Polytechnic campus in Fort Worth, with a college (but not a university) remaining in Georgetown. An exchange of letters with Hyer deeply disapproving the move to Fort Worth ensued, with three letters from Boaz to Hyer and two replies from Hyer. The public press got wind of the brewing controversy and reported it in the daily papers. This led G. C. Rankin, long-time editor of the *Texas Christian Advocate*, the official Methodist paper of Texas, to publish the letters in full in three editions of the *Advocate*.[32] A holograph of Bishop Boaz in the archives of Bridwell Library simply says he "raised a mighty row" in 1910.

Rankin wrote an editorial in the *Advocate* as follows:

> There has scarcely been a single year during the twelve that we have been editor of the paper that some one has not tried to break into these columns with an article upon the question of removing Southwestern University. But up to the beginning of this conference year we studiously declined to permit the question to be discussed in the *Advocate*. Yet we felt all along that it was only a question of time when this battle would have to be fought to a finish in the *Advocate* and before the Annual Conferences.[33]

The Decision: Begin a New University

Previous to this open dialogue in the *Advocate* in 1910, Nathan Powell, member of the Southwestern University Board and pastor at Brenham, attempted to get a commission appointed to study the matter of higher education in Texas, as mandated by the Convention of 1906.[34] A year later such a Commission did come into being, with two clergy and two lay members from each of the five annual conferences in Texas.[35] Bishop James Atkins, of North Carolina, was made chair of the Commission which met first on 18 January 1911 in Austin.[36]

From this time on the Commission provided leadership for the establishment and early supervision of the new university.

In the meantime Hyer had not been inactive. He proceeded with his discussions in spite of the fact that the Commission had still not made a decision or even been organized. Dallas citizens became concerned with Fort Worth's offer to move Southwestern there; so in 1910 Hyer arranged a meeting between Mayor Hay of Dallas, Dr. John P. McReynolds, dean of the medical school, and Mr. Babcock, the secretary of the Chamber of Commerce, with Wallace Buttrick of the General Board of Education. Out of this meeting, held in Little Rock, Arkansas, grew the action which led to Dallas's raising $300,000 and the securing of land north of the already developed Highland Park as the site for the university.[37]

On 10 June 1910, the Southwestern Board voted not to move Southwestern. The Commission, therefore, had to make a decision whether and if so where to establish a new university. In ensuing months Fort Worth made a valiant effort to outbid Dallas for the university, but in the end the Commission voted, on 3 February 1911, to locate a new university just to the north of Highland Park, in what eventually was to become the town of University Park.[38] In a later meeting in April the Commission, after considerable discussion, decided on a name. Bishop Atkins urged that the school be named Texas Wesleyan University. He was voted down, partly because members of the commission felt there were already too many Wesleyan universities, and Southern Methodist University became the preferred name. Hyer was elected president, Boaz vice-president (to raise money), and Frank Reedy, who was at Southwestern, as bursar.[39] The Commission also awarded the medical school to SMU. There is a bit of irony, to say the least, and perhaps some unpleasantness, in the fact that Hyer and Boaz who had argued so strongly for Dallas and Fort Worth as sites of the university should now be colleagues.

Obtaining the Money

How much money and land did Dallas actually provide for Southern Methodist University? Mrs. Armstrong provided the land for the campus. The four major donors were W. W. Caruth, R. S. Munger, Alex Sanger, and Mrs. Alice Armstrong.[40] The $300,000 figure, with more coming later, is probably accurate, though $325,000 is sometimes given. There is no record whether all of it was paid, but apparently most or all of it was. The land deal is more difficult to assess. Thomas's figure, based on various sources, is probably as nearly right as any. She gives the figure as 662.5 acres, following Hyer in his handwritten copy of the founding of SMU.[41] She does not speak of the 725 acres in which W. W. Caruth gave a half-interest to the University. Caruth owned 7,000 acres just north of the proposed campus site.[42] According to the Executive Committee Minutes, located in the office of the Secretary to the University, officials of SMU spent a great deal of time selling lots both singly and in groups, until in the 1940s.[43] In fact, prior to the establishing of the town of University Park, SMU served as the chief developer of the fledgling community which became University Park.

Hyer was convinced that the University could not be established without drawing upon three sources of income: the General Board of Education, the city of Dallas, and the Methodists of Texas.[44] We have seen that Dallas came through generously and quickly. The General Board of Education pledged $200,000 of matching funds if $800,000 could be raised for endowment in other ways.[45] It was a number of years before the Board was satisfied that the matching amount had been raised, though it paid part of the pledge early.

Texas Methodists were enthusiastic about the new University but, either because they could not or would not, were slow in raising their portion of the endowment. The *Advocate*, from 1911 to 1915, gave generous space to the raising of the money. Hyer gives considerable credit to Bishop Atkins for the campaign, even though his episcopacy was in North Carolina. John M. Moore and Vice-President Boaz, along with three special "commissioners" for raising funds—L. S. Barton, J. T. McClure, and J. D. Young—were also active.[46] Sunday School rallies, a rally at Fair Park during the State Fair of 1911, and various other methods—even gimmicks such as a trip to Yellowstone National Park—were used.[47] By November 1914, the bursar of the University could report to the West Texas Conference that 15,000 people had made subscriptions, with the average pledge being $70.00.[48] It is difficult if not impossible to determine how many of these pledges were never paid.

In the meantime, H. D. Knickerbocker, perhaps the greatest fund-raiser among Methodist ministers in the early years of this century, had been brought into the team of fund-raisers. He called his campaign "the Knickerbocker Special," and publicity for it included a train steaming down the track. He himself gave $1,000, and sought for ninety-nine other people to do likewise.[49] Thomas states that he did in fact secure 125 pledges of $1,000 or more.[50] In spite of all these efforts, however, the University went into operation short of its goal of $1,000,000 for endowment.

These financial campaigns were for the University as a whole, though much of the money would benefit the school of theology indirectly. The General Board of Education money could not be used for theology, however, and the leadership of the University soon realized that funds had to be raised directly for that area of work. As early as 1 June 1913, H. A. Boaz and J. D. Young were made responsible for raising a special endowment fund for the school of theology.[51] There is a record of a gift of $25,000 from Mrs. W. D. Haynie of Rice, Texas.[52] On 10 July 1913, the Building Committee authorized the raising of $250,000 for what is still called the Theological "Department."[53] In January 1914, a campaign was launched to endow the theological department,[54] and in June 1914, the *Texas Christian Advocate* reported that $66,000 had been received by Theology in cash and subscriptions.[55] A Mackenzie Chair of Moral Philosophy was projected, named for "Old Master Mackenzie."[56] In 1914 there was also a proposed chair in Religious Education, to be raised by Texas Sunday Schools,[57] though it is not clear whether this was for Arts and Science or Theology. The *Advocate* reports that $30,000 was subscribed for the MacKenzie Chair,[58] and $25,000 of the proposed $50,000 for the chair of Religious Education.[59]

These early financial problems persisted over the years, and budget cutbacks have been necessary within recent years. Over the years a great deal of money has been raised for buildings and a substantial amount for endowment, but SMU had a late start in relation to the older universities of the nation. The School of Theology existed on a modest budget until 1946 when the magnificent gift by the Perkins family made possible the building of a first-class school of theology.

Planning for a University

During this time of preparation, Hyer served as the chief instigator and designer of the new university: everything from the securing of a faculty to the design of the campus and its buildings, from the general supervision of financial drives to the details involved in curriculum and the first registration. Hyer's proposed design proved far grander than most people could conceive. If the beginnings of a university are a portent of the future, Hyer set a goal which has always been better than the realized situation.

Hyer's duties also included the supervision of the Medical College, which continued to have financial problems that led to the withdrawal for a time of its accreditation. In any case the Medical College lay claim to the first academic activities of Southern Methodist University[60]—and also to its first recorded borrowing of money to tide the institution over a difficult time.[61] After a few years of such problems, the Executive Committee decided to close the Medical College, and in 1918 sold the building to the Dallas Dental College, a state institution.[62]

In the meantime the Board of Trustees had been organized and began functioning under the chairmanship of Horace Bishop, on 12 March 1912. Bishop held the position until 1916. Bishop, not to be confused with the C. M. Bishop of the faculty, was a "leading" pastor and presiding elder in the North

Texas area. Beginning his ministry in 1868, he served well into the twentieth century. Twenty-four years of his ministry were spent as presiding elder, including the Fort Worth district.[63]

One of the first responsibilities of the newly appointed Board was to think about buildings for the emerging school. By 1912 Hyer had done the preliminary work on the main building and secured plans from a Chicago architectural firm. The building committee, of which Horace Bishop was also chair, asked for bids at its meeting on 6 May 1912.[64] Hyer had done his planning well. After a survey of college buildings, he decided on the Georgian style.[65] Herbert Gambrell, in a 1951 article, in order to indicate Hyer's close attention to details, says that Hyer asked the architects to make low risers in the steps of Dallas Hall, and that he then cut them an additional inch lower than the architects had proposed.[66]

Since Dallas Hall is still a striking building, it is easy to imagine the effect it had on viewers as it was being built, and as it finally stood, almost alone, in the center of a broad prairie still replete with Johnson grass. Accompanying it, of course, was the North Texas Building, later called Atkins Hall and now Clements Hall, to be used temporarily as a women's dormitory. But Dallas Hall was Hyer's great joy. The *Texas Christian Advocate* called it "an enduring monument as those of the Roman Empire and as beautiful as the classic structures of the age of Pericles." Another issue of the *Advocate* provided its dimensions: 258 x 109 feet at its greatest extremities, with the dome 83 feet above the first floor. The capitals of the front columns, says the writer, weigh more than four tons each, and were replicas of the Roman Pantheon's capitals.[67] According to James F. White, the building reflects the Georgian revival architectural style in vogue at the time (and used with greater and lesser success for the University's later buildings); Dallas Hall's basic form was that of the Roman Pantheon (built under the Emperor Hadrian in about 120 A.D., as mediated through Thomas Jefferson's classic Library at the University of Virginia (built in 1817–26).[68]

Hyer had in fact had the architects lay out the entire campus, on as grand a scale as the 1988 campus has turned out to be.[69] He described the two permanent buildings, Dallas Hall and what became Atkins/Clements Hall, as buildings "built for the ages."[70]

The laying of the cornerstone of Dallas Hall took place on 27 November 1912, coinciding with the opening day of the North Texas conference.[71] The builder was Fred A. Jones Construction Company, which submitted the lowest bid of $212,902.00.[72] The H.&T.C. Railroad built a special spur from east of the campus to transport building material, a track which remained for many years and eventually became Fondren Street.

Robert S. Hyer

Who was this remarkable man whose vision helped to create Southern Methodist University and whose persistence and driving force led to its opening in September 1915? There is no definitive biography of the man, and perhaps none would be possible since his daughter says that he kept few personal records. His daughter's *Robert Stewart Hyer: The Man I Knew* is by her own admission not an objective biography.[73] The man must have had serious flaws, for he was after all a member of the human race: but it is difficult to find any derogatory remarks against him.

The basic facts of his life are: He was born in Oxford, Georgia. At Emory, then located at Oxford, he "received every honor which the school and the student body could give"[74] and received both the B.A. and M.A. degrees from that institution.

He came to Southwestern University in Georgetown in 1882 as professor of science, and is often called the first scientist in Texas. According to Herbert Gambrell's sketch for the *Dictionary of American Biography*, "his interest in science appears to have been awakened by Darwin's *Origin of Species*, which he considered the greatest scientific work in English."[75] He saw no conflict between Darwin and Christianity and was a devout Christian and Methodist, doing a great deal of lay preaching. His daughter notes that one of his former students said that the greatest sermon she had heard him deliver was entitled "Why I as a Scientist Believe in God."[76] Although he was criticized for his beliefs, no one could ever touch him significantly by such criticism.

When John McLean resigned as president of Southwestern in 1898, Hyer was made regent (or president). That same year he received his first honorary degree, from Baylor University,[77] an exceptional act at the time—a Methodist university president receiving a degree from a Baptist university. Although burdened with the demands of his office, Hyer continued his scientific work and designed the first Texas wireless station, which could transmit one mile.[78] He also made an X-ray machine which was "borrowed" by Georgetown doctors until they had access to a commercially made one.[79]

We have already seen how Hyer's vision caused him to turn toward Dallas as a place where a great university could be built. In 1911 he became president of this fledgling university. As Herbert Gambrell later describes what he did in these early years: "Hyer planned the campus, determined the architectural design, supervised the erection of its first five buildings, and obtained an endowment of about $300,000."[80] In addition, he obtained a faculty, set up the organization of a university, and moved the new institution along so that it could enroll its first students (other than medical) in September 1915, one year later than many people hoped and a year after the Candler School of Theology at Emory University in Atlanta, Georgia, had begun its operation.[81]

Hyer never claimed to be a money raiser, though raising of money for buildings, operating expenses, and endowment was a necessity for the new school. With the help of others, he did rather well. But by 1919, the situation had become sufficiently desperate that the Board asked Hyer to step down, since the university owed $207,601.34. H. A. Boaz was elected president; Hyer served as President Emeritus and Professor of Physics until his death on 29 May 1929.[82] He thus served the university he designed and loved for eighteen years.

To Build a Great University

Hyer had planned well, but in the winter of 1915 there was still no place to house male students. A hasty campaign was begun, and by the opening of school three temporary dormitories were in place. One was named for G. C. Rankin, editor of the *Texas Christian Advocate,* who died in January of 1915. The other two bore the prosaic names of North and South Halls.[83]

Integral to this university was its department, or school, of theology. Surprisingly little is said in the sources during its founding years about this part of the school. Near the opening time an attempt was made, not too successfully, to provide an endowment for theology.[84] Yet most of what concerns the university as a whole also concerns the school of theology, for it was never thought of as a separate entity but rather as part of the whole.

Hyer's dream, and that of such leaders as John M. Moore and of many rank and file members of the Methodist Episcopal Church, South, far exceeded the reality of that first college with music and theology attached. As Hyer himself said in this very early period, "We have only thus far laid the foundation for a university."[85] His idea of a university was founded, as was that of John M. Moore and Frank Seay (both having attended European universities), more on the German university than any other pattern. Hyer knew that SMU had only begun to be such a university, but he believed that the church *could* build such an institution and that his dream would eventually be realized.[86]

As I have surveyed the records of Southern Methodist University, I have been struck by the fact that this dream of Hyer's has guided its subsequent leaders. Their reach has always exceeded their grasp, but in their reaching, steps have been taken toward the goal which Robert Stewart Hyer set for Southern Methodist University in those founding years.

Marshall Terry, professor of English and sometime member of the administration, said this to the Board of Trustees on 6 November 1964: "The founders had no 'run of the mill' institution in mind; there was from the first a sense of great potential for SMU."[87]

2

The Early Years: 1910–20

The final days before SMU's first registration were feverish days of preparation. Bishop Mouzon, the dean of the School of Theology, was away on episcopal duties. President Hyer had asked Mouzon to assemble a faculty and guide the new school of theology in its first months in spite of his other responsibilities. Mouzon and Frank Seay had taught together at Southwestern, and so it was Seay who was drafted to make preparations for the organization of classes and the registration of students.[1] Earlier during the summer Seay and John McGinnis had assisted President Hyer in the preparation of the University's first bulletin or catalog.[2]

A hasty, last-minute campaign had produced sufficient money to build but not pay for the three temporary men's dormitories completed just before classes began: Rankin, North, and South Halls.[3] The waterworks which served both the University and the fledgling new but still unincorporated town of University Park were completed just in time for the opening of the University.[4] Until the incorporation of University Park in 1924, the community was for all practical purposes an adjunct to the University. In one Executive Committee meeting, for example, the bursar of the University was authorized to visit with several people in the neighborhood to advise them that unless they connected with the University's sewage system, their water and gas privileges, also furnished through the University, would be denied.[5]

The trolley car line had been extended to the northern part of the campus, and its operation began on 1 January 1915. By September 1, the physical facilities for the University were in place, and now the more subtle work of building its academic life began.

There is no indication of this fact, but it seems likely that the fourteen graduate theological students were fewer than had been expected. To be sure, the grand total of ninety theological students, including undergraduates and those in special programs, out of a total student body of 706, was impressive.

Those hectic first days, presided over by and large by people who were inexperienced in registration, were partly compensated for by the warm welcome which the University received from the church and the Dallas

13

community. The Dallas Epworth League Union arranged a banquet at the Scottish Rite Cathedral, attended by more than one thousand.[6] Gus Thomasson, often called Mr. Epworth League of Dallas and even of Texas, chaired the occasion, and it was indeed a gala evening. Two hundred Dallas citizens attended an opening faculty reception on September 4, and a parade was held downtown on September 9.

University Resources

What kind of school did those first students discover? It is tempting to deride the University in those first years; yet there were some excellent faculty: for example, J. H. McGinnis in Arts and Science and Frank Seay in Theology. Miss Mary McCord, who developed a superb theatre program, began her work in 1915 and continued until 1945. Hyer knew how to assemble a faculty, and he did a rather remarkable job in view of the obstacles he faced.

Other resources were less impressive. No one developed an adequate library prior to the opening, and Frank Reedy, the bursar, was asked to confer with the City librarian about the use of books from that source.[7] At the end of the first year, the theology library, which was incorporated into the total, had 1,488 volumes, secured largely through gifts from individuals and from the Methodist Publishing House.[8]

The University, through the School of Theology, offered a standard B.D. course, taking three years for completion, including one of the biblical languages. But it was also possible for students to take theology courses as undergraduates, up to 45 quarter hours, and then to apply part of that work on the B.D. degree later, in the form of double credit.[9] It was also possible to take the regular theological course excepting language without an undergraduate degree and receive a certificate.[10]

From the beginning the School of Theology recognized a corresponding responsibility to those who could not attend regular courses in any of the three ways listed. Extension work was therefore set up beginning in January 1916. Through this process pastors and others came to the campus each Tuesday for special one-day-per-week courses offered by the regular faculty. Between 10:15 A.M and 3:15 P.M., four courses were offered,[11] with SMU students and visitors also being allowed entrance to the classes.[12] This practice continued in some form for many years.

The Curriculum

The process of curriculum revision began early in the history of the School of Theology, a process that has continued to the present. The original curriculum was fairly simple, with six quarter hours being required in both Old and New

Testament (twelve altogether); thirteen quarter hours in one of the biblical languages; nine hours in Church History and Missions; six hours in the psychology and philosophy of religion; twelve hours in Religious Efficiency (practical theology), and six hours in public speaking and voice. A major had to be selected during the student's second year with thirty quarter hours required in the major subject and fifteen in the minor department.[13]

A few years after this initial curriculum was adopted, another took its place, not radically different but not identical either. Nine departments were established: Old Testament, New Testament, Church History, Philosophy of Religion, Ministerial Efficiency, Religious Education, Sociology, Christian Missions, and Christian Doctrine.

The three years were outlined as follows:

First Year

Fall	Winter	Spring	Quarter hours
Old Testament	Old Testament	New Testament	9
General Church History	General Church History	Methodist Doctrine	9
Religious Education	Religious Education	Religious Education	9
Sociology	Sociology	Sociology	9
Ministerial Efficiency	Ministerial Efficiency	Missions	9
N.T. Greek	N.T. Greek	N.T. Greek	9
Public Speaking, 1 hour throughout the academic year			n. c.

Second Year

New Testament	Homiletics	Homiletics	4 ea.
General Christian Doctrine	Phil. or Psych. of Religions	Phil. or Psych. of Religions	4 ea.

The remainder of the work was elective, with the same major and minor requirements as previously.[14]

The Faculty

The work of implementing the first curriculum was the task of five full-time and four part-time faculty during 1915 and 1916.

Bishop Edwin D. Mouzon was the first dean, in addition to his episcopal responsibilities which, after 1914, took him away from Dallas. Mouzon, it will be remembered, began the theological department at Southwestern University in 1908. He was elected bishop in 1910, but agreed to Hyer's request to help organize the new School of Theology. Mouzon was a widely respected churchman and educator, with his most distinctive academic achievement being the delivery of the Lyman Beecher Lectures at Yale, published under the title *Preaching with Authority*. He served until mid-1916 when he returned to his episcopal responsibilities full-time.

Ivan Lee Holt was the chair of the faculty,[15] professor of Old Testament, and chaplain of the University. Holt was the youngest member of the theology faculty and the only one possessing the Ph.D. degree, from the University of Chicago. He had had six years of pastoral experience prior to coming to SMU. One remembered event of his chaplaincy was his daring to wear a pulpit robe in the university chapel. The outcry was so great, however, that he backed down, and it was many years before this "popish" custom took root on the SMU campus (the mid-1950s).[16] Holt went on to St. John's Church in St. Louis in 1918 and remained there until his election to the episcopacy in 1938.[17] In later years Holt was active in ecumenical matters.

Paul B. Kern was professor of English Bible first and later of Homiletics and Ministerial Efficiency (Pastoral Administration). His father had been a professor at Vanderbilt and at Randolph-Macon College; so Kern was at home in an academic setting. After his graduation from Vanderbilt, he taught there for two years, and then served churches in Tennessee until he was called to the SMU faculty. He used his father's textbook, *The Ministry to the Congregation,* and as William C. Martin (later a bishop) put it: "We soon learned that the price of a good grade in homiletics was the virtual memorization of this book."[18] Kern became Dean of the School of Theology after the resignation of Hoyt M. Dobbs, and remained in that position until 1926 when he returned to the pastorate of Travis Park, San Antonio. He was elected bishop in 1930.[19]

James Kilgore, the senior member of the faculty, was an M.A. graduate from Southwestern University and attended the University of Chicago for five summers. He had been a pastor for more than twenty years, and was presiding elder of the Houston District when he was called to the seminary. He was first connected with Southern Methodist University as a member of the Education Commission which called for its establishment.[20] He then became a member of the Board of Trustees and remained a member even after beginning to teach. During his first year he taught Pastoral Theology and Religious Education, but later changed to Philosophy and Psychology of Religion, and often taught courses in Christian Doctrine. He was acting President of the University between Boaz's and Selecman's tenures, and was acting Dean of the School of Theology from 1926 to 1933.[21]

Frank Seay was the acknowledged star of the faculty. Seay came to the faculty of Southwestern in 1909, and was Hyer's first choice to follow him to

Southern Methodist University. His father, Thomas Seay, was the governor of Alabama from 1886 to 1890, and was generally considered a progressive one.[22] Frank was graduated from Southern University at age 17, studied law for two years, and later did his theological work at Vanderbilt and additional graduate work at the University of Chicago, Harvard, the University of Berlin, and Oxford University. He was professor of New Testament and New Testament Greek until his untimely death in February 1920.

Two other members were selected but did not serve. Gross Alexander was to have taught Church History, but he died just prior to the opening of the University.[23] Fitzgerald Parker, from the Methodist General Board of Education, was scheduled to teach in the field of Christian Doctrine, but decided that he could not leave his position in Nashville.[24]

Frank Reedy, University bursar, taught in the field of Sunday School organization, and during the first year of classes, the Rev. J. L. Bell, pastor of East Dallas Presbyterian Church, taught Church History, and George M. Gibson, a Dallas Methodist pastor, taught Christian Doctrine during the winter and spring quarters.[25]

Others took part in the life of the School of Theology. For example, A. Frank Smith (later a bishop), in addition to his responsibilities in a men's dormitory and his pastorate of the University Church, served as "secretary" to handle inquiries during the summer of 1916.[26] He is also listed as a lecturer in Religious Education.[27] Some theology faculty members also taught undergraduate classes. Although classes were usually small, the teaching load was heavy as these SMU pioneers labored to set the new University, including its School of Theology, on its proper academic course.

Sometimes, faculty minutes are characterized by a failure to give a later reader the details needed to know what exactly happened, and the School of Theology faculty minutes are no exception. But perhaps the strangest set of minutes is the first recorded, in the handwriting of Frank Seay who served as first secretary to the faculty. Dated 22 October 1915, the minutes begin:

> The faculty of the School of Theology of Southern Methodist University met informally on the banister railing of Mr. Kern's residence on October 22, 1915, with Ivan Lee Holt, Chairman of the faculty in the chair. Present, Messrs. Holt, Kern, Kilgore and Seay.[28]

During the following four years, new faculty were added and a change of deans occurred. Bishop Mouzon resigned as dean in mid-1916, and Hoyt M. Dobbs succeeded him a few months later[29] and taught Christian Doctrine. Horace M. Whaling became Professor of Church History and Missions in the fall of 1916.[30] Jesse Lee Cuninggim, father of Merrimon Cuninggim (later Dean), came to teach Religious Education in January 1917, at which time he set up the

Correspondence School (Department of Ministerial Supply and Training), which he had first established at Vanderbilt. Comer M. Woodward occupied a new chair in Sociology, with equal responsibility for undergraduate teaching, at about the same time.[31] After Ivan Lee Holt's resignation in 1918, John A. Rice was added to the faculty to begin his work in 1920. Miss Mary McCord, who was a part of the larger faculty from the beginning and who produced the first Shakespearean drama, *As You Like It*, in 1916, began giving non-credit work in speech in 1917.[32] J. W. Hubbell of the School of Music also taught Church Music.[33]

Space for Theology

The School of Theology had its own space in Dallas Hall. Its classes and offices shared the east end of the third floor with Miss McCord's public speaking department. Somewhere on the third floor were also the piano studios, and most of the west end was utilized by the university chapel. (Theology had a small chapel of its own.) We can only wonder now how all the activities of the fledgling University could have occurred in one building. Herbert Gambrell, who graduated in 1921 while this condition still persisted, describes it many years later in this bit of nostalgia:

> It all seemed pretty grand, that University under a single roof. Of course, fumes from the chemistry laboratory and hamburger grill in the basement had a way of rising and penetrating: and sounds of pianos, lungs and brass instruments at work on the third floor floated downward. Odors from the cooking laboratory beneath the library made hungry students drool, and some complained that the embalming fluid in which biology specimens were preserved was unpleasant to smell in adjacent rooms. But it all seemed right and proper to us pioneers.[34]

University Life

The organization of university and theology school life began shortly after the opening of school. Umphrey Lee, later University President, was elected president of the student body, and Robert Goodloe, a later long-time professor in the School of Theology, was made president of the graduate class.[35] E. W. Bridges was chosen as president of the theological student body[36] and became the first B.D. graduate in 1916. J. Coy Williams was awarded the first certificate at the first graduation.[37]

University chapel was compulsory, of course, and held in the west end chapel of the top floor of Dallas Hall. The School of Theology held its own chapel according to various patterns—weekly during the day or in the evening, and later daily.[38]

Student organizations quickly came into existence, and theology students were often active in them. The earliest were the YMCA and the YWCA, with the former given responsibility for student employment.[39] A Ministerial Association was organized in February 1916, with E. W. Bridges as president and George Gibson as secretary.[40] It was not until 1919 that a ministerial club of both graduate and undergraduate students was organized.[41]

Social gatherings of theology faculty and students were held occasionally, the first of record being in December 1915.[42] Perhaps the sporadic nature of such matters was partly due to the school's being an integral part of the total university. Ivan Lee Holt, in his first report to the Board of Trustees, listed as the first distinctive aspect of SMU's School of Theology that its students were in close touch with other students.[43] (They could hardly be otherwise since they attended classes in the same building and lived in the same dormitories.) Also, there was little time for campus life. Twenty-two students held student pastorates,[44] and many others worked at other kinds of jobs.[45]

"Take the School of Theology to the Church"

From its beginning, the School of Theology felt a responsibility to provide opportunities for theological study to clergy and laity already active in the Methodist Episcopal Church, South. We have already seen how during the second quarter of our school's existence, an extension day was begun on campus. Other campus activities were also quickly put into effect. Holt's report to the Board whose first article we have already noted contained a second which included this injunction: to take the School of Theology to persons already in the pastorate.[46] One means of doing this was to provide work by correspondence, some of which counted on a degree.[47]

A major thrust was made in the summer of 1919 with the combined Preacher's Assembly and Western Training School for Sunday School Leaders, planned jointly with the General Sunday School Board.[48] The Sunday School conference continued for several summers, and the Pastor's School became a fixed tradition for many years until it was replaced by the longer Supply Pastors' School, of four weeks' duration.

There were also plans to go into district conferences for theological education, but no record has been found concerning whether this was carried out.[49] Faculty were asked to give "popular lectures" in the community as part of the school's extension work.[50]

Also during this early period, in 1918, the Correspondence Course of Study School was set up in Dallas. Previously this work, required for ordination without the B.D. degree, had all been done at Candler School of Theology. Now, the work for states west of the Mississippi was done at SMU, continuing for many years, into the 1950s.[51]

Near the end of this period a major breakthrough in what is now called "continuing education" was made in the establishment of the Fondren Lectureship in Christian Missions. In 1919 Mr. and Mrs. W. W. Fondren of Houston, who became one of the half-dozen major benefactors of Southern Methodist University, provided $10,000 as an endowment to bring eminent scholars and church leaders to the campus for a series of lectures.[52] Always to be related to the mission of the church, this series led, as we shall later see, to the beginning of Ministers' Week with eventually two other series of lectures.

The Location of Scarritt College

Another example of SMU's reach exceeding its grasp occurred very early in its history in its attempt to secure Scarritt Bible and Training School for SMU. Scarritt was located in Kansas City where it was founded in 1892. When it sought a new location, the Executive Committee of the Board of Trustees decided to try to locate it on the SMU campus. They instructed Dr. Boaz, then Vice-President, "to use every means suitable to bring Scarritt Bible and Training School to Southern Methodist University."[53] The invitation was repeated on 6 January 1921, and the Committee agreed to provide a satisfactory site for the school.[54] Later discussion occurred in what appears to be a significant effort of the Executive Committee to effect the change.[55] The desired result did not materialize, however, and eventually Scarritt was moved to Nashville in 1924, where it formed a three-way relationship with Vanderbilt University and George Peabody College for Teachers.[56]

Previous to this move, the Board of Trustees had presented a plan to the Boards of Missions and Education for establishing a School of Missions in connection with the School of Theology. Since neither SMU nor the board had the $500,000 needed to begin such a school, this too became an unrealized dream.[57]

In these and other ways, attempts were made to broaden the experience of resident students and also to extend the benefits of the School of Theology to both clergy and laity in the field. When the attempts to get a major school of missions failed, for example, missionaries were brought to the campus for brief teaching stints. We shall see more of this in the following chapter.

Finances

For many years, most of its life, the School of Theology operated on a modest budget with little endowment and with the University thinking of it as a separate entity to be supported by the Methodist Episcopal Church, South. The School demanded much of its small faculty and probably expanded beyond its ability to do so, especially through its extension work. The church did provide funds,[58] never as great as projected, however. Somehow, the School of Theology seemed usually able to operate within its budget.

Students paid very little of the cost of their education. Fees were $10 per quarter. Room rent was free, except for heat and light which averaged about $2.00 per month. Board could be had for $4.00 per week.[59] Not until many years later, when two generous people from Wichita Falls, Texas, Mr. and Mrs. J. J. (Joe and Lois) Perkins, provided for the seminary's future, was it possible to build the kind of school of which John M. Moore and others dreamed in these early years.

A Matter of Interest

The account of the first University Church and later the founding of Highland Park Methodist Church is only a peripheral concern to this history of Perkins School of Theology. It does seem appropriate, however, to recount briefly its story, however difficult it is to understand some parts of it.[60]

During the fall of 1915 the University provided church services on Sunday, considered as an offshoot of the Oak Lawn Church. Sunday School and worship were begun as soon as registration was completed, with Horace Bishop preaching on the first Sunday.[61] The sermons were regularly reported in the campus newspaper, and more than 400 students enrolled in Sunday School classes.[62] From the beginning it seems to have been assumed that the SMU congregation would become, in Methodist terms, a "charge" of its own.[63] According to Ivan Lee Holt, Chaplain, there were regular services but no organized church on campus during this first semester.[64]

Then SMU asked the presiding elder, O. F. Sensabaugh, on 28 January 1916, to form a duly constituted congregation on campus, and up to April 27, 150 members had been received.[65] The first quarterly conference was conducted in February 1916.[66] In the meantime, A. Frank Smith had been appointed to the Forest Avenue Methodist Episcopal Church, South, on 13 December 1915, located near the Fair Grounds. In a later letter to J. J. Perkins, Bishop Smith tells of enrolling in the School of Theology but having to give up his courses when he was made pastor of the University Church.[67]

But University Church persisted for less than six months. For reasons not explained, in May 1916 University Church was merged with First and Trinity downtown to form a new First Methodist Episcopal Church, South, and First Church was moved from its Commerce and Prather site to the Trinity Church building on McKinney at Pearl.[68] The new university church, later named Highland Park Methodist Episcopal Church, South, was therefore not a continuation of the campus church but rather a completely new congregation.

Land for the new church was set aside at the 27 June 1916 Board of Trustees meeting.[69] Frank Smith was appointed pastor of the new church but he remained only until the fall conference before he was sent to University Church, Austin.[70] The only hint which is given to explain why University Church was not simply moved to a new location is that the new church from its beginning had hoped to appeal to Methodist families already living in the new suburb of Highland Park.[71]

Clovis Chappell was made the second pastor and a "little brown Church" was built. It grew rapidly to 412 members in 1917.[72] Chappell was transferred to Washington, D. C., and the pulpit was filled successively by H. M. Whaling, Paul B. Kern, Glenn Flinn, and C. O. Shugart, until Umphrey Lee was appointed pastor in November 1923, remaining until June 1936.[73]

SMU and World War I

World War I began on 14 July 1914, fourteen months before the opening of Southern Methodist University. America's entry was unthinkable at that time; and so the fact of entry on 1 April 1917 came as a shock to both individuals and institutions such as SMU. At the 7 June 1917 Board of Trustees meeting, President Hyer announced that SMU's attempt to secure a military instructor from the U. S. government had been denied. So the school had secured its own, a Major Conner, who had been in charge of cadets in Dallas High School.[74] He also proposed that military science be made mandatory for all male students.[75]

Even so, the reduction of male students was drastic, from 349 in 1916–17 to 245 in 1917–18.[76] The School of Theology, its students not being automatically subject to military service, had actually increased slightly.[77] By February 1918, according to the *Campus*, 143 students and faculty were serving in the armed forces.[78] All of this, of course, made SMU's financial situation even bleaker than it already was.

A future theology professor, Robert Goodloe, finished his B.D. at Yale and entered the chaplaincy soon thereafter.[79] A later report was that eleven SMU students had been killed in military service.[80]

Among other disasters which befell the University in 1917 was the partial destruction by fire of South Hall, on November 27. No one was injured since the fire occurred during chapel and only two people were in the building.

A New Dean and a New President

Hoyt M. Dobbs succeeded Bishop Mouzon as Dean of the School of Theology in late 1916. A graduate of Vanderbilt Divinity School, Dobbs was Dean for less than three years. During this time a new curriculum was put in place, and there is a record of the Dobbs family's entertaining the student body in their home.[81]

Dobbs became ill in the summer of 1919, and James Kilgore, for the first of several times, was made acting Dean. Six months later, in March 1920, Dobbs resigned, and Paul B. Kern became acting Dean.[82] Dobbs returned to the local church and was elected a bishop in 1922. Kern, of course, was soon made permanent Dean of the School of Theology.

Under more unhappy circumstances, SMU also acquired a new president. For all of Hyer's genius in other areas of university administration, he was not an active fund raiser. He said so at the beginning of his presidency, and though he was instrumental in seeing that money was raised, the efforts were not adequate, and by 20 February 1920, an indebtedness of $207,601.34 had been incurred.[83] This was a large debt for a small school, and obviously something had to be done.

In a letter to Judge E. Cockrell, who had followed Bishop Mouzon as chair of the Board of Trustees in 1919, Ivan Lee Holt proposed two "heads of the University" based on a plan he knew at Washington University. There would have been a President who would conduct business and administrative affairs and a Chancellor who would direct student life and activities.[84] But this was not done.

The natural candidate for the job was H. A. Boaz, the greatest long-term money-raiser in SMU's history (both before and for many years after his brief presidency). Boaz had left SMU's vice-presidency to head the church's Church Extension work in Louisville, Kentucky, and was reluctant to leave that work so soon.

In the end, however, Hyer's resignation was accepted and he was made President Emeritus and Professor of Physics.[85] The Board then lost no time in electing Boaz, who by pre-arrangement had agreed. It was May 1920 before he could complete his work in Louisville, and he then began his urgent task of putting the school on a sounder financial basis.[86]

Hyer's daughter, Ray Hyer Brown, recounts the incident with a certain bitterness. "In the presence of accolades from the academic world for having accomplished the impossible," she writes, "a fabrication of petty criticism had enmeshed him in an incredible web."[87] She recognizes the financial straits of the University but believes that jealousy over a lay person's being President of the University was at the base of the matter.[88] And who knows but that this may be the case: stranger things have happened in the church. One can only wonder, for example, why a fund raiser could not have been employed to work with Hyer. In any case a great man felt humiliated,[89] and in retrospect one can only wish that some other plan, perhaps Holt's, could have been implemented.

Boaz did ameliorate the financial situation, partly by selling land which Hyer wanted to hold on to for the future.[90] But Boaz remained in office only a little more than two years as he was elected to the episcopacy in 1922, the year in which Hoyt M. Dobbs was accorded the same honor.

Fortunately, later years have recognized both President Hyer's greatness and the contributions which he made to Southern Methodist University. Perhaps someone else could have done what he did between 1911 (and even earlier) and 1920, but there is no obvious candidate for the honor. His contributions have been memorialized by a building on campus named Hyer Hall, and a bust presented by his daughter, Mrs. Ray Hyer Brown, in 1956.[91]

A Tribute to Frank Seay

Almost simultaneously with the forced resignation of President Hyer occurred the death of the School of Theology's star scholar, Frank Seay. His academic credentials have already been given. Although he did not have a Ph.D. degree, all indications are that in knowledge and wisdom he far outshone many of those possessing this academic distinction. Perhaps the Board of Trustees summarized his qualities best when the framers of his obituary wrote: "He was one of those rarely gifted and specially called of God to be a teacher."[92] The *Dallas Morning News*, in a front page article, declared him to be "one of the most prominent churchmen, lecturers, scholars, and authors in the United States."[93] The faculty resolution, written by Dean Hoyt M. Dobbs, included this sentence: "As a scholar, as a minister, as a teacher, and as one of the founders of the School of Theology, he has made a definite and permanent contribution to the history of the church."[94] And the alumni magazine, *The Mustang*, described him as "a man of exact scholarship, broad culture, intense honesty, and unquestioned courage."[95] In 1919 he had accepted a position at the University of Texas, but at the urging of his fellow faculty, he had changed his mind and remained at SMU.[96]

Seay wrote mostly for pastors and laity, especially those in the Conference Course of Study. His way of remaining true to his own biblical understanding without offending his conservative readers was to take the critical conclusions for granted. For example, in presenting the story of the Old Testament he neither affirmed nor denied the Mosaic authority of the Pentateuch. Yet what he wrote clearly assumed a non-Mosaic source for the Bible's first five books. His books were widely used and well received.[97]

Seay's scholarship was matched by his churchly and pastoral concern; he had served churches in Alabama for several years before coming to Southwestern University. One example illustrates his continued pastoral concern. O. W. Moerner, later a leader in the general Sunday School Board, tells that Seay found him one day standing on the balcony of the rotunda of Dallas Hall.

"Moerner," Seay said, "I'm ashamed of you. You know you ought to be in the Methodist ministry." That set Moerner thinking; he attended the School of Theology, and became a leader in the Methodist Episcopal Church, South.[98]

Seay died at his home on Haynie Avenue on 14 February 1920 at the age of 38.[99] He was survived by his wife Clara and two children, a daughter Hibernia, age 9, and a son, DeLesdernier, age 5.[100] Mrs. Seay returned to Alabama, and no record has been found of Seay's descendants. A collection of 400 volumes was given to the library in his honor[101] and the 1952 Committee on Building and Grounds was asked to locate an area on the campus to be designated as "Frank Seay Park."[102] For many years a sign stood in the parkway in front of Atkins (now Clements) Hall, but it has long since disappeared.

What Kind of School of Theology?

Three statements concerning the nature of SMU's School of Theology conclude this chapter. A pre-opening statement in the *Texas Christian Advocate* declared: "The opening of this department [School of Theology] foretells the spirit of the whole institution. It is to be Methodist but not exclusive. It must be decisively religious."[103]

The SMU catalog for 1916–17 stated: "It is the plan of the School of Theology not to segregate the theological students from the general life of the University or use separate buildings either for classes or for dormitories."[104]

The Board of Trustees was told on 7 July 1917 that the curriculum of the School of Theology was correlative in nature: "Studies which ground men in the fundamentals of Christianity and those which relate the student to the world in which he lives have been prescribed."[105]

3

A New Dean, a New Building:
1920–26

The halcyon (though sometimes hectic) early years of Southern Methodist University were a time of slow but steady growth and an increasing stability—except in one area, the financial. We have already seen that the financial crisis led to the request of the Board of Trustees for President Hyer's resignation and the election of H. A. Boaz as his successor. Boaz's introduction of better financial management and the work of a special group for raising money solved the immediate crisis, but the problem remained, worse some years than others.

The 1920s also brought a series of crises involving athletics, biblical understanding, and the administration of the University. We shall deal in this chapter with the ongoing life of the School of Theology, and in the next with the crises and their handling.

Administrative Changes

The first change, as we have seen, was the coming of H. A. Boaz to the presidency. Although he remained in office only two years before he was elected bishop, in 1922, he did by concentrating on the reorganization of the finances of the University put them on a sounder basis.[1] The process included a massive financial campaign chaired by Bishop John M. Moore, concluding in 1924. The results put the University in its first viable financial situation.

Part of the problem had been the unwillingness of the General Board of Education—John D. Rockefeller's foundation—to accept the accounting of SMU with regard to endowment. In fact, the Board felt that money for endowment had been used for operating expenses.[2] In 1920 the Board had pledged $333,000 toward a $1,000,000 endowment even though the original $200,000 bequest had not all been paid.[3] The Moore campaign began to secure larger gifts for the first time, partly because of the new prosperity in Texas engendered by the oil boom. S. I. Munger pledged $100,000 and J. J. Perkins and W. B. Hamilton of Wichita Falls each gave $50,000.[4] The campaign was greatly abetted by a gift in his will by Col. L. A. Pires, who had never set foot on the campus of SMU. His gift was by far the largest yet received, $500,000 in 1923,[5] with the total gifts for that year amounting to more than $1,000,000.[6]

The great effort by Bishop Moore and others who worked on the campaign meant that by 1924 (after Charles Selecman was President), the University's debt was paid, the endowment was reimbursed for money used for operating expenses, and the endowment was also increased to more than $1,500,000.[7] The General Board of Education forwarded a check for $247,013.37 in one sum, and $86,219.00 later.[8]

During Boaz's two years as President, he had not really become concerned with the academic life of the University but left this to the deans, A. S. Pegues of the College of Arts and Paul B. Kern of Theology.[9] Boaz's attempt to influence the University was through emphasizing religion on the campus. For example, he reported to the Board of Trustees on 13 June 1921 (the end of his first year as President), that "adjustment week" (previously called a "revival") had resulted in 300 reclamations, 100 professions of faith, and 94 who signed "life service cards."[10]

When Boaz was elected bishop, no immediate successor was in sight. As a consequence, James Kilgore of the Theology faculty was asked to be acting President. The Board requested that Bishop John M. Moore act as "Counselor to the Administration."[11] Five months later Charles C. Selecman was made President and assumed office on 2 April 1923.[12]

Dean Paul B. Kern

More important for the School of Theology was the selection of one of the original faculty, Paul B. Kern, first as acting Dean in March 1920,[13] and later as Dean, beginning in 1920, a position he held for six years. For the first time in its history, the School of Theology had stability in its leadership. Its faculty expanded during the next few years, and its breadth of curriculum was limited only by budget considerations. Dean Kern was squarely in the Methodist tradition, and he set forth the purposes of the School of Theology in three-fold terms: to keep the ideal of Christian manhood in the fore with all student contacts, to "train the mind," and to develop skilled workmanship. "We set as our goal," he added, "the equipping of a man spiritually, intellectually, technically for the work of a preacher of the gospel in the Methodist itinerancy."[14]

Faculty Additions

The two most auspicious appointments to the faculty early in Kern's term were Harvie Branscomb and John A. Rice.[15] Both, as we shall later see, became involved in controversies, and both were distinct losses to the University when they resigned.

Branscomb had first come to the University as head of the Department of Philosophy and assistant in the Department of Education.[16] After Frank Seay's death, Branscomb was asked to teach New Testament in the School of Theology. He had studied New Testament at Oxford University as a Rhodes Scholar,[17] and in latter years became known as a respectable New Testament scholar, in spite of his considerable administrative responsibilities.

John A. Rice had been in pastoral ministry and had been a respected member of that order. He was an early member of the Board of Trustees of SMU. While he was pastor at St. John's Methodist Episcopal Church, South, in St. Louis,[18] he wrote *The Old Testament in the Life of Today*, published by Macmillan in 1920. Soon after he began teaching at SMU, the book became controversial. The upshot of the matter was that he resigned his appointment in the School of Theology, and through the good graces of Bishop Edwin Mouzon was given a pastorate in Oklahoma, and later the Boston Avenue Church in Tulsa where he was pastor during the building of what became the first breakthrough in church architecture in the South.[19]

Other faculty members during the early 1920s were Dr. J. F. Pierce, who completed Dobbs's year as teacher of Christian Doctrine; Walter B. Nance who taught Missions in the fall of 1920,[20] and Mims T. Workman, the subject of another controversy to be considered later. Although Workman's primary responsibility was in the undergraduate college, he both studied and did some teaching of Hebrew and Greek at the School of Theology.[21] Robert W. Goodloe also taught on a visiting basis during 1920–21 but left at the end of the year to pursue Ph.D. work at the University of Chicago.[22]

J. L. Cuninggim resigned in October 1921 as Professor of Religious Education to become President of Scarritt Bible and Training School in Kansas City; he became President of Scarritt College in 1924, when the school was renamed and moved to Nashville, Tennessee. James Seehorn Seneker was nominated to succeed him at SMU and became part of the permanent faculty a year later.[23] J. Marvin Ormond, pastor of the First Methodist Episcopal Church, South, of Elizabeth City, North Carolina, came to the teaching position in Pastoral Administration.[24] W. D. Bradfield offered courses in Christian Doctrine in 1921–22[25] and became a permanent member of the faculty the following year.[26]

E. W. Alderson apparently completed Rice's work following his resignation,[27] and John H. Hicks became the permanent holder of the Old Testament teaching position in 1922,[28] remaining until his retirement in 1955. Thomas H. Hudson, Dean of Theology at Kwansei Gakuin, Kobe, Japan, was visiting professor of Missions in 1921.[29] Claude Eagleton, from SMU's history department, filled in in Church History for a time.[30] Additional missionaries brought to the campus for one quarter each included John W. Cline, from China; James W. Hitch, Korea; and Ben O. Hill, Cuba.[31]

By the beginning of 1922, a "core faculty" began to develop. Four members of that group were James Kilgore, a member of the first faculty; James Seehorn Seneker, Robert W. Goodloe, and John H. Hicks, the last three remaining until their retirement in the 1950s.[32] Other faculty were Paul B. Kern, Comer Woodward, Harvie Branscomb, J. M. Ormond, D. L. Mumpower (medical missionary from Africa), S. A. Stewart (from Hiroshima, Japan),[33] and J. C. C. Newton, Dean of Kwansei Gakuin College (also in Japan).[34]

Three new faculty members were added in 1924: J. Richard Spann in City Church, Ora Miner in Town and Country Church, and Henry G. Barnett in Missions.[35] Woodward, who had come in 1918, left to take a job with the Georgia State Department of Public Welfare.[36] Spann and Miner, together with Barnett temporarily, formed an expanded Missions department in cooperation with the Board of Missions.

Other part-time or temporary faculty included during the period were Paul W. Quillian, also a student;[37] R. E. Dickenson, whose primary work was as chaplain and teacher of Religion in the undergraduate school;[38] George M. Gibson, W. A. Smart, John C. Calhoun, George F. Thomas,[39] and Edmund F. Cook.[40] Prior to 1922, undergraduate Bible courses had been listed under "General Literature." In 1922 a separate department of English Bible was established with Mims T. Workman as Professor of Bible.[41]

Persons in the administration of the School of Theology during this early period included Lillian Jennings who, it would appear, served not only as registrar but also as Dean Kern's administrative assistant. She came to the staff in 1921 and became secretary of the faculty along with her other responsibilities.[42] She was also in charge of the newly opened Marvin and Pierce Halls.[43] There is very little in the sources about her personally, but one gets the impression that she could have operated, and to some extent did run, the School without the Dean's assistance. She died prematurely of typhoid fever on 10 July 1925.[44] She was succeeded by Miss Nell Anders who had been at the school earlier; Miss Anders remained as Registrar for more than thirty years.

Others in administration included Annie Mae Galbreath, the Dean's secretary; Louise Gillon, secretary of the Correspondence School, and Mrs. A. H. Anglin, secretary to the faculty.[45] Mrs. Kate Warnick became theology librarian upon the move of the library to the newly built Kirby Hall in 1924.[46]

One new full-time faculty member was added during Kern's last year as Dean, namely, C. M. Bishop to fill the place vacated by Harvie Branscomb's resignation.[47] According to an issue of the *Semi-Weekly Campus* of a later date, C. M. Bishop was the nephew of Horace Bishop, the first chair of SMU's Board of Trustees.[48] Additional short-term faculty consisted of James T. Meyer and Alfred W. Wasson,[49] the latter becoming a full-time faculty member at a later date. Of the total faculty of eleven full-time and two part-time faculty in 1925–

26, six remained until their retirements. When Kern left as Dean in 1926, James Kilgore was the only member of the 1915 faculty remaining. Kilgore served as acting Dean for the following seven years (1926–33).

A New Home for the School of Theology

For its first eight years the School of Theology shared facilities with the remainder of the University in Dallas Hall. In the fall of 1924, it moved into its own building, Kirby Hall, now Florence Hall in the School of Law quadrangle. Still not finished when the move was made, Kirby Hall was the gift of Mr. and Mrs. Harper Kirby of Austin, members of First Methodist Episcopal Church, South, of that city, and "militant Methodists" according to W. D. Bradfield, whose friendship with the Kirbys resulted in the gift.[50] They had previously provided a loan fund[51] and had also built a dormitory for women near the University of Texas campus. The gift of $100,000, not sufficient to cover the total cost of the building, was announced on 31 May 1923,[52] and plans were approved the same year.[53] Bids were let in January 1924.[54]

Kern envisioned this building as one of three or four in a quadrangle at the northwest corner of the campus.[55] The cornerstone of Kirby Hall was laid during the Fondren Lectures the last week of March 1924,[56] and the first classes were held on the only complete floor, the third, on 24 September 1924.[57] The dream of having its own facilities had come true, and one sad by-product was that the School of Theology no longer was, by geography, an integral part of the life of the University. This condition has continued through the years with periodic attempts to bridge the gap.

A further step in this particularizing of the School of Theology was proposed in a plan to strengthen the School of Theology Committee of the Board of Trustees. The organization of the administration was a Board of Trustees representing largely the Annual Conferences and responsible to their Annual Conferences and ultimately to the General Conference of the Methodist Episcopal Church, South. The group that provided the daily operation of the University was the Executive Committee which met monthly and was dominated by lay people in Dallas. Dean Kern, supported by Bishop Mouzon and Bishop Moore, believed that the School of Theology needed a stronger committee than existed. Such a committee was to be, though they did not use the term, a kind of "Executive Committee of the School of Theology."[58] Although their plan was not carried out fully, there was a gradual strengthening of this committee over the years, but it met only in conjunction with the Board of Trustees.

In spite of the separation from the remainder of the University, the new building provided a great boon to the School of Theology. The other buildings were never built, though as we shall later see it was only the vision of Bishop John M. Moore that moved the Theology quadrangle to the southern part of the campus in the late 1940s. The words of the Kirbys with regard to their gift is a fitting way to conclude this section:

Having profound faith in the Divinity of Jesus Christ, knowing God's guidance, and His Boundless love for mankind, and His great desire that all men shall be saved, and believing firmly in Christian education, we will give one hundred thousand dollars to the Southern Methodist University at Dallas, Texas, for a theological building.

Sincerely,
Mr. and Mrs. R. Harper Kirby[59]

Curriculum

If curricular change indicates the vitality of a school, then the deanship of Paul Kern was a vital period. In 1924 the University changed from the quarter to the semester system, and the School of Theology faculty saw this as a good time for curriculum revision. Five areas of specialization were established: General Pastorate, Town and Country Church, Social Service and City Work, Foreign Missions, and Religious Education. All the areas had the basic requirement of six semester hours in Old Testament, New Testament, Church History, Christian Doctrine, Philosophy of Religion, Religious Education, Ministerial Efficiency (including Homiletics), Missions, and Sociology, with three in Public Speaking for a total of fifty-seven semester hours. A biblical language was no longer required. The remainder of the students' work was elective, with a major subject, requiring a total of ninety credit hours.[60] Both an oral examination before the entire faculty with the Dean presiding and a thesis were also mandatory.[61]

Two years later the School of Theology requested permission to return to the quarter plan,[62] and to label courses as "majors" and "minors." A major was one-third of a quarter's work, ten per year, and a minor was one-half of a major. No longer were requirements uniform in the various areas. Four majors were required in New Testament, three in Old Testament, and one each in Christian Doctrine, Philosophy of Religion, Christian Doctrine or Philosophy of Religion, Church History, Homiletics, Ministerial Efficiency, Religious Education, and Sociology, with two minors in Church Music and four minors in Public Speaking. Both the oral examination and the thesis were retained.[63] Those majoring in one of the Testaments were required to have a reading knowledge of the appropriate language, and six majors were required in the major field.[64]

A new degree was begun in 1925, the M.C.A. (Master of Church Administration) under the direction of J. Richard Spann.[65]

Extension Work

As we saw in Chapter 2, the School of Theology saw its work from the beginning as including persons who were not registered in a degree program. Called "extension work," much of this work would now be considered "continuing education." There were several major forms of such work.

The Preachers' Summer Assembly and Western Training School for Sunday School had begun in 1919,[66] as we saw in the previous chapter, and the combined school continued for several years. This led to the formation in 1924 of the "Extension School," co-sponsored by the School of Theology, the Board of Education, the Board of Missions, and the Sunday School Board of the M. E. Church, South. The work could be done either in the extension school or by correspondence, and the first school was held in 1925.[67] J. Richard Spann was in charge of the Pastors' School[68] and Louise Gillon was in charge of the Correspondence Division. According to a report she made in January 1925, more than 400 students were enrolled for correspondence work, from as far away as Washington, Oregon, California, and Montana.[69] Sixty-nine enrolled in the Extension School for Pastors beginning 1 January 1925.[70] Undergraduate courses were conducted for those seeking to fulfill ordination requirements, and advanced studies for those already in the conference.[71]

The Library

For the first ten years of the University's life, there was only one library, housed in Dallas Hall. Space was limited however, and even if funds had been available, there would have been no place to house a larger number of books.

The core of the theology library was formed by the Shettles Collection and a Methodist Historical Collection.[72] The Whited Fund was given quite early and had reached the sum of $10,000 by February 1921.[73] The John A. Rice Fund for books in Old Testament was established in 1921, with the first gift coming from Trinity Church, Sumter, South Carolina, where Rice had been pastor before coming to SMU. It had reached a total of $4,500 in February 1921.[74]

Questions were raised concerning whether the theological library should be moved to the new building, Kirby Hall, or remain a part of the main library. At first only reserved books and periodicals were sent to the new location, but during the Christmas vacation of 1925 the entire theological library was moved to Kirby Hall.[75] Dean Kern asked that Mrs. John Warnick become the theology librarian,[76] a post which she accepted and occupied until 1950. After 1950, she served as Reference Librarian and later as curator of the Methodist Historical Library until her final retirement in 1979.

Student Housing

When SMU opened, it had a permanent building for housing women, the North Texas Building, later Atkins Hall and now Clements Hall. Three hastily built dormitories housed male students: Rankin, North, and South Halls. No housing was available for married students on campus, and very little in the immediate vicinity. Highland Park was a city of private homes, and University Park was not incorporated until 1924. Because forty percent of the theology students in 1923 were married,[77] housing was a critical need.

The first step in solving the problem was the purchase of a building just north of the campus at the corner of Airline and Rosedale, where a University Park water tower is now located. The Executive Committee authorized the purchase on 2 September 1920.[78] There is no record of why the building was there, but it required repairs when it was purchased and had so deteriorated by 1935 that it was no longer habitable and was sold to University Park.[79]

In July 1922 the Executive Committee authorized the building of two additional apartment houses.[80] They were wooden, two-story buildings located just to the east of the main campus. They were occupied in the fall of 1922.[81] Their official names were Marvin and Pierce Halls, but were popularly known as the Bee Hive. Many theological students lived there over almost thirty years before they too were demolished.

A third change in student housing, this time for singles, occurred when the three men's dormitories burned on 11 February 1926. A group of theology students who lived in Rankin, the middle building, helped to save possessions of students who lived in the first to burn, and then when Rankin caught fire were unable to save their own.[82] Before the incident was over, all three buildings had been destroyed along with University Park's new fire truck, which became mired in the mud and could not be freed.[83] A committee was appointed to help relocate the students, and money was received from a wide variety of sources to help those who had lost their possessions.[84]

Fortunately, plans were already under way for the building of two women's dormitories, Snyder and Virginia Halls. This made it possible for the women to move out of North Texas Hall when the dormitories were completed less than a year later, and for the men to occupy what later came to be called Atkins Hall, after Bishop Atkins, the chair of the Educational Commission which authorized the founding of SMU.[85] Male students, including theology students, lived in Atkins Hall until the new theology quadrangle was built twenty-five years later.

"The Search for Greatness"

Earlier, we noted that from its beginning SMU seems to have been pre-occupied with a "search for greatness." One small search for greatness appeared in the form of the new M.C.A. degree, for non-ordained church professionals. Like many such efforts, the degree did not draw a great many students, but Kern seemed proud of this attempt to increase the School of Theology's offerings.[86]

Earlier than the beginning of this degree a much grander plan was considered—but never carried out. In 1922, the Executive Committee of the University accepted a proposal to establish a "School of Christian Service" which would include the School of Theology but involve other sorts of work also. It was to be a joint effort with the School of Theology and the Boards of Missions and Education of the Methodist Episcopal Church, South, the Sunday School, the Epworth League, and the Woman's Missionary Council. The faculty was to be an integral part of the University.[87] Another facet of this plan was the establishing of a School of Missions at Southern Methodist and Emory Universities.[88] A few months later, the possibility of including Scarritt as part of the plan was revived.[89] The negotiations over Scarritt continued for some time but never materialized.[90] Nor did the special school become a reality, though the Board of Missions and the Women's Missionary Council did grant almost $10,000 yearly to the School of Theology for work in Missions. Unfortunately, it appears that they did not always provide the full amount and so their plan also did not persist.

What would have happened to SMU's School of Theology had either the joint enterprise with the Boards or the moving of Scarritt to SMU come about? The least one can say is that had either plan materialized, subsequent history would have been considerably different.

Students

The most difficult area of history of the School of Theology to secure information about is that of student life. There are occasional references to student activities—an annual picnic[91] for example. An undated document in the school's archives reports on the 1925 picnic and gives plans for the 1926 festivities. According to the report, 143 students attended in 1925 and thirty faculty, staff, and visitors. The *Semi-Weekly Campus* reported that about 150 attended, that Joe Connally won the men's beauty context and that Miss Nell Anders was winner of the "Prim and Precise Contest."[92]

Intramural sports were at first for fraternities only[93] but were later expanded to include other groups, including the School of Theology.[94] A myriad of organizations existed on the SMU campus, and theology students regularly participated in them.[95] Although Paul Martin was not a theological student at the time, his description of his own participation in the student life of the University is illuminating. He writes:

The small town boy entered heartily the activities. I was a cheer leader, a debater, the editor of the 1918 Annual *The Rotunda*. I sang in the Glee Club and played Shakespeare in the Arden Club on the steps of Dallas hall. As a sophomore, I sold chapel tickets to the freshmen. I did not participate in the tying of the calf to the piano just before chapel one morning, but I thoroughly enjoyed the strange sight.[96]

A Ministerial Association was organized in 1925 with W. A. Bonner, Walter Towner and Joe Connally among its officers.[97] There is little information about the Theology Students' Association, but we can infer that it was continued after its organization during the early part of the University's first year.

It is difficult—and risky—to select outstanding graduates, but a few stand out in terms of their later accomplishments. We have already noted two M.A. graduates in the first class who later assumed leadership roles in the University—Umphrey Lee and Robert W. Goodloe. Paul Martin, later a bishop, entered SMU in 1915, prior to his deciding to enter the ordained ministry.[98] He later felt his calling to the set-apart ministry and returned to SMU in 1922 for theological training.[99] His friendship with Mr. and Mrs. J. J. Perkins during his pastorate at Wichita Falls, and his continued close association with them after he became bishop, played a large part in their making of their magnificent gift to the School of Theology many years later. He later served as Bishop-in-Residence at Perkins School of Theology after his retirement from the episcopacy.

William C. Martin, later a bishop, graduated from the School of Theology in 1921,[100] and while he was Bishop of the Dallas-Fort Worth Area from 1948 to 1964 was a strong supporter of the School of Theology.[101] Kenneth Pope, later a bishop, came to SMU as a junior student in 1920, received the B.A. degree in 1923 and the B.D. in 1924.[102] Bishop Pope, like Bishop W. C. Martin, served both as Bishop of the Dallas-Fort Worth Area and later as Bishop in Residence at the School of Theology. While he was Bishop, at a time when the School of Theology was under periodic attack, he invited the District Superintendents of the North and Central Texas Conferences for lunch with the faculty, and in the course of his presentation noted that he was using Schubert Ogden's latest book for his devotions.[103] Ogden was the theologian most frequently under attack at the time.

Another bishop from these early days was Eleazar Guerra, bishop in Mexico, who received his Bachelor of Divinity degree in 1926.[104]

In fact, the School of Theology had rather quickly taken on an international flavor. In 1922 ten such students were in attendance: from Japan, Brazil, Korea, Mexico, France, Guatemala, and Russia.[105] Up through 1923 sixty-nine international students had received the B.D. degree and five Americans had gone to other countries as missionaries. The best known perhaps was Earl Moreland, who received the B.A. degree in 1918 and the M.A. and B.D. in 1921.[106] He soon went to Brazil to a college which Bishop John M. Moore had helped to establish in Porto Allegre. Later Moreland became its President. For many years the students of SMU in Dallas raised money to support what had become known as "Little SMU in Brazil."[107] Moreland concluded his college administration as President of Randolph-Macon College. Sam Hillburn went to Japan, Jalmar Bowden to Brazil, H. H. Washington to Cuba, and R. A. Taylor to Japan.[108]

The number of B.D. graduates remained small during this period. For example, the SMU Alumni Directory lists only seven for 1926 (though this may be an incomplete list).[109] Usually the graduate B.D. students were a minority in the student body. In these early years SMU's theological studies program was not, as it later became, primarily a graduate level program but rather included undergraduates, as well as those in special programs. Many of these students held pastorates,[110] and others held jobs as varied as waiting tables in the dormitories and selling shoes.[111]

Dean Paul B. Kern

All of what we have considered in this chapter occurred under the deanship of Paul B. Kern, later a bishop, and much during the presidency of Charles C. Selecman, also later a bishop. We shall have more to say about Selecman later, but what about Paul Kern? Kern took the deanship after five years of the school's existence, with two deans and an acting dean having served during that early period. Kern brought stability and maturity to the school. The impression one gets from the data is that he was a kind and considerate person who perhaps at times did not take as strong a stand as might have been desirable. Many years later, one of his colleagues talked of Kern as if he had really been the only Dean the School of Theology had had.[112]

Kern was essentially a pastor at heart. He returned to the pastorate in 1926, going to Travis Park Methodist Church in San Antonio, from which he was elected to the episcopacy in 1930. It is difficult to assess his contribution to the School of Theology. The least one can say is that he provided a sound foundation on which others later would build.

If he was a pastor at heart, he also believed strongly in the work of the School of Theology, as the following story from Kenneth Pope illustrates:

At one time I went to Dean Paul B. Kern of the School of Theology and expressed a desire to quit school in order to get to the firing line at once. The Dean said a word or two about the need for an adequate foundation for the ministry and then told me of a student who, like myself, wanted to quit school and start preaching. His advisor said that if the student would tell him where he, the student, would be preaching on Sunday, he, the advisor, would go out and preach for him if he would stay in school. The Lord gave me sense enough to take Dean Kern's advice.[113]

4

Controversy and Conflict

Southern Methodist University underwent an unprecedented series of crises and conflicts in the early 1920s. Although not all of these directly affected the School of Theology, two of them did and the others had indirect effects on that school. The first to be discussed, though not the first chronologically, was a football scandal. Harvie Branscomb, a new member of the Theology faculty, was a member of the Athletic Committee, and it is easy to surmise that the process of conflict with the administration which eventually led to his resignation began because of the stand he took on complete faculty control of athletics.

The First Football Scandal

Before H. A. Boaz was elected a bishop in 1922, he decided that it was time for SMU to undertake an all-out effort to develop a winning football team. In the fall of 1921, a superior freshman team was ready to take the field in preparation for their becoming part of the varsity the following year.[1] But Boaz was elected to the episcopacy in 1922, leaving the University without a permanent president during much of the ensuing controversy over football. James S. Kilgore of the School of Theology was acting President for almost twelve months, until April 1923.

The 1922 football season was SMU's most successful to that time, with the team's winning five games out of nine and tying one, with only three losses.[2] New rules had been set up by the Southwest Conference, however, including one that "No athlete was to be paid for work that he did not perform."[3] In December 1922 an investigating committee of the Southwest Conference recommended that SMU be suspended from the conference until the faculty gained control of athletics, in order to eliminate rule infractions including pay for work not performed. The major issue became whether townspeople or the faculty should control athletics. This led to a larger issue, the role of faculty and members of the Executive Committee (and ultimately the Board of Trustees) as the controlling factor in operating the University.

The issues were not really settled even after Charles Selecman became President. Branscomb concluded that the faculty "had gained a measure of

39

control but was not receiving full co-operation."[4] This was essentially where the matter lay when the Board of Trustees voted to close the affair, with at least a visible nod in the direction of faculty control and with the conclusions that "any irregularities that did occur were due to the rapid growth of the University."[5]

Background to Theological Controversy

The football scandal had touched the School of Theology only through Harvie Branscomb's participation as a member of the Athletic Committee. Other controversies directly affected that school, the first of which occurred in 1921. This grew out of the fundamentalist-modernist controversy whose development coincided with the founding of SMU.

The beginning of the fundamentalist movement goes back at least to the early twentieth century. Its basics were set forth in ten small volumes in 1910 entitled *The Fundamentals: A Testimony to the Truth.*[6] The five fundamentals were: (1) the verbal inspiration of the Bible (and its inerrancy); (2) the virgin birth of Jesus Christ; (3) Christ's substitutionary atonement; (4) his bodily resurrection; and (5) his immanent and visible Second Coming.[7] Fundamentalism went beyond most orthodoxy and seemed to say that one's salvation depended on accepting these beliefs. It was a reaction against the growing liberalism of the main-line churches and their tendency to emphasize the "fundamentals" of Adolf Harnack: (1) the Kingdom of God and its coming; (2) God as Father and the infinite worth of the human soul; and (3) the ethical message of the Gospel, especially the law of love.[8]

Methodism in both its Northern and Southern branches had been especially vulnerable to the inroads of an optimistic, nineteenth century liberalism. This approach, of course, included a non-literalistic view of biblical truth. Methodism's anti-Calvinistic roots and its emphasis on personal experience were simply inconsistent with the rationalistic approach of fundamentalism, which provoked a kind of "belief-righteousness" which would have had to replace the tendency of Methodism towards a "works-righteousness." In other words, fundamentalism tends to emphasize salvation by right beliefs while John Wesley's concern for holiness of heart and life had led Methodism to tend to assert salvation by good works. A gradual change occurred over a fifty year period. I once went through all editions of the Methodist *Book of Discipline* to see what they said about education and nurture. As I reflected on my reading, it became clear that the nurture ("liberal") side of education gradually came into prominence beginning about 1880 and reached its climax about 1930. Walter N. Vernon confirms this, though he does not use the exact period that I have suggested.[9]

This is not to suggest that all Methodists had become "liberals" theologically. On the whole the clergy was more liberal than the laity, but some clergy even joined the fundamentalist ranks. Perhaps, however, the two major controversies that rocked SMU would not have occurred had it not been for fundamentalists beyond the bounds of Methodism.

The situation in Methodism needs to be seen also against the environment in which SMU existed. We have already noted that not all of Methodism subscribed to the more liberal tone of official Methodism. This was especially true in the so-called "Bible Belt."[10] Here a conservative view of the Bible prevailed. Perhaps even more pertinent is the fact that the SMU of the 1920s did not actively encourage a spirit of free inquiry. Essentially SMU was a religious school. Revivals were held on campus; chapel was required; at times even attending Sunday worship was mandatory. Generally, the church expected all of SMU to be Christian-oriented, not just its School of Theology. As Kenneth Pope put it, "SMU was not only a Methodist 'owned' University, it was a Methodist 'run' University." In this conservative milieu, he adds, "Conferences made pronouncements on the affairs of [their] educational institutions."[11]

Even as early as the academic year 1917–18, an English instructor, Katherine Balderson, raised eyebrows and evoked an "inquisition" before the theological faculty. The point in question was a discussion of "biblical criticism" in a novel by Winston Churchill, *The Inside of the Cup.* She was exonerated but soon left the University.[12]

The Rice Affair

It is not surprising, then, that John A. Rice's book, *The Old Testament in the Life of Today,*[13] created a stir. The book was published shortly after he came to the School of Theology.[14] It was not something he produced in an academic "ivory tower." "The substance of its chapters," according to a pamphlet produced in his defense, "had been delivered upon innumerable platforms in Methodism and had been the means of strengthening the faith of many men and women in the Bible as the living message of God to modern life."[15] Rice had been a pastor all his ministerial life and came directly from a pastorate in Sumter, South Carolina.

The book was well received in many circles. S. Parkes Cadman called the book "the best book on the Old Testament."[16] Numerous commendations are included in the pamphlet supporting Rice.[17]

What is the book like? The impression one gets from reading it is that Rice was a person of great personal faith who had accepted the latest findings of what was unfortunately called "higher criticism."[18] In the introduction, he wrote:

[T]he Bible must be judged in the light of its purpose, which is to bring God and men into such satisfying relations with each other as that they shall work together in blessed fellowship for the creation of a new social order characterized by righteousness, peace, and the joy of holy living over all the earth. Should errors in history, science, philosophy, or in any other field of inquiry be found, they need not disturb us. The infallibility of our inspired book depends not upon these, but rather upon the effective achieving of the end it sought and still seeks.[19]

And at the end of the book he wrote:

This marvellous collection of booklets, more than half poetry, mostly anonymous, seeks no defence, shuns no attack, asks only that we test the pledge it brings of God's saving and satisfying touch upon the human spirit, and venture upon its promise of a world redeemed through Jesus Christ our Lord in whom dwelt all the fullness of the Godhead bodily.[20]

In between these statements is a great deal of material dealing with both the content and form of the Old Testament. He begins with the earliest poetic fragments from 1400 to 1200 B.C.;[21] goes through the JEDP origin of the Pentateuch;[22] writes an extensive analysis of the prophets from 750 to 500 B.C. (and includes Deuteronomy in this discussion);[23] discusses further the priestly sources and compilations, including the Psalms;[24] provides an overview of the "sages and their philosophy" (which for him includes more than what we usually call Wisdom Literature);[25] and includes a brief section on apocalyptic literature (in which he puts Haggai, Zechariah, Malachi, Isaiah 24–27, Isaiah 34–35, Joel, and Daniel).[26] The final section deals with text and canon.[27] Not on a par with Bewer, Muilenberg, and von Rad, the book nevertheless summarizes the best sources of its time and was a viable text for beginning Old Testament students. It pulls no punches concerning the critical analysis of sources and form, however, and it is easy to see how it would be upsetting to many people even today. Perhaps the amazing fact is how widespread at SMU and among his other students the support of Rice was.

The book's critics used the usual methods of quoting out of context, misinterpretation, and similar ways of proving their point. For example, he was quoted as saying, "The Bible cannot survive as a fixed rule of faith and practice, for which it was never intended."[28] The sentence occurs in a paragraph where he discusses the finished Torah at the time of Ezra and Nehemiah. The Torah, he asserts, became severely binding and "was in the strictest sense a rule of faith and practice." This resulted in the "complicated, lifeless pharisaism prevalent in Jesus' time." "The letter killeth," he writes. "It always does." But there are some even in Protestantism who subscribe to this attitude toward the Bible, those who insist on a literal interpretation of the Bible.[29]

> They do not seem to realize that they are seeking to enforce ideas Christ came to explode. The Bible cannot survive as a fixed rule of faith and practice for which it was never intended. It is rather the world's greatest book of religious experience on whose pages, inspired because inspiring, we meet God face to face and find rest unto our souls.[30]

He was accused of calling the prophets "roving dervishes."[31] He does use this term, but for the early "prophets," or the pre-prophetic movement. I Samuel 10:12 is cited as seeming to describe the prophets of that time as "peripatetic clairvoyants, teachers, preachers, entertainers, religious enthusiasts, dervishes roving about, often in groups, from the centers where they lived together."[32] In another place he spoke of Saul as raving "among the prophets who were little more than roving dervishes."[33] Of course, Rice is referring to the pre-prophetic movement which existed centuries before those great ones of the Old Testament—Amos, Hosea, Micah, Isaiah, Jeremiah, and others.

The pamphlet defending Rice continues with other examples of misinterpretation and other ways of provoking a negative impression of the book.[34]

Who were the critics? There were Methodists who wrote to the *Texas Christian Advocate*,[35] but the most vocal critic was a person whom the pamphlet identifies only as "a Baptist preacher."[36] From other sources, we know that the Baptist preacher was J. Frank Norris, an early fundamentalist, pastor of First Baptist, Fort Worth. Norris actually withdrew his congregation from the Southern Baptist Convention, was involved in a much publicized murder case, and purposively sought out "liberals" and attempted to destroy them. Norris called Rice agnostic, atheist, and infidel, and concluded that the devil had decided that Bob Ingersoll was not effective as an attacker of Christianity from outside and instead had secured Rice as an inside emissary.[37]

Many people also came to Rice's defense. A group of students wrote a defense in which they said that "Dr. Rice has made the Bible a living book to us and that our ideas of its divine inspiration and value have been greatly strengthened."[38]

A faculty statement signed by Branscomb and concurred in by Dean Kern and Professors Woodward, Kilgore, Seneker, and Workman contains these sentences:

> That we do not accept the judgment of Dr. Rice revealed in the articles of his critics in recent issues of the *Texas Christian Advocate,* and that we insist that in view of Dr. Rice's statement of faith and conformity with Methodist beliefs it is not proper for us to pass judgment upon his orthodoxy as a Methodist preacher and teacher. We insist that the admin-

istration shall say very frankly to our constituency that the University is conducting a theological seminary upon the recognized principles of the modern historical method of biblical interpretation, always in conformity with Methodist and Christian fundamentals.[39]

The minutes of the Executive Committee of the Board of Trustees contain a long statement on 4 October 1921, including these words: "It is to be feared that some of Dr. Rice's over-zealous critics reveal a lack of robustness in their own faith when they seek to suppress freedom of thought and speech in matters pertaining to the Bible."[40]

The faculty of the School of Theology in the document quoted above recommended that the matter be held in abeyance until the meeting of the Board of Trustees in June 1922.[41] The Executive Committee, however, in spite of their words of commendation, accepted Rice's resignation on 11 October 1921. Rice did not back down on his conclusions in the book but reported that he was resigning for the good of the institution.[42] Six weeks later the Executive Committee asked S. B. Perkins and A. D. Schuessler to work out a financial adjustment for Rice,[43] and in December they authorized that he be paid the amount due him on the full year of his salary, and that he be compensated for the $8,000.27 he had spent in building his house, less $100 per month rent during the time he occupied it.[44] As we saw in Chapter 3, Bishop Mouzon, a supporter of Rice, provided an appointment for him in Oklahoma, later assigning him to Boston Avenue Church where he was pastor when the church selected its present unique architectural style.

Why did the administration of the University and the Executive Committee give in when neither appears to have favored Rice's leaving? There is no clear answer to this question. Thomas's answer is really no answer at all, that they simply surrendered to a vocal fundamentalist element in Texas Methodism. Perhaps the ability of J. Frank Norris to get publicity for the causes he espoused also contributed to this result. But the question remains, why did they do this? Perhaps it was to avoid further controversy, to offer, as it were, a sacrificial lamb to the opposition. Bishop O. Eugene Slater has told me that, as he prepared to enter the School of Theology as a student, one person let him know that it was all right for him to go since they had got rid of the troublemaker, Rice. It was many years later, during the administration of President Willis Tate, that the battle for academic freedom was fought and won. For the time being, in the 1920s, the faculty desired such freedom but it simply did not exist.

Mims T. Workman

The lack of protection for faculty members is illustrated once again in the case of Mims Thornburgh Workman a few years later. Workman's work was primarily in the undergraduate school though he had a continuing relationship to the School of Theology. Since Thomas has given full account of the Workman case, the presentation here will be less detailed than for the Rice case.[45]

The Workman case began in May 1923 when the World Christian Fundamental Conference met in Fort Worth and "tried" SMU and other Methodist schools "for the dissemination of rationalistic instruction, of evolutionary thought, of higher criticism, of teaching alleged to be inimical to the Bible as a book of Divine inspiration."[46] Workman, who came to SMU in 1920, was the principal target of criticism at SMU. One of his students, Margaret Pelley, testified that what she had been taught at SMU weakened her faith.[47]

Other students countered the charges. One was Charles Ferguson, then editor of the *Campus* and later one of the senior editors of *Reader's Digest* and the author of a number of substantial books. Another, Mary Vaughn Morgan, said: "While at SMU I have learned to exalt Him [Jesus Christ] as never before. I have come to trust Him more surely as my personal Savior and to more fully dedicate my life to the spread of His Gospel."[48]

The Board of Trustees asked Bishop John M. Moore and the newly elected President Charles C. Selecman to look into the matter, and no action was taken against Workman at this time. The action changed two years later, in 1925, when Selecman requested Dean Jennings of Arts and Science to encourage Workman either to take a leave of absence or resign.[49]

Students again rallied to Workman's defense. One said: "If those of us who disagree with his [Workman's] teachings would live as close to the Master as he does, and could shed as much of Christ's love as he does, perhaps we could come to know that it really means to live what we believe."[50] Another commented: "I have seen as much of the spirit of Christ in the life of my teacher [Workman] as I have seen in any man."[51] The student body presented a petition to the Board of Trustees asking that he be allowed to remain at the University,[52] and a *Campus* editorial supported him.[53]

None of this support deterred the Board of Trustees, however, and so when the Board met on 1 June 1925, his resignation was asked for and accepted.[54] Thomas concludes, rightly, I think, that his "career never quite recovered from these events."[55] Good and faithful Bishop Mouzon secured a teaching post for him, and he later taught at Vanderbilt. After a few years he changed to the pastorate but never quite seemed to make it there.[56]

Again we may ask, why did President Selecman not support Workman? Just two years earlier he had declared fundamentalists as "religious misfits." He had also declared that "hide-bound liberalism had no place in true Methodist doctrine."[57] Thomas, who is not always kind to Selecman in her history of

SMU, concludes that he feared what controversy might do to the raising of money (probably a legitimate concern but a dangerous one), and that his love of "inner harmony" in the University was well known.[58] Whatever the cause—legitimate or not—academic freedom suffered another setback on the SMU campus.

Harvie Branscomb and the Administration

The occasion which prompted Harvie Branscomb's forced resignation was criticism that he made in the press of the University's administration concerning the Workman case.[59] As Branscomb later liked to tell it, he was "fired before breakfast in his pajamas" after Selecman had read the story in the morning paper. President Selecman's exact words, as Branscomb reported them to Thomas in 1971, were: "I have just read your gratuitous letter in the morning *News* and want to say to you that the sooner you leave this campus the better."[60]

The conflict between Branscomb and the administration actually began before Selecman became President. As we have seen, Branscomb was a member of the Athletic Committee when the football scandal occurred. The committee criticized the administration for its favoritism toward athletics. A conflict between the committee and R. H. Shuttles, later chair of the Board, led to Shuttle's resignation from the Board, a resignation that was not accepted.[61] This conflict with Shuttles, strangely enough, foreshadowed a conflict with President Selecman some years later and was based on Shuttles's belief that businessmen ought to run the university.

The athletic problem occurred in 1922–23. Shortly after, Branscomb went on leave to work on his doctorate at Union Theological Seminary and Columbia University. The Rice affair was still fresh in his mind, and the football scandal had apparently raised questions for Branscomb about the security of faculty at the new University.

In late 1923 (or perhaps 1924) Branscomb wrote a letter[62] to Dean Kern which Kern interpreted as questioning his integrity in supporting faculty members who received outside criticism.[63] The tenor of Branscomb's response is that what he was questioning in the letter was not Kern's personal desires in such matters but what Kern could *in fact* do. Branscomb had felt the pressure of the Shuttles affair (in the conflict between "town and gown"), and expressed his feelings in these words:

> What I tried to ask in my letter was not about your personal motives nor intentions but rather what policy you could maintain. Of course I know the difficulties under which you labor. That is the simple reason why I asked my question and what I meant by it. What we would like to do we cannot, because of the responsibilities and accountabilities of office, always

accomplish. Thus in the Rice case referred to above you will remember that
tho we felt that the charges were unfair and we unconditionally stood for
Dr. Rice, at the same time it was felt that all we could ask for was a trial
before the complete board. That is why I asked for the "dean's administrative policy." Much has happened since the memorable Rice fight. Among
other things the tables have turned some what and I feel the chairman of
the board of Trustees and member of the administrative committee my
avowed and implacable opponent. I therefore merely tried to ask what the
dean had come to feel that he *could* stand for in such a case.[64]

Kern's response is enlightening but not altogether clear since I have not been
able to ascertain to what committee Judge Cockrell had been appointed, nor is
it clear concerning the situation of which he is speaking. The intent of the letter
is the purpose for quoting part of it here:

I sincerely regret that the incident regarding Judge Cockrell's opponent on
the committee occurred as it did. I can now, only with difficulty, place
myself back in the mental attitude of those distressing days when it looked
as if our faculty would split into a sullen majority against an illogical
minority. I was deeply distressed. I have laid all of my plans before the
faculty in great detail and I now have no recollection whatever of
purposely withholding from my colleagues the matter of the Judge's
coming on the committee. In fact, I think now that most of them understood
it and understood the reasons prompting it; and if the matter was not
discussed with you, it is chargeable to the distraught condition of my mind
and not to any deliberate purpose to conceal. I am really surprised to learn
that the matter went through to its consummation without every member
of the faculty knowing what was being done; and I shall always regret that
you feel that I withheld this information, however guileless may be the
purpose which you are willing to attribute to me for withholding it.

  Perhaps, after all, you ought not pin too much dependence upon me or
any other single individual, but come down and join hands with us and
work together in faith and good spirit to make a better world around us and
a better ministry for the church. Certainly we desire the same great ends;
and the matter of the individual who leads may be both temporary and after
all only a part of the great effort to bring in a new day.[65]

Branscomb did return to the campus for the fall semester of 1924, and six
months later was offered a position teaching at Duke University.[66] Kern immediately responded to Branscomb and offered a raise in salary if he would
accept a new position for which Kern had already received approval, Dean of
Students.[67] Branscomb did not accept the position at Duke nor is there any

record that he became Dean of Students at the School of Theology. A letter to
Kern from Branscomb dated 18 January 1926, after Branscomb had gone to
Duke, reveals that Branscomb's orthodoxy was being investigated.[68] The letter
is in Branscomb's handwriting.

> Has the discussion of "is" or "contains" in the findings report died down?
> If it hasn't I wish to call to the attention of all who are interested the
> following fact: my wording is that of John Wesley and the Articles of
> Religion. If you will look at article five of the latter you will find that the
> phrase there is that the "Holy Scripture contains . . ."[69] Now I do not aspire
> to be more orthodox than the Articles of Religion. I don't think that greater
> orthodoxy should be insisted upon in ephemeral documents such as our
> findings. Please pass this on to my friends, if the occasion arises.[70]

Apparently this investigation of Branscomb's orthodoxy was under way
prior to his accepting a position at Duke. Thus, the event which led to his leaving
SMU must be seen as only a part of a series stemming back to his reaction to
the football scandal. That catalytic event was Branscomb's criticism of the
interpretation of a faculty vote of confidence in the administration, in a letter
which he wrote to the *Dallas Morning News* and which was published on 30
May 1925. In part, Branscomb said:

> If the faculty members of good training, acknowledged orthodoxy and
> wholesome influence are to be discharged because of the no doubt sincere
> objections of those outside the University who misunderstand them, I see
> little hope of building here in SMU the spirit necessary to a great
> university.[71]

If Thomas is correct that President Selecman cherished "inner harmony"
above all else,[72] it is easy to see how Branscomb would be a problem to him.
In any case, Branscomb resigned and went to Duke to continue a distinguished
career as New Testament scholar and administrator.

Outside Investigation

As early as 1922, the Texas Conference was so tired of hearing about heresy
in Methodist institutions that they appointed a committee to try to put such
rumors to rest.[73] A year later the North Texas Conference also appointed such
a committee,[74] and SMU, Texas Wesleyan College (formerly Polytechnic), and
Southwestern were exonerated from charges of heresy.[75] In 1925 the West
Texas Conference appointed a similar committee.[76] There is no record that any
formal charges were ever brought against SMU's School of Theology or any
other Texas Methodist educational institution.

A special committee on orthodoxy in educational institutions was appointed by the General Conference of the M. E. Church, South. Arthur J. Moore (later a bishop) wrote to the School of Theology saying: "Permit me to thank you for the statement regarding doctrinal standards signed by yourself and other members of the theological faculty."[77]

Perhaps it was partly to offset criticism that Dean Kern reported near the end of his tenure as dean on the "fruits" that graduates of the School of Theology had produced.[78] The statistics are rather startling and one can only wonder if some degree of "ministerial estimation" is not involved. According to Kern's report, the graduates had received 2,595 new members by letter and 1,642 by profession of faith, or an average of 75 additions per person. Thirty of the fifty-six respondents had raised conference claimants (the general funds assigned to local churches) in full. Every former student answered "No" to the question, "Has any charge of irregularity in doctrine been made against you . . . ?"[79]

Although the modernist-fundamentalist controversy abated after the 1920s, in one form or another it has always been present, and still is. The underlying question remains: "What degree, if any, of control should the General Conference exercise over its Methodist theological schools concerning what is being taught?" The most common answer in practice has been, "None." Other denominations have taken a different stance on the question. The discussion (when it has taken place) is a part of the larger question regarding the relationship of systematic religion and liberal learning, between Jerusalem and Athens.

Perhaps the question can never be settled. That it should be a question for open dialogue (which it usually has not) seems clear. SMU and its School of Theology have had their share of problems stemming from the unanswered question. Its resolution, if such there is, remains for the future.

5

The Kilgore Years: 1926–33

The seven years of James Kilgore's deanship are relatively uneventful. The circumstances under which he carried out his responsibilities were not conducive to an aggressive administration. He apparently did not know from year to year how long he would be continued as Dean. Mrs. Kilgore was ill during the first years of his term of office, and died on 7 April 1930 after a long illness.[1] During the final years of his deanship, he was facing retirement which occurred in 1934, one year after he had ceased to be Dean.[2] And, of course, there was the Great Depression which became more acute for Texas during the early 1930s. The depression brought increasing problems to the University,[3] and although the School of Theology seems to have fared better than the remainder of the University, it felt the effects of the malaise which struck America as a result of extremely difficult financial times.

James Kilgore was born in the small town of Clinton, Texas, southeast of San Antonio, in 1865. His father originally lived in Maryland and later moved to Ohio.[4] The younger Kilgore became a Methodist minister in the Texas Conference and was serving as Presiding Elder (District Superintendent) of the Houston District when he was asked to serve on the first faculty of the School of Theology in 1915. His relationship to SMU, however, had begun earlier. He was a member of the Educational Commission which established the University, and was a trustee from 1912 to 1935. (Faculty and administrators were permitted to serve as regular members of the Board in those days.)

Herbert Gambrell describes Kilgore as of average height, round-shouldered, and inclined to paunchiness. But he had a firm chin, and his dark hair never turned gray. He was not especially gregarious, but could tell a good story to his friends.[5] When he was asked to be acting President after H. A. Boaz's stormy two years, he requested otherwise, but he was appointed nonetheless.[6] Gambrell urged him to write his recollections of the early SMU. His response was "Oh, no. I know too much."[7]

He brought to both the University and the School of Theology stability, not assertiveness. He was willing to step in and keep the University or the School of Theology operating effectively even when he did not know how long his term would be. He was one of those stable people who help to keep the world, or some part of it, on course, through faithful and stable leadership.

Why was Kilgore never made Dean? There is no evidence that a search was going on all these years for a permanent Dean. It is possible that Selecman had Eugene B. Hawk in mind all the time but had to wait until Hawk was willing to leave the pastorate. Gambrell speculates that a strong permanent Dean might have been a threat to Selecman's election as bishop. He also indicates what I think is true, that at least one and perhaps more on the faculty desired to be Dean. Whatever the cause, Kilgore provided the kind of leadership which kept the school going—and also carried on his responsibilities as a member of the faculty. He actually served as Dean longer than any other person had up through his deanship.

President Selecman

Charles Selecman, who became President of the University in 1923 and continued until 1938, was cut from different cloth. Mary Martha Hosford Thomas concludes that he dealt with the faculty in high-handed and dictatorial ways.[8] She believes that his "concept of what a university should be was often at variance with that of the faculty members who were educated in the liberal arts tradition."[9] He encouraged the development of the practical courses such as business, education, and engineering, and hoped for a winning football team as a way of receiving support from the Dallas business community.[10] I find some of these conclusions difficult to reconcile with the man I knew as a retired bishop living in the former President's home on Hillcrest Avenue across from the Theology quadrangle. There is no question, however, that he was an aggressive President who did not always listen to his faculty.

His background was on the one hand inadequate to prepare him for the University's presidency; he had no undergraduate degree[11] though he had attended Central College in Fayette, Missouri. Yet he had studied social work in England, and had worked for a year at Kingdom House, a settlement house in St. Louis. During the latter part of World War I, he was in France working with U. S. troops, and was pastor of First Church, Dallas, when he was elected President of SMU. He remained as President until he was elected to the episcopacy at the General Conference of the Methodist Episcopal Church, South, meeting in Birmingham, Alabama, in 1938.[12]

The growth of the University during Selecman's administration is significant, almost spectacular. During his first six years, according to a 1929 issue of the *Semi-Weekly Campus*, the value of the buildings increased from $622,000 to $2,000,000, and endowment from $823,000 to $2,700,000.[13] Not all of this was his doing, of course. For example, Kirby Hall, the new theology building, was a result of the friendship between W. D. Bradfield, Professor of Christian Doctrine, and Mr. and Mrs. Harper Kirby. By the time of Selecman's election to the episcopacy eleven new buildings, including Kirby Hall, Hyer Hall, McFarlin Auditorium, Snider and Virginia Residence Halls, Ownby Stadium, and an engineering building had been constructed.[14] The Association of American Universities recognized the University in 1919, and two new schools were begun, Law and Engineering.[15]

Selecman did not wait until all the money for a building had been pledged before beginning construction. As a consequence, the indebtedness in 1931 was $643,505 with $439,763 owed on buildings.[16] An intensive financial campaign in the middle of the Great Depression led to a reduction of the debt to $330,594 by the time Selecman resigned to become bishop in 1938.[17]

In the meantime, Selecman had faced, in 1931, threats to his presidency by both faculty and Executive Committee, especially its chair R. H. Shuttles. Faculty conflict was intensified in 1927 when Joseph D. Doty was terminated because he had allowed a page critical of Selecman to be included in the 1927 *Rotunda* (yearbook).[18] The conflict surfaced again in 1931 when Chairman Shuttles, supported by almost half the faculty, attempted to force Selecman's resignation. They did not succeed, however; the Board of Trustees gave him a vote of confidence; and the Methodist church at large also supported him.[19] During this period, conflict between the business community and Selecman arose over the dismissal of R. N. Blackwell, Business Manager of Athletics. Selecman based the dismissal, to which many Dallas business people objected, on Blackwell's use of alcoholic beverages.[20]

The faculty won a partial victory for a greater share in the control of the life of the University in 1933 with the establishment of the University Council which met first on October 6 of that year.[21]

No further evaluation of President Selecman is necessary except to say in his defense that he inherited a shaky situation from his predecessor and acted with sufficient boldness during his administration that a sounder foundation was laid for his successor in 1938, Umphrey Lee.

The Theology Faculty

The School of Theology faculty was reasonably stable during the Kilgore years. A "core" faculty—consisting of those who remained until retirement or at least stayed for a substantial block of time—consisted in 1926–27 of the following: James Kilgore as Acting Dean and Professor of Philosophy of Religion; James Seehorn Seneker, Religious Education; W. D. Bradfield, Christian Doctrine; Robert Goodloe, Church History; John H. Hicks, Old Testament; Ora Miner, Town and Country Work; J. Richard Spann, City

Church; and C. M. Bishop, New Testament. Mary McCord taught speech part-time (she was in the Speech and Drama Department of the University) for many years, and J. Abner Sage, from the School of Music, taught Church Music. Frederick D. Smith, from Arts and Sciences, was Professor of New Testament Greek.[22]

Spann resigned in 1927, and Umphrey Lee, Pastor of Highland Park Methodist Church, replaced him temporarily in Homiletics.[23] Harold G. Cooke replaced Spann in the City Church in 1928,[24] and remained until 1931. Kilgore inquired of W. C. Martin (later a bishop) in June 1928 if Martin would be interested in a faculty appointment,[25] but it was only later, after he became pastor of First Methodist, Dallas, that he did in fact teach homiletics for a brief period.[26] Olive Donaldson, Professor of Art, also taught a course in Art History beginning in 1930.[27] Ora Miner remained until 1934.

Faculty members had little time for research and writing. In addition to teaching a gradually growing student body,[28] faculty were expected to be active in local churches. At one point they were assigned names of churches to visit in a program set out by President Selecman "for bringing the School of Theology to the attention of the people."[29] Goodloe was pulpit supply at Highland Park Church during a leave of absence of Umphrey Lee.[30]

Several faculty members were still working on Ph.D. degrees. Goodloe received his degree from the University of Chicago in 1929, and Hicks was in the process of completing his at the same time.[31] A. W. Wasson who had joined the faculty completed his Ph.D. degree at the University of Chicago in 1931.[32] Faculty did do some writing. For example, C. M. Bishop was asked to do the volume on First Corinthians and J. H. Hicks on Isaiah in the "Living Bible Series."[33] Faculty also participated in professional societies. The Southwestern Society of Biblical Study and Research originated on the SMU campus on 29 December 1929. C. M. Bishop was elected President, and the Society included Brite Divinity School at Texas Christian University, Southwestern Baptist Theological School, Oklahoma University, Howard Payne College, SMU's School of Theology, and others.[34]

Curriculum

A record of some kind was probably set during this period by the fact that there was not a single change in the curriculum from 1926 to 1933. A new curriculum had just gone into effect when Kilgore became acting Dean, and a new one was begun immediately after his stepping down with Dean Hawk as the new Dean. The requirements during Kilgore's deanship were: one major each in Christian Doctrine, Philosophy of Religion, Church History, Homiletics, Ministerial Efficiency, Missions, Religious Education, and Sociology, with an additional one in either Christian Doctrine or Philosophy of Religion; four majors in New Testament and three in Old; two minors in Church Music and four in Public Speaking. Six majors were required in the major subject, with the appropriate language if the major was one of the Testaments. What was called a "dissertation" was an additional requirement as well as an oral examination before the entire faculty.[35]

"Double credit" on courses taken in the School of Theology by undergraduates—credit toward a theological degree as well as toward an undergraduate degree—continued to be a matter of debate (as it was even later). Apparently at one time up to thirty semester hours of such work were allowed, but in 1930–31 this amount was reduced to four and one-half majors (or about fifteen semester hours).[36] One year later the provision was changed to allow upper class undergraduate students to take courses in the School of Theology but not to receive double credit, a move which it was hoped "would remove friction which now exists between the School of Theology and the Department of Religion in the College of Arts and Sciences."[37]

Apparently this provision did not hold, however, for the April 1932 *University Bulletin* still provides for double credit provided the student had had six semester hours of preparatory work in the field and sixty semester hours of general course work (that is, it was open only to juniors and seniors).[38] Perhaps it is true that if a faculty does not revise the curriculum, it will find some other curricular problem to discuss!

Continuing Education

Continuing education, known then as "Extension Work," continued to be an important part of the work of the School of Theology. One type that persisted was the Pastors' School, which had begun in its current form in 1922. The school lasted for ten days and was under the direction of A. C. Zumbrunnen, Professor of Religion and Dean of Students for the College of Arts and Sciences. (It was probably thought of as an activity of the University in general rather than the School of Theology in particular, but was widely staffed with theological faculty.) It offered work in the Course of Study for those preparing for ordination without a seminary education, and gave courses on a "graduate" level for those already ordained.[39] The courses could also be taken by correspondence, and often were.

The Conference Course of Study, it should be remembered, was the basic way in which one was made a member of the Annual Conference and ordained, and this remained the case for many years. A Bachelor of Divinity degree was an alternative means at that time of seeking ordination, a substitute for the Conference Course of Study. To indicate what a small number of Southern

Methodist ministers possessed anything like an adequate formal education, the following statistics from Stonewall Anderson of the Board of Education at Nashville are illuminating. Only four out of 100 Methodist ministers in 1927 were seminary graduates. Ten out of 100 had received some theology school training; 22 out of 100 had received some college training, and 31 out of 100 had received only an elementary education.[40] With so few candidates for ministry eligible for the School of Theology at this time (a fact which began to change in the 1930s), it is no wonder that SMU's School of Theology had problems in obtaining students for its degree work and offered in its place so much non-credit work.

The Winter Short Term was a second form of extension work—"for the benefit of pastors and church workers, directors of religious education, church secretaries and Sunday school teachers."[41] The school conducted Missionary Institutes,[42] and other forms of continuing education, including the Fondren Lectures, were regularly carried out. The School of Theology still took quite seriously its responsibility for its larger constituency, the M. E. Church, South, and especially its clergy.

Student Life

If the records are accurate, the extracurricular life of theology students increased considerably during the Kilgore years. A significant aspect of this increase was the beginning of the Interseminary Movement (called "Association") during this early period.[43] The earliest record of this group, which gathered students from the various participating denominations in colleges and universities together for study, worship, and fellowship, is in 1927. A brief article appeared in a 1927 edition of the *Semi-Weekly Campus* about students from Texas Christian University coming to SMU to discuss the organization.[44] Meetings subsequently occurred with both graduate and undergraduate students taking part.[45] Dr. James Moffatt, Fondren Lecturer for 1929, addressed a meeting of this group on the SMU campus on 16 April 1929.[46] Students from state universities also participated, unlike a later day when only seminary students attended.[47] As many as four meetings were held yearly.[48]

Perhaps this increase in student activities was due in part to a gradually increasing student body.[49] In any case more and more events are recorded in the *Semi-Weekly Campus*, the chief source for a description of student life. For example, the annual picnic was held in 1927 at Summit Point on White Rock Lake, on May 6. A description of the activities indicates that the seniors had planned and directed the picnic for the first time. Students won the baseball game over the faculty, and Acting Dean Kilgore accompanied Professor and Mrs. Abner Sage's duet.[50] The picnic was held at Doran's Point the following year, on March 23.[51]

What is more interesting is that the first banquet was held on 4 May 1928. Walter Towner was chair for the event, and Kate Warnick assisted, as she did for many years following. Seventy-five attended the event at which the speaker was Honorable Wallace Hawkins, former Assistant Attorney General, with Mrs. Warnick providing piano music.[52] This event, except for 1932 because of the Depression, and 1947 for unstated reasons, has continued to the present, having taken many forms. Speakers were a part of the program until 1965. The first dance was held this same year, and those attending celebrated with an Agape Meal in 1977. Panorama, which became a faculty "take-off," was featured at some later programs, and since 1970 there has been little or no program. Each year since 1969 the students have presented the Elsa Cook Award, named for the long-time secretary of student life, to an outstanding student.[53] Usually the faculty take-off has been done on another occasion. For example, it was done at a Christmas party at Highland Park Church in 1929,[54] and many years later it was carried out as the spring "Panorama."

The first record of the theologs' receiving an intramural pennant is in 1928, when they received the pennant in the Independent Basketball Tourney.[55]

Two pre-theological students were elected president of the SMU student body during this period: O. Eugene Slater (later a bishop) in 1930[56] and Ennis Hill in 1932.[57] Slater actually served his term after he was in the School of Theology. Another bishop coming out of this period was Sante Barbieri, a graduate of "Little SMU" in Brazil, who received his B.A., M.A., and B.D. in 1932, and was later made a bishop in Brazil. Lance Webb received the B.A. degree in 1933 and the B.D. in 1934, and was elected to the episcopacy after serving in North Texas and Ohio.[58] All three future bishops were members of the same prayer-fellowship group while at SMU.[59]

The School of Theology continued to maintain an international flavor. For example, out of thirty-three graduates in 1932, five were internationals, from Korea, Brazil, and Mexico.[60] Two years earlier, SMU graduates were in ministry in seventeen countries outside the United States, with sixty representatives.[61]

School of Theology Worship

One would think that chapel in a school of theology would be universally attended, that students would adjust their schedules to fit the chapel schedule, and that few problems would exist in regard to seminary worship, but such is not the case. And so, numerous changes occurred in these early days with regard to chapel, and they have continued throughout its history. In 1929, the time for chapel was 12:00 to 12:30 P.M., four days a week.[62] The faculty was periodically roused to assume more responsibility for community worship, as it was at the opening faculty meeting in 1931:

> Dr. Bishop spoke concerning the efforts to improve our chapel services, appealing for greater interest and fervor. Dr. Bishop then moved that the Dean arrange the chapel programs for the first few weeks in line with the above idea, and that on the first day of school there be held a Communion service, followed one day each by the several professors and four students.[63]

Four weeks later Bishop reported favorably on the increased attendance at chapel. The faculty then appointed a committee, with, of course, Bishop on it along with A. W. Wasson and Nell Anders, to continue the good work.[64] In December the faculty gave a vote of thanks to the committee and asked it to continue its work, and they apparently did such a good job that they were asked in April to continue for the third quarter of the academic year.[65]

In 1933 the chapel time was changed to 8:30 A.M., Tuesday through Friday. Apparently some time between 1931 and 1933 a one hour per week arrangement had been tried.[66] So has run the course of chapel—a concern for low attendance, experiments with different schedules, and attempts to improve the quality of worship. It has probably been better since students took it over in the 1930s, but the problems have continued in various ways to the present.

The School of Theology Library

One of the questions a university faces is whether it has one library or separate libraries for the separate schools. The decision was made, as we have seen, in 1925 to set up a separate theology library. That library grew steadily from almost nothing in 1915, but it grew exceedingly slowly. Kate Warnick continued as librarian with student help, on the second floor of old Kirby Hall. By 1930 Mrs. Warnick reported that Kirby Library had 10,715 books, 1,285 bound periodical volumes, and 2,000 pamphlets, and was receiving 82 periodicals.[67] It had its own card catalog, and was supported by 75,000 catalogued volumes in the General Library.

At the heart of the Theology collection were the Methodist and the Shettles collections, provided during the first year of the University, and the Whited Research Fund, worth $10,000, and the John A. Rice Old Testament Fund, at a similar value. Other individual donors included Jesse H. Jones of Houston.[68]

The Mustang Band

An interesting and historically significant episode has to do with the place that theology students had in the development of SMU's Mustang Band. Although Cy Barcus was not yet a pre-theological student when he began making history with the Band, he continued as its director through his theological study and even maintained some relationship with it after graduation. It was he who began the "jazz band" tradition—which appears to have been a truly unique development for the time.[69] He received his local preacher's license in 1919 and began his theological work in 1924.[70] One of the many traditions for which Barcus is responsible is the adaptation of a song he heard on a phonograph record to become SMU's "Peruna," a song which still remains the school's principal "fight song."[71]

Robert E. Goodrich, Jr. (later a bishop) became a member of and eventually assistant conductor of the band when he entered the School of Theology. He continued and refined the Barcus tradition when he took over as conductor in 1933.[72] Goodrich initiated a special band program in 1932, and the following year the program was called "Pigskin Review."[73] This program featured singers, magicians, and other entertainers as well as the band,[74] and in 1934 Goodrich and Charlie Meeker[75] produced a review which played to more than four thousand paid admissions in Dallas and elsewhere.[76]

Goodrich showed his concern for media, later put to work for the church, by beginning a series of radio programs.[77] Barcus had already taken the band on several trips in addition to those with the football team,[78] and Goodrich expanded this tradition by, among other things, taking the band on a European tour.[79] In 1935 the tour included the Chicago Palace Theater,[80] and Lowe's Circuit booked the band for seven consecutive weeks. They did not fulfill the engagement, however, and as I have always understood it was due to Goodrich's realization that he had to make a choice between entering the entertainment field or the Methodist ministry.[81] He chose the latter, of course, and became one of the outstanding preachers of at first Southern Methodism and later the entire Methodist Church after unification.

Heresy Hunts

Heresy hunts were not over after the stormy 1920s. In 1930, for example, Dr. Frank Onderdonk wrote to Dean Kilgore to say that he thought "Br. Bishop was not orthodox." Kilgore defended Bishop by citing specific instances of his piety and devotion and by saying that a well-known fundamentalist had said that Bishop's talk to a Sunday school class was one of the best he had ever heard.[82]

Incidents such as this continued during the Kilgore and later the Hawk administrations. Students sometimes agreed with the criticisms but more often supported the faculty whom they had come to know and often to love as genuinely Christian human beings.

Financial Support

We have already seen how the aggressive policy of President Selecman, while it led to considerable growth in the University (new buildings, two new schools, and increased endowment) also led to an increased debt, to more than $600,000 at one period.[83] Endowment grew, as we have seen, as well as plant value.[84] The truth of the matter, however, is that SMU was still not tapping the newly made fortunes in oil to the extent needed. Gifts of hundreds of thousands of dollars were considered significant, whereas the University needed millions in order to be able to become what it envisioned itself to be. It was decades later before gifts in the millions of dollars began to be provided.

But what about the School of Theology? University presidents have sometimes complained that individual schools can raise money more easily than the University as a whole, and this is probably true. In the case of the School of Theology, however, the tendency for the University was to treat it from the start as an independent financial entity responsible for its own budget. This was partly due to the fact that the M. E. Church, South (and later the Methodist Church) did provide at least minimum support for the School of Theology. Bishop John M. Moore's files contain a startling statistic for 1927–28. Out of the theology budget of $49,130.39, the church provided $33,942.89 and gave endowment to the extent of $15,187.50.[85] The manuscript continues:

> In the past two years, under the efficient management of Acting Dean James Kilgore, the school has operated without a deficit. This result has been obtained by:
>
> 1. Paying salaries that are scarcely half what the professors would receive in the pastorate.
>
> 2. Limiting the number of students.[86]

The money which came through the church consisted not only of gifts from official bodies (annual conferences, national boards, the General Conference), but also from church *people*. The most significant of the latter, used for endowment in 1927 from Mrs. Emma Lehman, amounted to $84,959.19.[87] Mrs. Lehman was born in Cincinnati, Ohio, 16 August 1854, but moved to Louisiana with her family in 1869. Her father died, and her mother took her two brothers back to Ohio. Emma stayed with her uncle, H. N. Meir, and his wife, at first in Louisiana, and then in Dallas beginning in 1876. In 1890 Emma married Edward Lehman, and both were charter members of Grace Methodist Church. Mr. Lehman died in 1919, and Mrs. Lehman seven years later, in 1926.[88] The Edward and Emma Lehman Foundation was incorporated in the School of Theology endowment with the freedom for the School to use it as the School determined.[89] In 1931 the money was designated for the Edward H. and Emma Lehman Chair of Christian Doctrine,[90] first held by W. D. Bradfield.

Whereas the Lehman money had come to the School of Theology without any known solicitation, a fund-raising campaign began in the fall of 1929 in an attempt to increase the School of Theology endowment. Called the "Ministerial Million Fund," it was aimed toward people in churches, with clergy being enlisted as fund raisers. John M. Moore was the chair of the campaign.[91] The fund was to begin by soliciting names from the presiding elders (district superintendents in modern parlance).[92] In one publication, Bishop Hoyt M. Dobbs, former Dean of the School of Theology, pointed out that SMU's School of Theology had enrolled 800 students during its 15 years of existence, including thirty-six from other countries, and that therefore the M. E. Church, South, had the obligation to provide better support for it as well as for its other school of theology, at Emory University.[93]

I have found no record of how much was raised in this campaign—probably not a great deal. The campaign coincided with the increasing pressure of the Great Depression on the South, in the early and middle 1930s. Later endowment amounts do not reflect a large amount of money having been raised during this drive.

And so we can conclude that the School of Theology simply got along, poorly financed and unable to expand its program significantly, until 1946 when the Perkins family's money came to the School for both building and endowment.

The A. V. Lane Museum

From its beginning, various people donated collections of one kind or another to the School of Theology. One of the chief donors, with continuing interest, was A. V. Lane, a Dallas physician. He presented an original gift of archaeological items from the Belgian Congo, Japan, China, Mexico, India, and the Holy Land, and he continued to give other materials. In 1937 he provided $1,000 for the equipping of a museum.[94] The most popular item, still in Bridwell Library, was an Egyptian mummy brought to America by Judge A. W. Terrell of Austin. A minister plenipotentiary during Grover Cleveland's Presidency, he helped solve a problem for the Egyptian government, and the government in turn presented him with the mummy, presumed to be a princess from the time of Ramses II, the Pharaoh of the Hebrew Oppression.[95]

Others have added to the collection, and the museum was named the A. V. Lane Museum in March 1928.[96] Between the opening of the still-unnamed museum in January 1927 and 1933, according to the *Semi-Weekly Campus*, 1,700 visitors signed the museum's registry.[97] Dr. J. H. Hicks served as director during this period and Mrs. John Warnick as curator.[98] Mrs. Warnick was always a gracious hostess to the swarms of children who came to see the mummy. Although not a significant museum as museums go, it brought thousands of visitors to the SMU campus over the years.

Campus Religious Activities

Although our focus is on the School of Theology, it is appropriate to note briefly the scope of religious activities on the total campus (of which, of course, the School of Theology was an integral part). For many years an annual revival was held on campus, sometimes called "adjustment" and later "Religious Emphasis Week." In 1929, for example, Clovis Chappell was the preacher,[99] and in 1932 J. N. R. Score began the revival at Highland Park Church on Sunday morning and continued on campus throughout the week.[100] The university sponsored other religious services,[101] and beginning in 1933 chapel was reduced to only once a week.[102] Also, the Religious Activities office held early morning Holy Week services during 1932.[103]

A special social service class (for carrying out helpful projects) had begun in 1922,[104] and continued for a number of years, later moving to Highland Park Church.[105] A Christian Council was organized in 1926 for coordinating campus religious activities,[106] later becoming the Student Council of Religious Activities (SCRA). Gordon Gay served as Director of Religious Activities until 1928, to be followed by Robert E. Dickenson who also remained for some years.[107] A Pre-theological Association functioned on campus for many years.[108] It persisted at least into the 1950s when for several years I served as faculty member and the junior member of by then the Perkins School of Theology faculty.

A great many university religious activities have persisted into the 1980s. More of them are independent, however, not directly related to the University as in the earlier years. The major exception, of course, is the office of Chaplain to the University, which has existed since 1949.

Conclusion

The impression one gets from reading about the 1920s and early 1930s is that SMU was still very much a religiously affiliated school. As a student in the School of Theology from 1937 to 1940, I can attest to the reality of this fact at that time. There was a strong secular bent on campus, however, and it was becoming even then increasingly difficult to maintain a direct Methodist connection. We shall see in the next chapter some of the steps in this breakdown of Methodist control. Although this did not directly affect the School of Theology, it did change the atmosphere in which it operated and gradually separated the "preacher" or "angel" factory (School of Theology) from the remainder of the University, an increasingly secular institution.

6

The Hawk Years: 1933–51

The dual purpose of the School of Theology was affirmed at a faculty meeting on 23 January 1936, two and one-half years after Eugene B. Hawk became its Dean. Its primary duty, the faculty affirmed, is "the training of a pious and learned ministry. This work is usually carried on through regular class instruction or through supervised study by correspondence." This covered both degree students as well as those qualifying for Methodist ministry through the Conference Course of Study, a series of courses, often done by correspondence, set up by the Methodist Episcopal Church, South, for qualification for ordination. This work was done either through the Emory or the SMU "correspondence schools."

The second responsibility, the faculty went on to say, is in regard to the larger church, and they gave as an example the recently begun Bible conferences for which the General Board of Education wanted seminary faculty to provide teachers.[1]

There was no question, therefore, that SMU's School of Theology was a part of the M. E. Church, South, and the efforts of that church to provide for itself an educated ministry. The primary agency responsible was the larger church; the seminary was an agency of the church for helping make that possible. A secondary purpose was to extend that Christian education to the larger church through such enterprises as Bible conferences, aimed primarily at the laity. The mandate of SMU was changed somewhat when the two Episcopal branches of Methodism (North and South) and the Methodist Protestant Church united to form the Methodist Church in 1939. The domain of Southern Methodist University had been Southern Methodism west of the Mississippi. Now it became the South Central Jurisdiction of the Methodist Church consisting of Texas, Louisiana, New Mexico, Oklahoma, Kansas, Arkansas, Missouri, and Nebraska.[2]

Eugene B. Hawk

Eugene Blake Hawk was ideally suited to administer a *church* institution. Pastor of Fourth Avenue M. E. Church, South, in Louisville, Kentucky, at the time of his selection as Dean in June 1933,[3] he was not in the strict sense of the word an educator. Born in 1881, he had served churches in the Central Texas Conference including First Church, Fort Worth, had been a presiding elder (district superintendent) of the Waxahachie District, and was a thoroughgoing Methodist. With an A.B. from Emory and Henry and a B.D. from Vanderbilt,[4] he had basic theological education but no advanced degree. His vision for the School of Theology appears not to have extended much beyond Methodism, but he made that service increasingly more efficient during his almost eighteen years of service as Dean. Some faculty felt that academic standards were sacrificed, perhaps because of an open admissions policy and because of the increasing size of the student body without the addition of sufficient faculty.[5]

Hawk was elected Vice-President of the University in 1938, and was acting President between Selecman and Lee,[6] from 1 September 1938 to 1 March 1939.[7] He remained as Dean until 1 September 1951, and stayed on an additional year as Vice-President of the University, until his retirement in 1952.[8]

After his brief tenure as acting President, a committee drew up a resolution of appreciation including these words: "So thorough and capable has his work as an administrator been that no unrest of dissatisfaction or hesitancy in the program of the institution has occurred."[9] Perhaps his administration as Dean can best be summarized by words he wrote in 1945, when he said that the faculty "believes that the men who go from the Seminaries must be better trained for an effective ministry."[10]

The events contained in this chapter are one way of describing the accomplishments of and during his administration.

Umphrey Lee as President

The first five years of Hawk's deanship were under the presidency of Charles Selecman. Umphrey Lee was named President in November 1938, and assumed his duties early the following year.[11] This means that the majority of Hawk's term was spent during the presidency of Umphrey Lee, with Hawk also serving as Vice-President during most of this period.

Umphrey Lee was the second *educator* to hold the presidential office at SMU, the first having been Robert S. Hyer. Lee was ordained, and served in the pastoral ministry, much of the time at Highland Park Methodist Church on the SMU campus.[12] He also completed his graduate work while a pastor,[13] and served for two and one-half years as Dean of the Vanderbilt School of Religion before returning to Dallas.[14] Lee, according to Herbert Gambrell, long-time member of the History Department, was not a preacher dubbed educator but an educational statesman. "In every relationship of life, in every task to which he set his hand, Umphrey Lee was an extraordinary man."[15]

The campus had changed from Lee's time as a student during 1915–16 when he was student body president. In those days, according to a historical note in the *Semi-Weekly Campus*, SMU kept hogs and butchered them on Bishop Boulevard for use in the dormitories.[16] The character of the school had changed much less; it was still essentially a humanities college with other schools attached. Dancing was still prohibited, and the church was still in control. Lee's educational statesmanship began to change this so that by 1951 he could report to the Board of Trustees, "What has happened is that we have a University on our hands."[17] It was not, I think, that Lee wanted to wrest SMU from the church, but rather that he understood that changes were necessary in order to create a university. Thus, Hyer's dream began to come true some thirty-five years after the start of the institution.

Few people have ever enjoyed—and kept—the respect of so many different people as Umphrey Lee had maintained. What John W. Bowyer of the English faculty said in the alumni magazine in December 1938 is representative: "The city of Dallas is pleased, the alumni are pleased, the student body are jubilant, and the faculty, who should know more about the University than anyone else and probably do, constantly reveal their satisfaction and their hope for the future."[18] At Lee's death in 1959, the *Dallas Times Herald* wrote:

A great and good man is gone.

A community, a state and a nation suffered inestimable loss. Dr. Lee was one of the most beloved citizens of Texas. The popularity of Dr. Lee, his skill as an administrator, his charm of personality, his broad tolerance and hard work were important factors in winning for SMU the goodwill and support, not only of Dallas residents of all faiths, but of public-spirited citizens of all Texas and other states.[19]

It was not in educational attainments alone that Lee contributed substantially to the development of SMU. By 1945 he could report to the Board of Trustees that all debts having to do with operating expenses had been cleared.[20] The beginning of an annual financial campaign, under the leadership of a now-retired Bishop Boaz and called the Sustentation Campaign, increasingly made a financial contribution to the University (but not directly to the School of Theology).[21] Before the close of Lee's presidency, twenty new buildings stood on the campus,[22] and the endowment, while still inadequate, at least had increased.

The price which the church paid for this transformation was the loss of control of the University, and the control, even the influence, became less over the years. It was not so much that Lee wanted to preside over the secularization of SMU; rather, as he developed an educational institution in a secular world, the control, and finally the influence, of the church tended to lessen. For example, a drastic reduction in compulsory chapel to once a month[23] eventually led to no compulsory chapel at all. The process Lee used to counteract this secularization was to spend more money on campus religious personnel[24] and eventually, in 1949, to secure a chaplain for the University to direct its religious affairs.[25]

Underlying all of this is the problem to which earlier reference was made: the problem of relating a religion which calls for commitment to a particular point of view and the spirit of free inquiry supported by education.

World War II

Hawk came to SMU's School of Theology in the midst of the Great Depression, and before the new oil riches of Texas were tapped significantly for the University. By the time Lee arrived war clouds were beginning to overshadow but not dispel the Depression, and World War II began six months later. Although it was several years before the war began to affect the United States directly, the loss of students soon became apparent. The Board of Trustees heard the report on 26 January 1943 that SMU continued to lose students to the war effort.[26] The *Semi-Weekly Campus* indicates the evidence of girding for the war effort as early as 1942,[27] and the School of Theology faculty received reports from Wesley Davis of defense plans for the University in January 1942.[28]

During 1943, the Navy V-12 program was expanded to train doctors, dentists, and chaplains for wartime service. Pre-theological and theological students accepted for chaplain's training would be assigned to theological seminaries on campuses which already had V-12 units. The SMU School of Theology was one of these.

In fall 1944 the program was begun. Relatively few students were accepted nationwide. They had the lowly rank of apprentice seamen but were outfitted with impressive cadet-style uniforms. The SMU contingent consisted of Kenneth McDowell of Oklahoma, Neill McFarland (later a Perkins faculty member), Walter Lee Underwood (later a bishop) and a fourth student who was transferred out of the program at an early stage.

Of these, only McDowell, a senior, was commissioned as a chaplain. With the end of the war, the program was cancelled and the remaining participants were discharged in December 1945.[29]

Following the war, of course, the situation was reversed, and this also included the School of Theology. The President reported to the Board of Trustees in 1946 that Arts and Sciences had almost doubled since 1944, and that the other schools had such spectacular growth as 346 to 851 in Engineering and

79 to 152 in Law. Theology had grown from 152 to 238.[30] Temporary buildings for classes and offices, for housing, and as a student center were moved on campus (mostly from Camp Howze at Greenville).[31] By the spring semester of 1947 the student body had reached 6,712.[32]

This increase created problems of adequate faculty all over the campus, including the School of Theology. When I came to teach in 1949, the student body of the School of Theology had reached some 300 students, while the faculty had not increased significantly over what it was with half that many students. Faculty loads strained ability to give adequate guidance to students, and until 1950 the one building which had housed fewer than one hundred theology students in 1924 was now invaded by more than 300.

The Faculty

In the early years of the Hawk administration, a permanent faculty developed and remained into the years of his successor, Merrimon Cuninggim. This "core faculty" was supplemented by visiting faculty and by a few additional members who arrived later on in the Hawk years. Three retirements occurred during the first years of Hawk's deanship: James Kilgore and C. M. Bishop in 1934 and W. D. Bradfield in 1936.[33] A. W. Wasson went to the Board of Missions in Nashville in 1934.[34] Those remaining and immediate additions included Hawk in Homiletics and Pastoral Theology;[35] James Seehorn Seneker in Religious Education; Robert W. Goodloe in Church History; John H. Hicks in Old Testament; Wesley C. Davis in New Testament (beginning in January 1935); J. T. Carlyon in Christian Doctrine (first as visiting professor in 1934 and then as Professor of Christian Doctrine in 1936); and Paul A. Root, in Sociology of Religion, in 1935.[36]

Various other people taught on a visiting basis or for a brief period. N. C. McPherson was professor of the Philosophy of Religion and Christian Doctrine for two years. Harold Hart Todd continued to teach Church Music until the late 1930s. Mary McCord taught Public Speaking until she was replaced by a full-time professor of Speech, and Olive Donaldson taught Art History in 1936. Guy W. Sarvis was visiting professor of Missions in 1934–35; William H. Barnhardt, in Philosophy of Religion in 1934–35; and R. E. Edwards, in Counseling in 1937. J. Paul Reed was visiting professor of Missions in 1937–38. Fred D. Gealy came as a visiting professor in 1938, and remained on the faculty until his retirement (and after). During his career, he at various times taught Missions, Church Music, New Testament Greek, and New Testament (the latter being his major field). He also began in 1939 and for many years directed the Seminary Singers, and after 1951 was chapel organist. A. M. Serex was visiting professor of Philosophy of Religion.[37]

Since I attended classes taught by most of these faculty members between 1937 and 1940, I can attest to their competency as teachers.[38] There was little time for research and writing, however. Most of their time was consumed in preparing to teach, in teaching, and in grading together with committee work and the work they were expected to do in local churches.[39]

Brief sketches of the seven "core" professors seem appropriate, based largely on my knowledge of them first as a student and later as a teaching colleague.

James Seehorn Seneker was educated under the preeminent religious educationist of his time and still a respected educator of the "liberal" school, George Albert Coe. Seneker was a pastor before going to Union Theological Seminary in New York to do graduate work, and apparently was a much beloved one. Over the years, however, he tended toward eccentricity in his relationships. Former students have testified to me over the years that his experiential as opposed to a transmissive understanding of Christian education was of a great value to them. He was a fine colleague, a gracious host, and generous in his will, leaving an estate of more then $1,000,000 to Perkins for religious education scholarships and for a partial professorship in religious education. He began teaching in 1921 and retired in 1957.

Robert W. Goodloe, Church History, was the mentor for many generations of students. He gave of his time unstintingly to both school and larger church, and was active in the Central Texas Conference. He was a fine teacher and a caring friend. Rumor has it that he wanted to be Dean prior to Hawk's coming, and perhaps this was what tended to make him a little bitter during his latter years. This feeling did not detract from his teaching, however, nor from the generosity of his personal relationships. He began teaching on a visiting basis in 1920, was gone for a year of graduate work, and became a permanent member of the faculty in 1922. He retired in 1957 and taught at Hendrix College after his retirement.

John H. Hicks, Old Testament, was a truly great teacher who made the prophets live and who himself "became" the prophet Amos as he read from that book in his deep, sonorous voice. His eyesight was so bad that he read just a few inches from his book, but this never seemed to slow him in his work. His sense of humor stood him in good stead until he retired in 1957 after thirty-five years of service to the school. Afterwards he taught at McMurry College in Abilene where he died in office.

Wesley C. Davis was a careful scholar and teacher in New Testament, not so dynamic as Hicks but still an effective teacher. In addition to his teaching in the seminary, he taught a large class (up to five hundred members) at Highland Park Methodist Church for many years. The class was considered as "church" for many members and those attending had a good "sermon" from their teacher.

Davis chaired at least two curricular review committees, including that under Dean Cuninggim which led to a somewhat innovative "core curriculum." Davis and Gealy retired the same year (1959) and reversed procedures by talking about one another rather than themselves in their response to the evening.

J. T. Carlyon, Christian Doctrine, was a gentleman who in his gentle way encouraged people to think about their faith. Perhaps his greatest problem was his failure to recognize fully the new winds of theology blowing from Europe and the East Coast. No one was more loyal, nor more energetic, in his work in local churches. He and I taught in the same training school a number of times, and he never seemed to tire of driving back and forth from nearby churches. Both Davis and Carlyon served on staffs of local churches after their retirement, which for Carlyon took place in 1954.

Paul A. Root became my mentor during my first quarter at SMU through a wonderful course in "Social Pathology." I served as his assistant including the proof-reading of the book version of his Ph.D. dissertation. Later I assisted him in beginning and operating the Theological Circulating Library. He combined an early training in Methodist piety (later abetted by work at Asbury College) with the scholar's love of truth which he learned during his theological and graduate work at Duke University.

One amusing incident: I, like he, tended to be the "nervous" type. On one occasion he was telling me that I ought to contain my nervous gestures, during which time he continued to run his Phi Beta Kappa key up and down his key chain—one of his persistent habits!

He was elected to the deanship of Duke Divinity School in 1947, and had asked me to go with him as his assistant. Before I had made a decision, Root died of a heart attack, in May 1947. Root was a popular preacher and at one time First Methodist Church, Dallas, attempted to secure him as their preacher after he had served an interim pastorate there. Root was the second School of Theology professor, after Frank Seay, to die in office.

Fred D. Gealy, who came on a visiting basis in 1938, became a permanent member of the faculty the following year. Gealy was an extremely versatile teacher, and a person of many interests. He came to the School of Theology after teaching at Aoyama Gakuin in Tokyo, Japan, for twelve years.[40] He taught in such varied fields as Church Music and New Testament Greek. Later, during the Cuninggim regime he taught in his field of concentration, New Testament, until his retirement in 1959. After his retirement he taught at the Methodist Theological Seminary in Ohio, and after his second retirement and return to Dallas, he still taught occasionally at SMU. At the time of his death, he had not quite completed the grading of a set of papers for the course he was currently teaching.

Later Faculty

One of Dean Hawk's priorities was to enlarge the faculty to serve a growing student body. His budget was inadequate to make this fully possible, and during the 1940s the additions to the "core" faculty were augmented by a number of visiting faculty. This might not have been the best way to improve faculty quality, but a growing student body, especially after World War II, necessitated the additions regardless of how they were made.

The earliest of the permanent additions was A. W. Martin, who was brought to the campus in 1945 to establish a new Department of the Local Church (later "Church Administration"). Part of the reason for the emphasis on "the Local Church" was to offset the tendency of Professor Seneker's courses to be considered too theoretical.[41] Martin was also made responsible for "Field Work" (later "Field Education").[42] Martin, who had been an active pastor in North Arkansas, both enlivened faculty meetings with his acerbic wit and made things move in his areas of concern, because of high activism. He remained until his retirement in 1956, when through a gift from the second Mrs. Martin, the A. W. Martin Local Church Research Laboratory was established at Perkins in his honor.

Earl Marlatt, formerly Dean of the Boston University School of Theology, came as a visiting professor of Homiletics in January 1946.[43] He was elected Professor of the Philosophy of Religion in June 1946.[44] He also taught in the field of Religious Literature until his retirement in 1957. Marlatt had been educated partly in Germany, was a strong Personalist, and also became increasingly eccentric both in his teaching and his single personal life. He is remembered best for his composition of the words of the hymn "Are Ye Able?"

Thomas H. Marsh was also elected Associate Professor of Speech in 1946. Marsh, a graduate of Northwestern University,[45] did a great deal to teach his students better speech habits and performance, and taught classes in Homiletics. Active in the life of the school, he also produced the Methodist Men's Hour for radio for a number of years. This program featured Dr. Marshall T. Steel, pastor of Highland Park Church, as preacher. When the new Kirby Hall was built, the church provided the latest radio recording equipment for Marsh's studio so that he could record and edit the program at the school. He was the third faculty member to die in office (after Seay and Root) in March 1962.

Ben O. Hill, who had been a missionary in Cuba for a number of years, was brought to the campus as "overseer" (to use Umphrey Lee's word) of the Mexican-American Program.[46] His coming in 1948 was an early attempt to help the seminary serve the Hispanic churches in Texas, especially those of the Rio Grande Conference. He also directed the program by which SMU furnished the Religion faculty at Texas College, a black college in Tyler, Texas.[47] In addition he served as Visiting Professor of Missions in the School of Theology.[48]

William Warren Sweet was the last of the permanent additions to the faculty during the Hawk years. The pioneer in American church history, he had just retired from the University of Chicago. He was brought by President Lee as "Chairman of the Faculty" in Theology as well as Professor of Church History, in the fall of 1948. Exactly how the Chair of the Faculty was to work with the Dean was not made very clear, though rumor had it that the faculty could not meet with Dean Hawk without conflict arising because of the unresolved problems between them. There is no gap in faculty Minutes, however, and Hawk attended the first meeting in which Sweet presided.[49] When Umphrey Lee introduced Sweet to the faculty, his duties were stated as follows:

—to be presiding officer of the meetings of the faculty;

—to be ex-officio member of all committees having to do with academic policy;

—to be consulted by the Dean regarding faculty appointments;

—to be advisor to the librarian;

—to have access to all records in the registrar's office;

—to have no responsibility for business affairs; finances were to be completely in the hands of the Dean.[50]

One can speculate—and such appears to be the reality in this case—that a Chairman of the Faculty with no responsibility for finances is likely to be fairly impotent in the choice of faculty.[51]

Russell L. Dicks had a brief stint as a part-time faculty member in Pastoral Theology and part-time on the Highland Park Methodist Church staff, from 1941 to 1943.[52] Visiting faculty included Umphrey Lee, Floyd Poe, W. Angie Smith, Paul W. Quillian, Albea Godbold, Juan N. Pascoe, O. W. Moerner, Mrs. C. W. Kent, L. F. Sensabaugh, Douglas Jackson (who later became full-time faculty), Erwin Bohmfalk, Paul Cardwell, Leo Rippy, Mary Floyd, J. D. F. Williams, Norman Snaith, and W. B. Mahan.[53] Some were pastors; others were from the University faculty; still others were from boards and agencies of the Methodist Church; and a few were local lay people with special skills.

Paul Quillian, Pastor of First Church, Houston, had agreed to be full-time Professor of Homiletics in 1950[54] but died soon after the April 1949 announcement. Several other names were proposed but I find no record that they actually taught—for example, Roy L. Felder.[55]

Howard Grimes was elected to the faculty in May 1949[56] and taught in his major field, Religious Education. During his first few years he also taught courses in Counseling and Sociology of Religion, the latter having been a major emphasis in B.D. and S.T.M. degrees. Albert Outler was persuaded to come to the faculty in 1950 but is actually a part of the Cuninggim faculty.[57] Decherd

Turner became Librarian and Professor of Bibliography in the fall of 1950.[58] George C. Baker came to the University as chaplain in 1949 and taught Homiletics in the School of Theology,[59] until he became McCreless Professor of Evangelism when that chair was established. William A. Irwin joined the faculty in the fall of 1950, in Old Testament, after retiring from the University of Chicago.

The Curriculum

As soon as Hawk became Dean, the faculty began tinkering with the curriculum. The first changes had to do with changing the number of required courses in certain fields. A major was defined to be one-third of a term's (quarter's) value, while a minor was a course with half that value. The curricula of 1934 and 1935 are contrasted below:

	1934	*1935*
Old Testament	3 majors	2 majors
New Testament	4 majors	3 majors
Church History	1 major	2 majors
Philosophy of Religion	1 or 2 majors	1 major
Christian Doctrine	1 or 2 majors	2 major
Social Problems (Sociology)	1 major	1 major
Religious Education	1 major	2 major
Missions	1 major	1 major
Church Music	2 minors	1 minor
Homiletics	1 major	1 major, 1 minor
Pastoral Theology	1 major	2 minors
Public Speaking	4 minors	2 minors
Thesis	1 minor	1 minor[60]

Additional minor changes occurred until 1937 when a stable curriculum emerged that lasted for several years. Its requirements are as follows:

Of the twenty-seven majors necessary for graduation, nineteen majors are prescribed as basic courses, which each student is required to take, namely:

Old Testament	2 majors
New Testament	3 majors
Church History	2 majors
Christian Doctrine	2 majors
Philosophy of Religion	1 major
Sociology of Religion	1 major
Religious Education	2 majors
Missions and History of Religion	2 majors

Homiletics and Pastoral Theology:

Homiletics	1 major
Pastoral Theology	1 major
Public Speaking	1 major
Church Music	1 major

A comprehensive written examination over the required work completed the requirement. The thesis had become optional.[61]

By 1949, when I returned to begin teaching, an odd arrangement prevailed. Each professor had a single required course, and the rest were elective. The comprehensive examination was no longer in existence—with the number of students having almost tripled the grading would have been horrendous. A thesis was no longer an option. Except for a dozen or so required courses, the students made their own curriculum. Although our first reaction is probably one of horror, actually this may not be as bad an arrangement as one might first believe it to be.[62]

A new degree, the Bachelor of Religious Education (B.R.E.), was proposed and adopted in 1947. Professor Seneker's theoretical bias was seen as not meeting the needs of the church for practicing Christian educators. The B.R.E. was a kind of patchwork degree, and only one or two people actually received it.[63] Practitioners of Christian education were enlisted to help staff the degree, but it was discontinued in a few years when the Master of Religious Education was instituted in 1952.[64]

An addition to the B.D. degree was made in 1950–51 when Field Education became a degree requirement. This work was under the general direction of A. W. Martin with other faculty assisting in the supervisory process.[65]

Beyond the University

The extension work of the School of Theology faculty was still a high priority during the 1930s and 1940s. The annual five-day Pastors' School continued yearly (except for one year during World War II).[66] Later, in the early 1950s, a more formal school arose for non-seminary students often preparing for part-time pastoral work, sometimes for an affiliate relationship with the Annual Conference and usually not for ordination. There are several reasons why people go into the "supply" or "local pastoral" relationship. A practical one is that many small churches are not really able to support a fully trained pastor, and these local pastors therefore take up the slack.

So far as the persons themselves are concerned, they are likely to be men or women in a second career, older, unwilling to spend three or more years receiving a seminary education. Such persons feel called to the set-apart ministry, and this is one way they can fulfill the requirements for admission to that form of ministry. Although the work fulfilling these requirements can be done by correspondence, it is generally believed that much more can be learned from a two-weeks' concentrated course in a subject than can be acquired through self-study. In a real sense this work is not "beyond the university," for the local pastors often come with enthusiasm and consider themselves as alumni/ae of Southern Methodist University. No University credit is provided, however. A. W. Martin, Claus Rohlfs, and more recently Bert Affleck have been directors of the school.[67]

An earlier and less formal continuing education event was the introduction in 1936 by Dean Hawk of Ministers' Week. The Fondren Lectures as a University event began in 1919, but in 1936 they were incorporated into Minister's Week as the only lecture series available.[68] Eight years later a second lectureship came into being, established by Mrs. George L. Peyton (later Mrs. C. W. Hall) in memory of her husband as the Peyton Lectures on Preaching.[69] Then in 1946 the Jackson family established the Jackson Lectures on the Bible in memory of their parents Robert Malone and Ellie Jamison Jackson.[70] Thus Ministers' Week came to include three lectureships and eventually, in the 1970s, also a variety of seminars and workshops.

Another outreach to the constituency of the School came through Dean Hawk's establishing of the Theological Circulating Library in 1938. Directed by Paul Root with student assistance, the Circulating Library offered books for clergy to read beyond their own libraries or ability to buy them. In 1943 the Library contained 892 books with almost 1,500 books circulated that year.[71]

Still another outreach to the clergy of the South Central Jurisdiction was the beginning of the *Perkins School of Theology Journal* in 1947. At first a kind of house organ with some articles, it later became a more serious theological journal and has published over the years many distinguished articles.

These and other attempts to be in touch with its constituency led Walter N. Vernon to write in 1967:

> Perkins School of Theology is more deeply involved in the life of the churches than any other of the seminaries of the country, in the judgment of some who know this relationship at first hand. This situation augurs well for the future of both church and seminary, for they are dependent each on the other for strength and direction.[72]

The Library

Dallas Hall served as the site of the main library of SMU until 1939 when Fondren Library, the gift of the W. W. Fondren family of Houston, was completed.[73] Perhaps the most obvious lack of the University at the time was its library facilities, and the impressive Fondren Library building fulfilled this need. The per capita expenditure for books and library services, which had been disgracefully low, did not suddenly burgeon, but the library was at least on its way and changes did occur during the next years. But what about the facilities of Kirby Library, as the library of the School of Theology was usually called?

In prospect of the new Fondren building, the Theology faculty voted in 1936 to keep a separate reading room and an active reserve in Kirby but to move the remainder of the books to the main building.[74] This continued to be the request of the Theology faculty until October 1940 (after the completion of Fondren). At that time Professor Seneker, chair of the Library Committee of the School of Theology, moved that the previous action be rescinded and,

> That the regular library be held intact in the various rooms provided in Kirby Hall as far as possible, except such volumes as in the judgment of the Professors of the various departments, or fields, should go to the Fondren Library for proper keeping and use.[75]

The faculty approved the motion with the understanding that additional first-floor space be made available in Kirby Hall for the library. In this fashion the Theology library remained intact and the way was prepared for the development of the magnificent library resources which became the basis of the Bridwell Library.

Soon after this, Fred Gealy became chair of the faculty committee on the library. His committee tightened rules, and also stepped up the purchase of books so that by the time Bridwell Library came into existence in 1950–51, the total number of books had reached 39,699, and the budget for the year (Hawk's last) was $11,874.56.[76] This, of course, did not begin to approach the later years when $100,000 or more became common for book expenditures (first in 1964–65 when, because of special purchases, the total exceeded a half-million dollars).[77] Bridwell Library was on its way to the achievement of the distinction it now enjoys.

Student Life

As the University grew following World War II—up to 8,349 students including the evening school Dallas College in 1948—so grew the School of Theology. In 1949 the Theology student body had grown to almost 300, including eleven women, with 111 of the total being new students.[78]

The student body was also more active, with considerable evidence of participation, for example, in intramural sports. At least two theologs became University student body president in a decade—Jack Wilkes in 1940–41[79] and B. C. Goodwin ten years later, in 1950–51.[80] Chapel continued to change its time of meeting, and became more student oriented.[81] The spring banquet continued as a special yearly social event of a semi-formal nature.[82] The Student

Association of the School of Theology also became more active during this period.[83]

The student body continued to be international in flavor. One Chinese student, who returned to China in 1950, disappeared so far as his American friends were concerned, only to re-surface by writing to the Dean of the School of Theology at the close of the "Cultural Revolution" in the People's Republic of China to re-establish contact with his alma mater. D. J. Liu was a student in the late 1940s, and completed his M.A. degree in 1950.[84] He suffered as most professors did during the Cultural Revolution, but since then has resumed his teaching of English in the University of North China in Chengdu, Szechuan Province. Through the contacts of Ken and Iweeta McIntosh, who take many church groups to China, he has maintained a steady relationship with his friends in Dallas.

Perhaps the most noteworthy student achievement during the Hawk years was the establishing of the Seminary Singers in 1939. Previously Kate Warnick had directed male quartets, but under Dr. Fred Gealy the Singers grew and flourished during the 1940s.[85] It was at first a male chorus, but when the number of women students began to increase some twenty-five years later, it became a mixed chorus. The first year of the existence of the Singers also included a brief trip, which became an annual affair. The Singers' membership remained small for some years and only in the later years became the organization which students joined for fellowship whether they were good singers or not.[86]

The usual problem of scheduling chapel persisted, as times for classes and a time for chapel always seemed to conflict. In 1935 it was at 8:30 A.M.[87] In 1938-39 chapel was held from 9:50 to 10:10 A.M. with 10:00 classes ending at 11:00 and 11:05 classes ending at noon.[88] Four years later chapel was set for 9:35-10:00 A.M. with the first class commencing at 8:40 A.M.[89] In 1948 the time was changed to 8:30 A.M. only during examinations.[90] Perhaps it is not surprising that students did not always take chapel seriously when it appeared to be an addendum to the daily schedule.

SMU's School of Theology had been established as a school for the M.E. Church, South, west of the Mississippi. After Methodist unification in 1939, it became the theological school of the South Central Jurisdiction (the legal owner of Southern Methodist University). Its student body had never been completely homogeneous, but it remained largely male, and mostly from its own jurisdiction with Texas producing the largest number of its students. By 1942 its 195 students represented sixty-six colleges and universities, and it was increasingly trying to serve the Hispanic interests of the Methodist Church (the name of the united church). But the school remained largely a "provincial" school, with both its roots and in its primary concern for the Southwest. Thus it remained until the 1950s, when at least in principle it became a more nearly world-wide institution. These comments are not meant to be pejorative, only to suggest that up to about 1951—the beginning of the Cuninggim deanship— its orientation was largely toward its principal constituency, the Southwest.

Admission of Minorities

The two principal minorities in Texas during the first half of the twentieth century were blacks (generally called Negroes) and Hispanics, mostly at that time Mexican-Americans or Mexicans from Mexico. Hispanics were admitted to the School of Theology from its beginning, and in 1948 special arrangements were made by the Board of Missions to encourage work with the Rio Grande Conference (the Spanish-language conference in Texas and surrounding states). Ben O. Hill was the Board's representative, as we have seen; unfortunately he was the only person on the faculty at the time who spoke Spanish.[91]

Although the situation was quite different for black students, the process of their admission began early and proceeded slowly, with several arrangements for their engaging in class work over the years. It took almost thirty years for the process to be completed. The most common pattern in the early years was special classes.[92] Meanwhile, occasional black speakers appeared on campus,[93] but by 1940 an SMU poll indicated that only 17% of the students voting favored the admission of Negro students to SMU.[94] By 1952 the percentage had grown to 45%.[95] Another plan of classes allowed black students to sit in class but not receive credit (for which none of the plans had made provision).[96]

Then on 10 November 1950, Dean Hawk offered a resolution to the Board of Trustees that the policy be changed so that black students could be admitted to regular classes. The Board then passed the following resolution:

> The Board of Trustees of Southern Methodist University committed to the administration the matter of the admission of Negroes to Perkins School of Theology with the approval of the principle and with the direction that the administration be given power to act if, as and when it seemed to be timely and proper.[97]

At the next faculty meeting in January 1951, the faculty passed this resolution:

> The faculty expressed its delight at the official recognition of Colored men as eligible for admission to Perkins School of Theology upon the same conditions as white students, and that two Colored men are thus enrolled for work during the winter quarter.[98]

The *Campus* commented on this first entry of black students in the School of Theology in its 6 January 1951[99] issue with approval. The two students did not remain, however, and it was the fall of 1952, at the beginning of Merrimon

Cuninggim's second year as Dean, that the first five students to graduate were enrolled. But an important milestone had been reached almost two years earlier, in the final year of Hawk's administration, the decision to admit black students. It should be noted that this was prior to civil rights legislation, and therefore the School of Theology and Southern Methodist University had made what was then a courageous decision in the long road to equality of the races.

John M. Moore

One of the people who made a great contribution over an extended period to Southern Methodist University and its School of Theology is Bishop John M. Moore. Except for his time on the Board of Trustees, including eight years as chair (1932–38), Moore worked behind the scenes. He often assisted in the raising of money, but of equal or greater importance was his first-hand knowledge of what a university ought to be. He earned the Ph.D. degree at Yale University, and he pursued a year of study at German universities after he had completed the Yale requirements for the Ph.D. degree. All of this made him a major force in the exalted dreams and hopes for a great university and especially for the School of Theology in Dallas.[100]

This dream was born while he was pastor of First Methodist Church, Dallas, 1902–06. He advocated the founding of a medical college in Dallas as part of the Southwestern University in the hope that it would lead to a university in Dallas. (Later the medical college became a part of SMU until financial problems led to its closing.)[101] In his autobiography, Moore writes:

> I accompanied Dr. R. S. Hyer to see President David F. Houston of Washington University in St. Louis, a Trustee of the Rockefeller General Board, in 1910, on the possibility of a donation from that Board to a first-class Methodist educational institution in Dallas. He gave us encouragement. I urged by letter business friends in Dallas to act vigorously to get the university located in Dallas. I came from Nashville for the ceremony of the cornerstone laying of Dallas Hall. When in 1920 the deficit had to be guaranteed by twenty businessmen to enable the school to go on, under the influence of R. H. Shuttles, a close friend, a Trustee, and an ardent supporter of the university, I planned and opened the campaign for the necessary $1,000,000 endowment fund, and secured by personal effort $250,000 of it as a starter.[102]

Bishop Moore not only helped save the school financially on several occasions; he also insisted on a quality school. He helped form the pattern of the University under the influence of the German universities where he had studied, insisting that a good school of theology must be developed, and he helped to implement this dream.

Reflecting on his life, he wrote in his 1948 autobiography:

I have had two great predominant passions and objectives in my Church life: (1) The producing of an acceptable plan of Methodist Union, and (2) the establishment of an adequately endowed, thoroughly equipped, and prominent and ideally located School of Theology on the campus of Southern Methodist University.[103]

He then indicates how unification had been achieved in 1939 and how the gift of the Perkins family a few years earlier would make possible the realization of his other dream.

He, like Bishops A. Frank Smith and Paul Martin, worked with Mr. and Mrs. Perkins in securing their gifts to establish Perkins School of Theology. As we shall see in the following chapter, it was he who almost single-handedly persuaded both the University officials and Mr. and Mrs. Perkins that the plans should be expanded from those which had been made to fit the northwest corner of the campus, and that instead the school should be enlarged and moved to the southwest corner, where it stands today.

It may be that Moore's greatest contribution to SMU was what he stood for in regard to the uniting of knowledge and vital piety.[104] He was one of the few prominent pastors in the Southwest who had an advanced academic degree (Bishop Ivan Lee Holt was another). His insistence that Dallas needed a great university upheld Robert Hyer in his similar desire and kept the dream alive even when the academic leadership of the University was less than what it might have been.

A. Frank Smith

Unlike Moore, A. Frank Smith maintained a visible link with the University for many years. It began during his pastorate of the University Church in 1916, and resumed when Moore retired as chair of the Board of Trustees in 1938. It continued for twenty-two years with Bishop Smith as chair of the Board until November 1960.

Smith is probably generally thought of as more a conciliator than a bold leader, but often his conciliatory efforts required bold leadership. During his early years as pastor of First Methodist Church, Houston, he and Jewish leaders established an inter-religious brotherhood banquet in Houston in the face of strong opposition of the Ku Klux Klan. They did much to re-establish the interracial harmony of the city.[105]

His service to the University included the significant part he played in securing the Perkins family's gift for the establishing of Perkins School of Theology.[106] It was his combination of both conciliation and strength that provided the leadership that SMU often needed. Norman Spellmann, in his definitive biography of the Bishop, says this:

As chairman of the board of trustees of Southern Methodist University, Bishop Smith gave such leadership in times of crisis that he became a symbol of both conciliation and strength. Administrators praised him for the depth of his understanding, the certainty of his support, and the skill of his diplomacy. "Let me tell you again how much I appreciate having you as the one to head up this organization," President Lee wrote to Smith in 1943. "You know how to take things, make them go smoothly, and direct the board's thinking so that there is no waste of time in useless argument.[107]

Two incidents may be cited. One was his handling of the objections to blacks' living in the dormitory and especially to two of them having white roommates, to be discussed later.[108] Another was his handling of the publication by a respected English professor, John O. Beaty, of a clearly anti-Semitic book in 1951, *The Iron Curtain over America*. Joining in the paranoid pursuit of communists in the United States, Beaty attacked even the University. Spellmann gives in detail Bishop Smith's handling of this situation: the appointment of a wise committee to handle the matter, his speaking to the issue but in a conciliatory matter, and in general the way Smith's wisdom avoided what could have become a divisive issue.[109] The committee reported to the Board in May 1954, as follows:

1. The material facts do not bear out the allegation made by Doctor Beaty in his pamphlets.

2. It is deplorable that Doctor Beaty, an employee of the University, failed to present his allegations to the administrative officers. . . . Instead, he presented his allegations to the students, patrons, and the press.[110]

Perhaps it is not coincidental that it was this same board meeting which elected Willis Tate, who did so much to advance the cause of freedom on the SMU campus, as President of the University.

7

Building the New Quadrangle: 1944–51

When old Kirby Hall was occupied in the fall of 1924, it seemed (and actually was) quite commodious in contrast to the previously crowded quarters of the School of Theology at the east end of the third floor of Dallas Hall. In 1924 the student body was small (under 100); the library could be accommodated in one end of the second floor of Kirby Hall, and the administration and faculty were provided with adequate office facilities. Classrooms and the chapel, on the west end of the second floor, completed the arrangements for housing the School of Theology.

These conditions prevailed for more than a decade. There was, of course, a lack of adequate facilities for housing married students. After the demise of Asbury Hall at the corner of Rosedale and Airline, only Marvin and Pierce Halls remained—the "Beehive"—and these two wooden buildings accommodated fewer than twenty couples. Single students lived in the university's dormitory for men, Atkins Hall (now Clements Hall, an office-classroom building) along with the chemistry laboratory in the basement.

When I was a student in 1937-40, I was not aware of any deprivation in facilities. Some of the school's backers did not feel that way, however. Bishop John J. Moore writes following the Perkins family's gift in 1945: "Then one February day in 1945, Mr. and Mrs. J. J. Perkins of Wichita Falls, by a rare munificent and magnificent gift, made possible the complete fulfillment of my dream and yearning hope of twenty-five years."[1] Part of his dream was for adequate facilities. Moore knew that buildings alone do not make a school but that such facilities do make a great school possible.

Financing the School of Theology

SMU's School of Theology had never been adequately financed. Although the general church contributed to it, many of SMU's funds could not be used for the School of Theology. There were some endowment funds—for example, the $85,000 given by Mrs. Emma Lehman, which had been used for the endowment of a chair in Christian Doctrine. There were gifts from churches and from individuals, but no large gift had been provided.

The school had been run economically, with inadequate salaries for its faculty. Acting Dean Kilgore had been a good financial manager, and Dean Hawk proved to be even better. There was a reserve fund for five years running, for example, from 1933 to 1938, a total of $25,593 for this period.[2] Dean Hawk was especially good at raising funds (though in relatively small amounts) for scholarships, loan funds, and the like.[3] What was lacking was a major gift which would provide a sounder basis for operating the school and make possible the expansion of program and faculty to fit the growing student body. A major financial breakthrough seemed the only way the School was likely to have this kind of financial undergirding.

In a letter to Bishop A. Frank Smith, chair of the Board of Trustees, dated 20 September 1940, Dean Hawk laid out the financial situation of the school:

> As you know, we do not share in the general Endowment of the University. Also, during recent years we have had no part in the contributions made by the various Annual Conferences. Some years ago the contributions coming from the Annual Conferences came to the School of Theology. For example, the Southwest Texas Conference directed its entire amount to the Seminary. Conditions were so bad on the campus in the matter of the general University that President Selecman asked that this amount be turned over to the University and this was done. The only exception we have is the small amount, some $350.00 or $400.00, which comes from the Northwest Texas Conference. This has continued to be directed to the School of Theology.
>
> It seems to me that the Board of Trustees is going to be forced to rethink the whole financial program of the Seminary. For example, the School of Theology is the only School on the campus that is charged with an overhead and at the same time it is the only school that has provided its building. We pay annually $4,000.00. It is the only School which does not share in the Endowment Fund of the University other than the small amounts which have been specifically directed to ministerial training. It is the only School that is practically eliminated from Conference support. We are facing a situation which promises to be permanent. Of course, we have a set-up, so far as General Benevolences are concerned, for a quadrennium. There will be very little disposition on the part of a General Conference to raise the amount for theological education. Of course, after the Annual Conferences make their response to the Service Scholarship Appeal, we can go to the various District Conferences and the larger churches. But this is an endless matter and must be carried on from year to year. There is nothing permanent about it, and we shall not project the budget on such uncertainty.[4]

The Bishop's response contained these words:

I feel that the most urgent claim resting upon the Church in this Jurisdiction is that of the School of Theology, and I want us by all means possible to enlist our people publicly and privately in its support.[5]

A number of campaigns for endowing the School of Theology had been undertaken over the years but none had been successful. There was another begun in 1944,[6] but it too appeared to be a failure—at least until Joe and Lois Perkins decided to direct their money to the School of Theology.

Joe and Lois Perkins

Who were Joe and Lois Perkins? Joe J. Perkins was born in Lamar County, Texas, in 1874. After moving first to Montague, later to Bowie, he settled in Decatur, a small town, where he opened a store. In 1910 he moved to Wichita Falls, where he began to expand his business interests to include, among others, the oil industry and banking. He made a substantial fortune, especially in oil, and spent many years seeking ways of putting his money to good use.

Lois Craddock Perkins was a student at Southwestern University at the same time as A. Frank Smith (later a bishop) and his future wife Bess were there. She was a teacher when she met Mr. Perkins, a devout Christian, and was influential, as he always said, in helping her husband use his money wisely and well.[7]

Together in Wichita Falls, they were active members of First Methodist Church and also active in the higher echelons of the Methodist Church. They were not nominal but rather devoted Christians and members of the church, and contributed to its total welfare, not just its finances.

Together they selected charitable, especially Methodist, institutions to receive their substantial gifts—Southwestern University, the Methodist Home in Waco, Methodist Hospital in Dallas, the North Texas Conference Pension Fund, and many others—and especially Southern Methodist University.

Mr. Perkins was elected to the Board of Trustees of SMU in 1928, and attended his first meeting of the Board on March 20.[8] At his first meeting the Board gave attention to the special needs of the School of Theology and spoke of needing $1,000,000.[9] Earlier than this, in 1920, Mr. Perkins had made a substantial gift to the University in the form of an endowed professorship which at that time required only $50,000.[10]

An important milestone took place in 1938 when Paul Martin became pastor of First Methodist Church of Wichita Falls. Martin had already served for three years as Presiding Elder (District Superintendent) of the Wichita Falls district, and so he was no stranger when he became pastor. Thus began a deep and abiding friendship between Paul and Mildred Martin and Joe and Lois Perkins, a friendship which in part led to the Perkins family's gift to the School of Theology.[11]

Of all the Perkins family's philanthropy, the most far-reaching gift was to the School of Theology which now bears their name, the Perkins School of Theology of Southern Methodist University. The Perkins name is also honored at SMU in other ways, however. There is the Perkins Hall of Administration, the Joe Perkins Natatorium, and—in the Perkins School of Theology quadrangle—Perkins Chapel, Lois Perkins Auditorium of Selecman Hall, and the S. B. Perkins Dormitory (named after Mr. Perkins's brother whose activity at SMU pre-dated his own). The gift to the School of Theology was in the words of Bishop John M. Moore a "munificent and magnificent gift,"[12] at that time unusual if not unique in the annals of theological schools. When asked why he chose the School of Theology for his major gift, he responded, "Because, I believe, the future will be determined by the ministry of the church."[13]

The Perkins Gift

The records indicate that no single individual was fully responsible for the Perkins family's directing their money toward SMU's School of Theology. As we have seen, discussion of the School's need for major endowment went on for many years and was a topic for Board of Trustees discussion during Mr. Perkins's first term on the Board.[14] As we have also seen, Dean Hawk was effective in securing gifts for scholarship and loan funds. Leadership of the School, however, especially Bishops John M. Moore and A. Frank Smith, realized that a major gift was necessary if the School were to reach its potential.[15] A third person in the negotiations was Paul E. Martin (later a bishop) whose influence on Mr. and Mrs. Perkins was great and without whose approval the gifts would not have been made. Mr. Perkins's remark is well-known that if the gift helped to produce one more Paul and Mildred Martin, it would be worthwhile for it to have been made.

Bishop A. Frank Smith seems undoubtedly to have been the chief negotiator, however. Smith's recollection is that the first direct discussion with Mr. Perkins on his making such a gift took place in 1944. The Board of Trustees that year proposed a financial campaign to raise $5,000,000 for endowment for the University.[16] Mr. Perkins immediately promised $50,000 with no other offers being immediately forthcoming. Following this, Smith recalls that he talked with Mr. Perkins about giving the $1,000,000 that Bishop Moore had proposed to raise for the School of Theology.[17] Bishop Smith continued to write to Mr. Perkins over the next months and suggested that the school be given the Perkins name if he were to make this kind of gift. Mr. Perkins at first objected but later relented after Bishop Smith wrote:

It will mean something, Mr. Perkins. You exemplify in your life the very things that the school of theology stands for. The Perkins men and women will be all over the church, and the Perkins name will represent what you believe in.[18]

In the meantime Smith and Umphrey Lee had asked architect Mark Lemmon to prepare a sketch of three additional buildings—two dormitories and a chapel—to complement Kirby Hall on the northwest corner of the campus.

Bishop Smith, with a flair for the appropriate, decided that it would be better to wait to show Mr. and Mrs. Perkins the sketch at the Jurisdictional Conference meeting in Tulsa, Oklahoma, in June. Bishop Paul Martin describes the event which transpired in these simple words:

Then the climax was reached on June 13, 1944, in a hotel room in Tulsa during the Jurisdictional Conference when Mr. and Mrs. Perkins told a small group consisting of President Umphrey Lee, Bishop A. Frank Smith, and Mildred [Bishop Martin's wife] and me, that the matter of building a home for the School of Theology which had been under discussion for some time was definitely to come into being.[19]

The formal announcement of the gift was made at the Board of Trustees meeting on 6 February 1945.[20] Bishop Paul Martin then moved the changing of the name of the school to Perkins School of Theology. "It was a high and holy hour," Bishop Smith later declared. "No such gift was ever made to a school of theology in the South."[21] The public announcement was made that evening at a special convocation during Ministers' Week, in McFarlin Auditorium, and on that occasion Mr. Perkins gave credit to Bishop Smith for having the idea and guiding the decision.

The legal document concerning the gift begins with these words:

Actuated by the belief that the future Peace of the World is dependent upon the work and influence of all the Churches of all Peoples and of all Nations, and knowing that there is not now an adequate number of Ministers in any of the Churches, and especially in the Methodist Churches, and desiring to do all we can toward relieving this crisis, we, J. J. Perkins and wife, Lois Perkins, are creating the Perkins Endowment Fund for the purpose of developing and enlarging the School of Theology of Southern Methodist University at Dallas, Texas in the hope that it will become one of the really great Theological Schools of our Nation.[22]

The original gift was $1,350,000, for building and endowment. During the years before the buildings were completed, the Perkinses increased the total on several occasions. The most important of these followed the decision to move the quadrangle from the northwest to the southwest corner of the campus. In the proposal of this change, the chief person responsible was Bishop John M. Moore.

The process leading to the relocating of the quadrangle began in the spring of 1947, when Bishop Moore first proposed to Mr. Perkins and Bishop Smith the need for a larger space than the land adjacent to old Kirby Hall. At first Mr. Perkins was cool to the idea, but Bishop Moore persisted. He drew up a tentative plan for the building on the new site. The location of the buildings in Bishop Moore's plan was rather like the final plan, except that his plan opened to the south, with the space beginning farther north than the actual location.[23]

In a long hand-written letter to Bishop Moore dated 14 September 1947, Bishop Smith says in effect that the expectation from Mr. Perkins at first had not been great enough when the plans called for adding to the old Kirby Hall quadrangle. Since then Mr. and Mrs. Perkins had expressed the intention of giving more to the project, which Bishop Smith as one of the trustees of the Perkins Foundations believed they could afford to do. He goes on to write, "I am convinced that we will make the change—but I want it to be done in proper fashion. I also want the Perkins to catch the vision of the possibilities of the School."[24]

Bishop Moore acknowledges the letter with "great joy and exultation," and commends Bishop Smith on what he had done in guiding the Perkinses in the project. "You have rendered a service that far exceeds anything the rest of us have done or could have done."[25]

In the meantime Bishop Smith had conferred with President Lee and Dean Hawk about the plan, and Bishop Paul Martin had encouraged the Perkinses to approve Bishop Moore's proposal. Bishop Smith waited until he met the Perkinses at the Methodist Ecumenical Conference which convened in Springfield, Massachusetts, on 24 September 1947. The story is told—and I think it is a true one—that the Perkinses had been taken to New Haven, Connecticut, to see the quadrangle of Yale Divinity School, also Georgian in design, and that Mr. Perkins had said, "That's what we want." In any case Bishop Smith could write in his journal for 27 September 1947, after he had left the Conference early: "Talked to Mr. Perkins just before starting to train. He is enthusiastic about the enlarged program for the School of Theology."[26]

On the following October 10, the Committee on the School of Theology agreed to recommend the larger site to the Board of Trustees.[27] The Board met on October 31 and authorized the relocation of the School of Theology to the new area of the campus.[28] Mr. Perkins wrote to Bishop Smith after the groundbreaking ceremonies saying he did not have a fourth building to name. That building became a reality a short time later by an additional gift from the Perkinses of $450,000, and the building was named for Bishop A. Frank Smith.

The new site and the buildings it would accommodate required additional gifts. The original gift was $1,350,000, with Bridwell's $500,000 for the library and the assets of Kirby Hall over and above this figure. The total Perkins gift had been increased gradually, and the amount given at the dedication of the buildings in 1951 announced as $2,000,000 for buildings and $3,000,000 for endowment.[29] The projected amount for the future was widely declared to be some $10,000,000 when the oil was sold from the oil runs presented. In 1988 information from the business office indicated that the market value of the Perkins assets was then in excess of $12,000,000.[30]

There had been wide speculation as to what school in the university should receive the use of the northwest corner of the campus. At one time Bishop Smith suggested it might be turned into a graduate school quadrangle. The School of Business Administration was also a possible occupant. But it was the School of Law that was actually given a home on that spot. And eventually a remodeled and renamed Kirby Hall (now Florence Hall), a main law school building, and one dormitory were built. Later, the magnificent Underwood Law Library was built, completing the Law School quadrangle.

Joseph Sterling Bridwell and Margaret Bridwell Bowdle

The other significant gift was for the library, with J. S. Bridwell and his daughter Margaret Bridwell Bowdle, also from Wichita Falls, as donors. The original gift was $250,000, later increased by another $250,000 to $500,000.[31] Subsequent gifts from the Bridwell Foundation, for the enlargement of the building in 1962 and for the purchase of rare collections of books such as the Bridwell-DeBellis Collection of Incunabula (the earliest printed books), and a still later gift for the redesigning of the building, have added substantially to the original amount.

Mr. Bridwell was also active in the petroleum industry. As Mary Basham Loggie put it:

> He felt that each generation held only a life-time interest in the great range of natural resources available to it and that the responsibility of each generation was to expend their resources sparingly and wisely and with due regard for future inheritance.[32]

The School of Theology Quadrangle

The seven buildings of the new Perkins School of Theology quadrangle were occupied on several dates beginning in the fall of 1950. At the center of the group of buildings was Perkins Chapel, a Georgian gem with such details as curving staircases leading up to the balcony and down to the bride's room. Both staircases had hand-carved railings.[33] To the left and in front of the chapel was

Kirby Hall, in a new building but still bearing the name of Harper and Annie Kirby. Across the quadrangle was Bridwell Library, which was later enlarged (1973) and still later (1988) redesigned for greater library efficiency and security.

Behind the chapel were four dormitories—Hawk Hall, named for Dean Eugene B. Hawk, for married students with children; Martin Hall, named for Bishop Paul Martin, for married students without children, S. B. Perkins Hall, named for Mr. Perkins's brother, and Smith Hall, named for Bishop A. Frank Smith, the latter two being dormitories for single students. Still later a third apartment house was built for the University through a federal loan and named Moore Hall for Bishop John M. Moore. Although a University building, it has always had a preponderance of theology student residents, and is like Martin Hall a building of efficiency apartments.

The buildings were dedicated during Ministers' Week of February 1951. The chapel was completed a few months after the dedication. As the faculty and administration began to expand under the deanship of Merrimon Cuninggim, Kirby Hall was soon inadequate for classroom and office space, and at that point, in 1951, the Perkinses gave the additional money for building Selecman Hall (with faculty offices and classrooms) with its Lois Perkins Auditorium. The latter has proved to be one of the most versatile and most used rooms in the quadrangle. Selecman Hall was named for the former President of Southern Methodist University, Charles C. Selecman.

Mrs. George L. Peyton gave $25,000 for the installation of the organ in Perkins Chapel.[34]

The Transformation of Perkins School of Theology

It is fair to say that the new quadrangle was the beginning of the transformation of Perkins School of Theology. When Merrimon Cuninggim took over as Dean-designate in early 1951, his first job was the enlargement of the faculty to take care of the increased student enrollment which had reached almost 400 by that time.[35] Cuninggim was essentially an educator and took advantage of the new facilities to begin the process of building a first-class institution for theological education. We have said that buildings do not make a university (or any kind of institution of higher education), but without buildings and other resources it is difficult if not impossible to build a first-class educational institution. Bringing Perkins School of Theology to wide recognition as being that kind of institution was Dean Cuninggim's task.

In 1985, I wrote these words for the fortieth anniversary of the giving of the Perkins name to the School of Theology:

Joe and Lois Perkins need no monument to attest to their greatness, but they have one which provides the material basis for the legacy which they have provided for theological education and for the United Methodist Church as a whole. The Perkins Story did not end with the end of their lives on earth; it goes on, and will go on through unknown members of generations of clergy, musicians, scholars and teachers, and lay people who are touched by the teaching ministry of Perkins School of Theology. For the Perkins, and for all those who have provided the rich legacy of piety and learning at Perkins School of Theology, we give thanks.[36]

8

The Cuninggim Years: 1951–60

When Merrimon Cuninggim officially took office as Dean of Perkins School of Theology on 1 September 1951, the school was still mainly oriented to its own area, the South Central Jurisdiction of the Methodist Church, and the southern part of that jurisdiction (not including Kansas and Nebraska). Its student body had grown almost to its maximum size of 400—with fourteen full-time faculty members! It had always welcomed international students in its student body, many of whom became leaders in their own countries, and some students came from outside the Jurisdiction, consisting of Texas, Louisiana, Arkansas, Oklahoma, Kansas, Nebraska and New Mexico.

It had never been so inadequate a theological school as some of the new Cuninggim faculty tended to think. According to one faculty member when I came back to teach in 1949, it was not as good a school as it had been when I was a student in the later 1930s. He was probably right, if for no other reason than the fact that the faculty teaching load was horrendous. Such a student-faculty ratio would militate against quality education regardless of what other factors were involved.

Yet the school was ready to reach toward greatness. It had a rich heritage, with a small faculty who in my experience were by and large good teachers—but not authors of books. To be sure, the dream that Robert Hyer, John B. Moore, and Frank Seay had for SMU's School of Theology had not been fully realized. The influence of the school, nevertheless, between 1915 and 1951—only thirty-six years—had been considerable.

During the Hawk administration of eighteen years, a financial base had developed for the immediate future. The cornerstone of this base was the magnificent gift of the Perkins and the Bridwell families for both buildings and endowment. Much of it was in the form of smaller gifts for scholarship, but several other substantial gifts were in place. Ruel G. Gilbert of St. Petersburg, Florida, gave almost $90,000 in 1946, the Nicholsons of East Texas had made a substantial gift to both SMU and Perkins which was not yet available, and the Crosbys of New Mexico had done likewise. So also was the gift of Mrs. Annie B. Hughey not yet available to the library.

91

Perkins School of Theology now had the buildings and the endowment to implement its continuing desire to become a first-class seminary. And Merrimon Cuninggim was eminently qualified to implement this dream.

Who Was Merrimon Cuninggim?[1]

Merrimon Cuninggim, Dean of Perkins School of Theology from 1951 to 1960, brought impressive Methodist and academic credentials to the post. Born in 1911, he had spent four years in Dallas, from 1917 to 1921, while his father, J. L. Cuninggim, was professor of what at first was called Religious Pedagogy, later Religious Education, at SMU's School of Theology. His years from ages six to ten were spent near the SMU campus where he could run in and out of his father's office in Dallas Hall. Dr. Cuninggim left Dallas in 1921, and, after a period as President of Scarritt Bible and Training School in Kansas City, he became President in 1924 of Scarritt College in Nashville, Tennessee, where he remained until he retired in 1943. (He died seven years later in 1950.) Most of J. L. Cuninggim's career was spent either in an educational institution or at the General Sunday School Board of the M. E. Church, South, also in Nashville. For a brief period, he was a pastor and a district superintendent.

The younger Cuninggim's academic preparation carried its own sterling imprint: an A.B. from Vanderbilt (1931), M.A. from Duke (1933), A.B. and diploma in theology from Oxford (1935 and 1936), B.D. (1939) and Ph.D. (1941) from Yale. His doctoral dissertation was published in 1947 by Yale University Press as *The College Seeks Religion*. He was a Rhodes scholar at Oxford for three years; while in England he was British intercollegiate tennis champion and was a Wimbledon tennis contender. Although an educator first of all, he was also an ordained Methodist clergyman.

Before coming to SMU, he had been director of religious activities at Duke (1936–38), and had taught religion at Emory and Henry (1941–42) and Dennison College (1942–44). Dean Cuninggim served as a Navy chaplain on the battleship *Tennessee* (1944–46). Following his chaplaincy he taught at Pomona College in Claremont, California (1946–51), and served as chaplain for the Associated Colleges of Claremont (1948–50).

Merrimon married Annie Whitty Daniel in 1939, and she became a partner with him, especially by her work at Perkins with faculty and students' wives during his deanship. She also worked indefatigably on various community enterprises, and became a national leader in some of these causes. The Cuninggim home during their years at Perkins was a center of social activities for the seminary community, for the larger community, and for their three children, Jessica Lee, Penelope Ann, and Margaret Merrimon (known as Terry).

Merrimon Cuninggim was President Lee's choice to be Dean of Perkins School of Theology, and so far as I can find, solely his choice. The faculty (of which I became a member in 1949) was not consulted, and apparently neither was Dean Hawk. A story may illustrate this statement. Dean Hawk was said to have had another candidate in mind to succeed him as Dean when Hawk retired in 1952, and had even talked with his friend about the prospects. The story goes that, when Hawk saw this man on a train, the friend said, "I thought I was going to be your successor at Perkins." To Hawk's surprise, the friend told him of Cuninggim's appointment.

Lee had obviously consulted other people, and probably more was known across academe than was known in Dallas. Lee, by and large, made decisions carefully. But the appointment was his, and for a very specific reason. Lee wanted an educator, not a clergyman-turned-educator as the previous deans had been. Lee's intention was that the new buildings and the new endowment be used to develop a first-class school of theology, and all the signs pointed to Cuninggim as the person within the Methodist Church who could make this transition most expeditiously. It was not, as I have already noted, that Perkins was not a good school; Lee, however, believed that only an educator could help realize its potential.

The faculty first met Cuninggim in the spring of 1951, just a few months before he took over as Dean. (Hawk was continued as Vice-President of the University for one additional year.) I remember almost the exact spot where I first met him—out-of-doors, between Kirby and Martin Halls.

Merrimon Cuninggim's distinguished academic background, his relationship to the Methodist Church, his knowledge of the national and international world of theological scholarship, and his entrepreneurial nature led to the transformation of Perkins School of Theology into a school widely known and a theological force of considerable significance.

A Change of Presidents

Umphrey Lee, on his doctor's advice, resigned as President of SMU, effective as of 11 May 1954. Bishop A. Frank Smith, chair of the Board of Trustees, immediately appointed a committee to seek a successor to Lee. In the meantime, Willis M. Tate, Vice-President of the University, and Hemphill Hosford, Vice-President and Provost, shared the responsibility as acting president.[2]

Lee had done a remarkable job as President (as we saw in a previous chapter). His chief concern had been to improve the academic life of the University, but in doing this job he also brought to the campus money for new buildings, increased the endowment, and managed to please both town (the city of Dallas) and gown (academe) in a most extraordinary way. The tribute to Lee at the

Board of Trustees meeting on 30 March 1954, contains these words: "Seldom has the head of any school been so admired and loved by all factors involved. *Time* magazine has called him 'the first citizen of Dallas'."[3]

The Board recognized the need for an appointment as soon as possible, and therefore the committee set to work quickly to examine the possibilities. They set up six criteria: the President should be a Methodist; have an appeal for young people; be enthusiastically acceptable to the alumni; have the capacity to become a leading citizen of Dallas; be someone whose educational accomplishments made him at home with the faculty; and be young, strong, healthy, and vigorous.[4]

Their choice came from inside the ranks of the University, Willis M. Tate, who was named President at the Board meeting on 6 May 1954.[5] Tate had been a student at SMU, having received his B.A. degree in 1931 and his M.A. in 1935. He was a football regular during his undergraduate days and played in SMU's appearance in the Rose Bowl.[6] Tate had been a member of the SMU staff and had also taught since 1945, first as Assistant Dean of Students[7] and later as Dean of Students. In 1950 he was made Vice-President of Development and Public Relations,[8] a post which he held until Lee's resignation. When Tate became President, he was writing his Ph.D. dissertation; Bishop Smith advised him to cease work on his dissertation, and Tate followed the advice.

During his presidency of more than twenty years, the University continued to make strides academically, to secure additional buildings, and to increase its endowment. Although this account concerns only one school of the University which he headed, a few remarks about Tate's presidency seem appropriate. Introducing a book of President Tate's speeches, Marshall Terry affirms Tate's conscious support of the two strains of SMU's history: the "idea of a liberal arts oriented university whose every graduate would participate in a core curriculum of the humanities" and "the idea of a university whose chief aim was 'to serve society,' especially through the establishment of strong professional schools."[9] Terry observed that neither Tate nor the rest of the University quite knew how to bridge the two strains of development. In any case, Perkins School of Theology was one of its professional schools "to serve society"—more specifically the church in general and the Methodist Church in particular.

Perhaps the greatest contribution of Tate to SMU, however, and this included Perkins School of Theology, was his active devotion to freedom of all kinds—specifically, to academic freedom (in the classroom) and to a larger university freedom having to do with who could speak on campus, what faculty could do and say outside the classroom, and so on. This aspect of his contribution was tested early, when in 1954 he had to deal with Professor John O. Beaty's anti-Semitism and his attacks on SMU as being "soft" on Communism.

Beaty was not discharged, as many thought he should be, and I suspect that academic privilege had been sufficiently breached that he could have been. But, as we shall see in more detail later, the charges were investigated concerning the University, and the incident allowed to die for want of a more dramatic disposition.[10]

This was only the first of a long series of incidents, including the student unrest of the 1960s and 1970s, with which Tate had to deal. His approach to a Dallas business community always suspicious of what was happening on the University campus proceeded in this way: if one believed in free enterprise in the economic realm, one also had to believe in the free enterprise of ideas. His power of persuasion prevailed enough times that the business community continued its support of the University. In 1965, the American Association of University Professors conferred upon him the coveted Meiklejohn Award for support of academic freedom.[11]

Tate did not always understand what was happening at Perkins under Merrimon Cuninggim, and he constantly wrestled with budget proposals from Perkins School of Theology whose anticipated expenses exceeded projected income. But he did not hold the reins too tightly, and in the integration crisis, which we will consider later, gave Cuninggim his full support.[12]

Faculty Additions

The first need to which Cuninggim addressed himself as Dean was the faculty. The student body had grown to almost 400, but the regular faculty remained at about the same size as when half that many students were enrolled. The core faculty of the 1920s and 1930s remained: Seneker, Goodloe, Hicks, Davis, Carlyon, and Gealy.[13] Four additions had been made to this original group: A. W. Martin, Earl Marlatt, Thomas H. Marsh, and William Warren Sweet.[14] George C. Baker had come to the University in 1949 as chaplain with a joint appointment in Homiletics, and Howard Grimes came the same year in Religious Education.[15] William A. Irwin came in 1950 to teach Old Testament. Albert Outler was persuaded to come to Perkins by Dean-designate Merrimon Cuninggim in the winter of 1951. He left his prestigious post as the Timothy Dwight Professor of Theology at Yale Divinity School to come to Perkins in the summer of 1951.[16]

A word should be said at this point concerning Albert Outler. His joining the Perkins faculty from Yale Divinity School was not only significant *substantively*: his presence added one of the finest academic and theological minds of the century to Perkins, SMU, and the Southwest. His coming was also important *symbolically*: it symbolized the coming of age of Perkins School of Theology. Theologians throughout the world could no longer ignore Perkins after Albert Outler chose to move from Yale to Perkins.

His contributions to the academic life of both Perkins and the entire University can hardly be measured. His participation in the ecumenical movement, including Vatican Council II, was important not only for that movement but also for the quality of Perkins life and its becoming known throughout the world-wide church. During the later years of his academic career, his main work was with the John Wesley corpus of work, especially the sermons. His determination that Mr. Wesley would be recognized not only as an evangelizing preacher, but also as an able theologian, and the care with which he edited the sermons, may well turn out to be Albert Outler's most lasting contributions to the church.[17]

Decherd Turner began his long career as librarian in 1950,[18] a fact which led to the development of a major theological library.

Not including Turner, who later did some teaching, this adds up to fourteen permanent members of the faculty, two of whom (Baker and Sweet) had other responsibilities.

This group was supplemented by eleven visiting faculty who taught one or more courses during the academic year of 1951–52. These included W. B. Mahan, Ben O. Hill, Marshall Steel, Rabbi David Lefkowitz, Edmund H. Steelman, A. W. Wasson, Allen Lamar Cooper, Clyde L. Manschreck, Robert E. Goodrich, Jr., and Mary Fisher Floyd.[19] Six of the eleven were either full-time in the undergraduate school or pastor or rabbi of a church or synagogue.

Faculty Participation

One of the changes which Cuninggim introduced into the procedure of operating the school was more faculty participation in decision making. This included visits by prospective faculty, with full opportunity for faculty members and some students to interview the person, and later a vote by the faculty on whether to recommend that the Dean present the name of the prospect to the President. The President, in turn, if he approved, made the recommendation to the Board of Trustees for their confirmation. Early on in the process, the faculty voted to extend the interview time to three days.[20]

New Faculty: 1952–53. William Warren Sweet retired in 1952, but three full-time faculty were added—those who had been interviewed during Cuninggim's first year as Dean: Edward C. Hobbs in New Testament, Marvin Judy in Church Administration and Field Work, and Joseph W. Mathews in Christian Ethics. Hobbs (an Episcopalian) was one of the first non-Methodists to be appointed to a full-time teaching position. Judy had been an active participant in the St. Louis Conference in Missouri, and later was recognized as one of the leaders of the Town and Country movement in the church.

Mathews was a unique character who liked to shock students out of their complacency and made a strong impression on the school in the few years that he taught at Perkins.[21]

The Dean also increased the visiting faculty for 1952–53, to sixteen. These included, in addition to those who remained from the previous year, E. Ahmad-Shah, William M. Elliott, Paul B. Kern, Charles T. Thrift, and Lance Webb (later a bishop). For the summer only, Philip H. Ashby, John L. Casteel, Floyd V. Filson, Robert E. Fitch, Paul Hutchinson, and Douglas Jackson joined the ranks.[22]

During the academic year, a number of invitations were issued to established faculty in other institutions and were declined. The faculty showed enough concern about this to discuss the matter in one of its meetings.[23] No definitive answers were given. Perhaps the reason was that Perkins still did not have the stature in theological education to lure older faculty to its ranks, Albert Outler, of course, being an exception. In future years the situation was somewhat different, but what is more significant, I think, is that the Dean used his knowledge of graduate theological institutions to secure younger faculty just completing their graduate work. Many of these turned out to be the core of the Perkins faculty that has persisted to the present (1989).

A signal honor which bore much later fruit was the appointment of Albert Outler as one of the eight Methodist delegates to the Faith and Order Conference in Lund, Sweden, during the summer of 1952. This was by no means Outler's first participation in the ecumenical movement, but did lead to increasing participation over the next few years. He attributed this and other nominations to the influence of Bishop William C. Martin, who was himself an active ecumenist.

1953–54. Because of the declinations, the regular faculty did not increase significantly for 1953–54. Allen Lamar Cooper joined its ranks as both Counselor to Students and teacher in the field of ethics. Decherd Turner and Dean Cuninggim were listed on the faculty for the first time. New visiting faculty included Gaston Foote, J. B. Holt, Charles W. Iglehart, Robert G. McCracken, Barney McGrath, Rabbi Levi Olan, John T. O'Neill, Thompson Shannon, and Olive Smith. Summer-only faculty involved Robert Hazleton, Ray C. Petry, Paul Ramsey, William L. Reed, and Seymour A. Smith.[24]

The Dean stated that Perkins was in need of and looking for four new faculty in Division I (Local Church), four in Division II (Christianity and Culture), two in Division III (Church History, Theology, and Ethics), and one in Division IV (Bible).[25]

The first faculty conference away from the campus occurred in September 1953. This practice has been continued to the present.

1954–55. Cuninggim made great strides in filling faculty gaps before the fall of 1954, with six additions. W. Richey Hogg was appointed in March 1954, but was on leave in India for 1954–55. It was a busy year for the faculty in the interview process just as it was for the Dean in the search for candidates. One retirement also occurred, that of J. T. Carlyon.

Four of the six newcomers began their teaching in the fall of 1954: Charles Johnson in Religious Education, H. Neill McFarland in History of Religions, Joseph D. Quillian in Homiletics and Worship, and Herndon Wagers in Philosophy of Religion (or Philosophical Theology). Robert Elliott assumed the post in Pastoral Counseling in January 1955.[26]

All of these were Methodists except Herndon Wagers. In the discussion of the possible appointment of Wagers, his denominational affiliation, The Christian Church (Disciples of Christ), came under question. He was not the first non-Methodist to be elected, but that discussion perhaps encouraged the faculty to recognize the benefits of including those from other denominations—as was done—eventually including the appointment of Roman Catholics as well. No one fit into the Perkins situation any better than Wagers, and when an opportunity came to him a few years later to return to an institution in his own communion, he chose to stay at Perkins where, I believe, he had come to feel thoroughly at home.

Visiting faculty in addition to some of those who had taught the previous years were Hans W. Frei of Rice University and Benjamin Petty of the undergraduate school. Summer faculty included Hiel D. Bollinger, Charles Braden, Elmer Leslie, Carl Michalson, and Roger Ortmayer.

1955–56. The year 1955 saw the retirement of W. A. Irwin, one of the translators of the Revised Standard Version of the Old Testament, who taught at Perkins after his retirement from the University of Chicago Divinity School. Three new full-time faculty arrived: W. Richey Hogg in World Christianity (elected a year earlier), Douglas Jackson in Sociology of Religion, and David Shipley in Historical Theology. John Deschner and Schubert Ogden were elected during 1954–55 but placed on leave to begin their teaching the following year. George C. Baker resigned as University Chaplain to become McCreless Professor of Evangelism. Umphrey Lee, Barney McGrath, and Sterling Wheeler assumed places on the faculty for part-time teaching. Visiting faculty numbered twelve with Richard C. Bush, William C. Martin, Kermit Schoonover, James N. Swafford, and Federal Lee Whittlesey as additions to those previously teaching. Robert E. Cushman, John Knox, and Willis C. Lamont joined the faculty for summer only.[27]

A shock to the community occurred in fall 1955 when Joe Mathews announced his resignation. Mathews was without doubt the most colorful, and perhaps the most controversial, person ever to serve on the Perkins faculty. (It has been suggested that Ora Miner, in the 1920s, matched him.) Mathews used the shock treatment with consummate skill. His classroom antics included such activities as throwing erasers at students and using colorful language (which I never heard him use outside the classroom). The period in which both he and Ed Hobbs taught—they egged each other on—was in my experience the most exciting in the history of Perkins. It was not the most comfortable, for Mathews never let us become complacent.

Having decided not to complete his Ph.D. dissertation—he was a perfectionist and never satisfied with what he wrote—Mathews left Perkins in June 1956 to lead a student community in Austin. After several years he moved the base of his operation to Evanston, Illinois, and took over leadership of the Ecumenical Institute, the forces for which emerged from the World Council of Churches' Second Assembly which had met in Evanston in 1954.

There, and later in Chicago, he developed a unique kind of adult education, led by a semi-monastic community (which did not forbid marriage). The group later produced a community development program by working in their own situation in a poor section of Chicago, during the racial strife of the 1960s. The Institute later became known as the Institute of Cultural Affairs, and has exported its community development plan to other parts of the United States and to various locations throughout the world.

1956–57. During a three-year period, five people retired from the faculty and were elected to emeritus status. These included the three pioneers who had joined the faculty in the 1920s: James Seehorn Seneker (1954), John H. Hicks (1955), and Robert W. Goodloe (1956). In addition two more recent members also retired, A. W. Martin and Earl Marlatt in 1956. Before the end of the 1950s, all pre-Cuninggim faculty except Marsh and Grimes had entered the emeritus ranks.

The fall of 1956 was the year of beginning for the two theologians John Deschner and Schubert Ogden. Perhaps no two people could have been less alike in their preparation and temperament than these two, but they worked out a unique team relationship. Deschner received his graduate training in Switzerland under Karl Barth, Ogden at the University of Chicago. Deschner was a native Texan, a pastoral professor who became the confidant of both students and colleagues over the years. Ogden tended to seem brash to many students, though in his personal relationships he was not nearly so demanding as in the classroom. There he believed that students should know what they were talking about and be able to express their thoughts logically and precisely. These two, along with Outler and Shipley, formed a formidable team of theologians who began to attract the attention of outsiders for both their variety and competence.

One additional full-time member, Kermit Schoonover, had taught the previous year in a visiting capacity. A member of the Society of Friends, Schoonover exhibited the kind of quiet personal style and attitude nourished by his Quaker traditions.

Twelve visiting faculty were listed in the catalog with new listings being Walter Bell, John Dillenberger, Carol Jones, John K. Kultgen, F. Gene Leggett, and Harald Lindstrom (from Sweden). New summer faculty included Douglas Chandler and John H. Otwell.[28]

1957–58. The academic year which began in 1957 was a banner year for faculty additions. Some were replacements for the five retirements of the previous three years. R. Floyd Curl succeeded A. W. Martin in Field Work and Church Administration. He brought with him C. Wayne Banks, who taught Christian Education and later became Director of Academic Procedures. In 1957, Banks suddenly found himself the only resident teacher of Christian Education. Grimes was on study leave, having received the first Perkins faculty fellowship offered by the American Association of Theological Schools. Unexpectedly, Johnson went to Garrett, his alma mater, to teach, but returned to Perkins after one year's absence.

Joseph L. Allen, a young Ph.D. from Yale, came to teach Christian Ethics. Richard C. Bush joined the faculty, teaching History of Religion part-time in addition to administrative duties. Emmanuel Gitlin came in Old Testament, and H. Grady Hardin, from Chapelwood Methodist in Houston, came in Worship and Preaching.

In 1957, Perkins first listed as an auxiliary the Institute of Religion at the Houston Medical Center, established to direct clinical pastoral education of both seminary students and pastors. Dawson C. Bryan was its director and LeRoy G. Kerney its first faculty member.[29]

Visiting faculty continued to fill gaps in the Perkins roster, providing enrichment for the curriculum. Although the number of visiting faculty for this period was unusually high, as Cuninggim proceeded in building a permanent faculty, this situation also brought greater breadth and depth to the faculty and enhanced the experience of both faculty and students. New visitors for the year included Maurice Culver, Lilla Mills Cunningham, Earl Cunningham, James C. Hares, Stuart Henry, Franklin Littell, and James N. Swafford. Summer-only faculty included Robert J. Arnott, Van Harvey, Roger Ortmayer, and Albert T. Rasmussen.[30]

1958–59. By 1958 nine formerly active faculty were listed as emeritus. Edward Hobbs resigned to go to the Church Divinity School of the Pacific. The Institute of Religion added two faculty members, Joseph W. Knowles and Edward E. Thornton. Only three new faculty were added to Perkins, and one returned. Roger Ortmayer was added to teach Christianity and the Arts. Lloyd Pfautsch, a joint appointment with the School of the Arts, began immediately in the work of developing a new degree, the Master of Sacred Music. Van Harvey came to teach Philosophical Theology, and Charles Johnson rejoined the Perkins faculty in Religious Education.

Eleven visiting faculty returned to supplement the teaching. Most of these had taught in a previous session. John B. Cobb and James S. Thomas were new for the 1958 summer session, and James Winton Gable and J. B. Holt taught during the year.[31]

1959–60. The academic year 1959–60 was Merrimon Cuninggim's final year as Dean. He left in 1960 to become the Executive Director of the Danforth Foundation in St. Louis. This year was also David Shipley's last year at Perkins; he transferred to the Methodist Theological School in Ohio in 1960.

Two members of long standing retired in 1959, Wesley C. Davis and Fred D. Gealy. Both Davis and Gealy, along with W. A. Irwin, were retained on a part-time basis to work in preparation for a graduate program in religion for the University.

Two New Testament instructors came to take the places of Davis and Gealy: William R. Farmer and Victor P. Furnish. Farmer had taught previously at Drew, while Furnish came directly from graduate school at Yale. A total of fifteen visitors completed the teaching staff. Newcomer visitors during the academic year were W. B. J. Martin, Thomas C. Oden, Kenneth C. Pepper, and Marion B. Richmond. The summer faculty included Markus Barth, Charles S. Braden, John von Rohr, and Ronald J. Williams.[32] J. B. Holt took Richard Bush's place as Director of Admissions in January 1960,[33] and taught in the field of Missions. Miss Nell Anders retired as registrar after serving in that position for some thirty-five years.[34]

1960–61. Although this was Quillian's first year as Dean, the faculty appointments had been made under Cuninggim's deanship during 1959–60. These final appointments brought a remarkable record of faculty appointments if not to completion, at least to a stage which provided a core faculty, still supplemented, as it should be, with visiting faculty with special expertise or with contributions in terms of character and knowledge. The new faculty for this year, found and recommended by Cuninggim, were Frederick S. Carney in Ethics, Franklin H. Littell in Church History, W. J. A. Power in Old Testament, William C. Robinson in New Testament, and James M. Ward in Old Testament.[35] Robert Anderson came in 1960, with his appointment actually being to the School of the Arts especially for the sacred music program, and soon became chapel organist for Perkins School of Theology, to the great delight of chapel-goers for many years.

Additional visiting faculty to make a total of twelve were Edmund Deane with John Trevor for summer only. Banks was moved from Field Work to become Director of Academic Procedures with part-time teaching in Christian Education.

Degrees

New faculty made new degrees possible. This did not change the fact that the basic degree had been from the beginning, and remained, the Bachelor of Divinity (B.D.), later renamed the Master of Theology (M.Th., in 1969) and still later the Master of Divinity (M.Div., in 1982). Rather early in its history a combined B.D. and M.A. (a graduate school degree) was set up with some double credit, making the time less than if the two degrees were taken separately.

We have noted the establishment quite early of the Master of Church Administration degree; it never attained the popularity its proponents hoped for it, and it was later abandoned. Much later the school set up the Bachelor of Religious Education degree (B.R.E.) as a stop-gap measure, but it was discontinued in 1951 after few takers had opted for it. Before that time the Master of Religious Education degree (M.R.E.) had come into being, the first graduate being Eloise Richardson in 1951. At first a twelve-month degree, it was strengthened a few years later when its requirements were lengthened to two academic years of full-time study.[36]

The Master of Arts degree continued to be offered, under the Graduate School, and a special M.A. in Bible was instituted, mostly based on examinations, but was never popular.[37]

The faculty adopted a new degree in 1956, the Master of Sacred Theology (S.T.M.). It was especially popular in Pastoral Counseling in connection with the Institute of Religion in Houston. It included a written project representing "an intensification of a major practical concern of the student."[38]

In the late 1950s, Perkins and the School of the Arts began to talk about a joint degree in church music (Master of Sacred Music). The committee presented the first proposal on 27 February 1959, and the degree went into effect in 1960 under the able direction of Lloyd Pfautsch, who had become director of the Seminary Singers the previous year.

The first step toward a doctoral level degree, the Ph.D. in Religious Studies, under the Graduate School with the leadership taken by Perkins, took place in 1959. The first report of a committee, chaired by Albert Outler, came before the Perkins faculty that year,[39] but several years passed before the degree actually materialized, with the first students in the program admitted in 1965.

Cuninggim's Record of Appointments

With the exception of Pfautsch and Anderson for the M.S.M. degree, the B.D. degree's curriculum was the basis for Dean Cuninggim's appointments. The record is truly remarkable.

Cuninggim made his first faculty appointment in 1951, when he persuaded Albert Outler to come to Perkins. His next appointments were in 1952–53, his last for 1960–61, ten academic years. The total was thirty-two, six of whom also had administrative responsibilities, with two being joint appointments with the School of the Arts. Ten were still on the faculty in 1989 (one of whom, Lloyd Pfautsch, had moved completely to the School of the Arts). Twelve remained until retirement. Four left Perkins while Cuninggim was Dean and six left or died later. The faculty rejected only one of Cuninggim's nominees. Probably six or eight invited to join the Perkins faculty declined to move from their existing posts.[40]

Cuninggim developed a core faculty which persisted for more than thirty years. This group still provided faculty leadership in 1989. As we shall see in the following chapter, some viewed Cuninggim's relationship with the church, which formed the immediate context for Perkins School of Theology, as occasionally lacking sufficient finesse; this led to problems greater than a seminary normally has with its constituency. But in faculty appointments and in other academic accomplishments, to be examined in the following chapter, Cuninggim's record may well be unparalleled in the history of American theological education.

9

The Quadrangle Comes to Life

From its beginning, SMU's School of Theology had had open admissions, accepting as students virtually all applicants. Indeed, at first upper-class undergraduates at SMU were allowed to take part of their theological work as undergraduates and receive credit on both the B.A. and B.D. degrees. In this way, the total for both degrees was less than the seven years otherwise required. Hawk made a brief effort to revive this practice, but apparently the faculty overruled the decision and if it was implemented at all it was for only a brief time. Upper-class undergraduates might still be admitted to complete their undergraduate degree while beginning their graduate work. Yet the American Association of Theological Schools frowned on this practice, and eventually Perkins received notations for it biennially from 1938 to 1944, the notations being removed in 1946.

In any case the admission standards required only an undergraduate degree from an accredited college or university, and some were admitted from non-accredited colleges. A fairly small percentage of such admissions did not jeopardize the school's standing with the AATS, but Perkins had sometimes exceeded the maximum percentage.

Cuninggim moved quickly to change the policy of open admissions in two ways: first, as Dean, he would no longer follow previous practice and be admitting officer. Instead, as in most seminaries, a committee would make the decisions. Second, admissions would become selective, with standards set so that not every candidate would necessarily be admitted.[1] He appointed an Admissions committee of five members, with Albert Outler as chair and the Dean a member *ex officio*.

The committee's task was twofold: first, to set admission standards that would be approved by the faculty; and second, to be the body that reviewed each application and either admitted or declined to admit each student. Although the grade point average was not high (a C+), the committee did reject a limited number of persons with inadequate grade averages. For example, in 1955 only ten were rejected but in 1959 twenty-five were not allowed admission.[2] It was much more difficult to determine when students did not appear to have the "gifts and graces" for ordained ministry, and this was set as another of the standards to be observed. The procedure for notifying the applicant of the committee's decision in the latter cases was even more trying than it was for grades.[3]

The consequences were soon evident: first, many people in the constituent Methodist Church, especially those who had sponsored a rejected candidate, were most unhappy with the school. Attempts were made to interpret the policy, and letters to sponsors sometimes helped; but it still remained that some people became disaffected with Perkins School of Theology. A second result was that fewer students were admitted, leading sometimes to a number of students under the unspoken maximum of 400.[4] What also became fairly common was that students began applying to other schools with lower admission standards.

In certain cases, of course, students with a lower grade point average were admitted if other factors were overriding grades. Some students proved decisively that they could do seminary work even though their undergraduate grades seemed not to warrant admission. Unfortunately, others could not do so.

Over the years the faculty, through the committee's recommendations, raised admission standards. Through psychological testing and other means, the school sought better ways of dealing with those whose psychological health did not indicate the likelihood of a useful ministry.

Curriculum

In 1951, the adequacy of the curriculum was probably at its lowest point in the school's history. The last revision before Cuninggim came as Dean resulted in a list of required courses based on each faculty member's having one required course. Students were then required to elect courses in the three divisions, and these varied according to the three types of ministerial preparation: pastoral, teaching, or social work.[5] Although hardly a sound way to build a curriculum, the result was not quite so bad as the method would suggest. Because the faculty had been selected with a view to what was considered a well-rounded curriculum, there was more curricular balance than one might expect.

Cuninggim's first move toward curriculum revision was to initiate a series of faculty discussions on the purpose of the school, what it needed to emphasize in order to fulfill that purpose, and the kind of curriculum that would support its goals.[6] The second move, on 8 October 1952, was to appoint a curriculum revision committee. Wesley Davis chaired it; members were Dean Cuninggim, Howard Grimes, W. A. Irwin, and Joe Mathews.[7]

A preliminary step was taken in the spring of Cuninggim's first year. The University had been on the semester plan for many years. The School of Theology had briefly tried the semester system but rather quickly returned to the quarter plan, with one quarter before Christmas, two quarters in the winter and spring, and one during the summer. At Cuninggim's recommendation, the faculty voted, with some negative votes, to change to the semester plan.[8]

The review committee worked diligently and quickly during the fall semester, and regularly reported to the faculty agreements it had reached. On November 21—and this must have been a record for committee action on such a major question—agreement took place by the faculty on basic points: the program was to cover six semesters, with a minimum of 90 semester hours for graduation (actually 96 emerged as the final recommendation). The four subjects per semester received four hours credit each, making each of the three years receive 32 semester hours of credit. Approximately one-third of the work would be elective, with two-thirds being required, for the B.D. degree.[9]

Throughout the work of the committee, Dean Cuninggim fully participated as a member of the group. Indeed, the curriculum which emerged, as I remember the process, was formulated largely on the basis of his proposals. Yet what emerged came through the committee process and by consensus. The Dean may have led the way, but the faculty could claim the new curriculum as its own. By 22 December 1952—just two months after the committee began its work—the results were presented to the faculty as "committee of the whole" and it was approved. It was ratified in a regular faculty session on 2 January 1953.[10]

Wesley Davis had described the new curriculum in the Spring 1953 issue of the *Perkins School of Theology Journal.* "We began," he writes, "with an effort to clarify in our own minds the task of the minister, to examine him at work in his parish."[11] The principles behind the curriculum, as Davis laid them out, were (1) pertinence (to the needs of students for ministry); (2) balance, between elective and required work, between practical and "content" courses; (3) sequence within each of the four divisions; (4) integration, so that the minister can see his task whole; and (5) flexibility within divisions, so that each division keeps on top of what future pastors need from that area of study.[12]

Cuninggim made a somewhat different emphasis in his report to the Provost for 1953–54. "The course of study," he writes, "is designed to provide an integration among the various disciplines and a sequence in their pursuit which traditional seminaries have lacked."[13]

This same quality is emphasized in the *Perkins Catalog*:

An understanding of the minister's task and of the ways of learning suggests that the separateness of, and often competitiveness among the various traditional disciplines give way to the difficult goal of synthesis and cooperative endeavor. These considerations, moreover, imply the need of orderliness, as well as of federation of activity; some proper sequence of study must be worked out. And since contemplation and activity must go together in the successful functioning of the minister, so also these two related aspects of living must find their joined embodiment in the curricular program.[14]

In order to implement these principles, a course of study based on three common cores of knowledge was set up: (a) the faith of the Christian community—that is the Scriptures and history and doctrine of the church; (b) the world (or culture) in which the Christian community has developed and its present context; and (c) the life of the world-wide and local church.[15] These common cores of knowledge (in the broadest use of the word, including practice) were organized into four divisions:

Division I: The Life and Work of the Local Church (Administration, Education, Preaching, and Worship; field and laboratory work)

Division II: Christianity and Culture (Philosophy, Missions and Other Religions, Social Ethics, and Counseling)

Division III: The Christian Heritage (Church History [institutional and doctrinal], Theology, and Ethics)

Division IV: The Bible (Old and New Testaments).[16]

Cuninggim emphasized the relating of the various aspects of the core to one another, a fact which required faculty cooperation. He believed there was a renewed emphasis on the Bible, and that Division II was genuinely new. The curriculum integrated classroom and "laboratory," and for Methodist students there was a new course on Methodist history, polity, and doctrine.[17]

The curriculum received a great deal of attention in theological circles.[18] There were assuredly unique aspects of it, for example, in the attempt to integrate practice into the curriculum itself. Divisions III and IV were fairly traditional, but Division II was genuinely innovative—a two-year attempt to relate Christianity and culture by dealing with such areas as philosophy, psychology, other religions, and human society as they impinged on the Christian faith. The attempt to build unity and sequence into the four divisions and to some extent between them was at least a more serious attempt than was common. The course of study served the school well, especially as it persisted in a modified form into the 1960s and later as some seminaries capitulated to students' demands and developed curricula which dealt more with current problems such as minority concerns than with the Christian heritage.

But did the curriculum really work? Insofar as it did not, whose fault was it? Slight revisions were made for 1957–58,[19] and for 1960–61 (with Cuninggim having been a member of the revision committee), with courses being reduced in the latter revision to three semester hours to provide more elective space.[20]

The answer to the two questions just raised can be sought in the reaction of the faculty to the reduction of courses from four to three semester hours (each course thus to be one-fifth of a full load rather than one-fourth, making the total requirement for graduation 72 hours). According to the really good students, the faculty by and large did not reduce the requirements in courses even though their percentage of a full load had been changed.

And so it was with regard to the original "New Curriculum": faculty tended to continue teaching what they wanted to teach rather than what a particular course represented in the entire curriculum and with scant regard for other parts of the course of study. Faculty members are by and large conservative when it comes to their teaching, and do not find it easy to adapt to new conditions. There are exceptions, of course, but it should be noted that teachers teach best when they are comfortable with the subject matter with which they are involved. Division II, Christianity and Culture, never really worked out. It really did require a new approach to education which sought to relate traditional subject matter to either a former culture or the present day. I do not mean that this is not done by many professors, only that the idea behind Division II was neither fully understood nor implemented.

Field Work (or Education as it was later called) received an incredible amount of faculty attention during the 1950s.[21] The intention originally was to involve the entire faculty in the enterprise and to relate Field Education to all aspects of the curriculum. Faculty minutes are replete with attempts to do this, but it never really worked. For some Parish Week, when faculty and students without churches went for a week to be with students who did, was a helpful experience. It was not until an intern program was instituted, with its own staff both in the seminary and in the field, that a workable plan emerged.

Perhaps the truth is close to what some faculty said even at the time: you cannot integrate a student's experience for him or her; the student must do that. The faculty by and large were oriented to a "classical" kind of seminary education with an emphasis on the Christian heritage, not unlike, I think, what Seay, Moore, Kern, and others had envisioned many years earlier. An even stronger attempt was made with the new curriculum to be sure that this classical heritage was made relevant to the present time, but in the course of time, the attempt to do this in a division was eliminated and that task was left to individual faculty members sensitive to the need and able to do it for their own field of thought.

New Buildings

It became apparent soon after moving to the new quadrangle that space for administrative and faculty offices, and even for classrooms, was inadequate in Kirby Hall for the increased size of faculty, staff, and student body. Early in

Cuninggim's deanship, therefore, he enlisted the Perkins family in the building of an additional building, just to the south of Kirby Hall. As an example of the new openness toward the faculty, Cuninggim appointed a committee to plan the building, with Earl Marlatt as chair.[22] (Incidentally, another example of this new faculty participation is that by 1956 there were eighteen faculty committees!)[23]

Marlatt was another of the faculty eccentrics. He had been Dean of the Boston University School of Theology earlier in his career, and attempted to operate the committee as apparently he had acted as dean. The committee had to be constantly alert to what he was doing outside committee action and occasionally step in to change decisions. What emerged from the committee, however, was an exceedingly useful building, named for the third president of SMU (not including acting President Kilgore). The auditorium, seating 300, was named for Mrs. Perkins, and the prayer chapel, later moved to a room in Perkins Chapel, for Earl Marlatt.[24]

One other building in the seminary quadrangle, but built by the University with a federal loan, was a third apartment building, named for Bishop John M. Moore. Opened in 1959, it has always housed mainly Perkins students, even though it is open to students from other schools.[25]

Several years earlier the University had demolished the two wooden apartment buildings on Airline Road, Marvin and Pierce Halls. They had served succeeding generations of students for more than thirty years, but were in need of such major repairs that it was not practical to continue them.[26]

Racially Integrating the School of Theology[27]

In a previous chapter we noted that SMU's School of Theology very early began offering courses to black students, but always without credit except when an occasional student took a course and received credit from his original seminary. Then during the final year of Hawk's deanship, in 1950, the Board of Trustees opened the door for the admission of black students to full membership in the Perkins community. It is reported that one influential member of the Board said: "I don't like this proposal. It goes against what I've always believed. But I can tell which way the wind is blowing, and I'm going to vote for it."[28]

For the sake of proper perspective on this matter, it should be remembered that this was more than four years prior to the Supreme Court decision of 17 May 1954, that declared "separate but equal" education unconstitutional. It occurred almost simultaneously with the earlier decision in 1950 that the Law School of the University of Texas at Austin must admit a black student because law school provisions for blacks were not equal to those for whites.[29] It was, of course, more than a decade before the Civil Rights Act of 1964. The process of desegregation in the South had scarcely begun and resistance to it was great. Street cars and buses, restaurants and public schools, all aspects of life, including some said especially the churches, were strictly segregated with whites clearly on top of the pile.

Two black students had been admitted to classes almost immediately but did not prove equal to academic demands. It was not until the second year of Cuninggim's deanship that five carefully selected black students were admitted to the Bachelor of Divinity degree program of the School, in September 1952. They represented three denominations, from five states. The real, and successful, pioneers of Perkins's desegregation were John W. Elliott, James A. Hawkins, James V. Lyles, Negail R. Riley, and Cecil Williams.[30] Four of the students sought and were provided rooms in S. B. Perkins Dormitory.

From the beginning, Dean Cuninggim adopted the policy of talking things out with the five black students in order to help them see the possible implications of any particular action they might take. He called them into his office the first day they were on campus, and they went, probably with misgivings, thinking that the law was to be laid down concerning what they *could* and could *not* do. To quote Cuninggim in an address given many years later:

> I said there were two things that I thought we ought to talk about. The first was as to how to handle this unusual and revolutionary movement. The Board had made it possible for them to be treated as regular students. "Within the bounds of the general University customs," I said, "regular students make their own decisions about where they go and what they do. So, you will have that privilege too. But you and I know that there will be a lot of questions and a lot of problems, incident to your being the first black students on a white campus. Can we share these problems as they arise, or even in imagination before they arise?" This wasn't going quite as they expected, so they gladly said Yes.
>
> I continued: "I'll promise to give you my understanding of any problems when I hear about it, and more, will give you advice about it. But then you'll be free to make your own decision—at least, as free as my advice, likely sometimes to be hard for you to take, will allow. Will you promise to share similarly with me the questions that you have or come to know about?" "O, yes indeed," they said. They didn't really believe me, of course, but it was a lot better than fiat. And what did they have to lose?[31]

There were a few problems at Perkins itself. The students welcomed the new students enthusiastically. They had raised a special scholarship on their behalf, and so far as I could determine at the time treated them simply as fellow students. Faculty and staff in general acted similarly. In some instances, to be sure, they practiced "segregation in reverse" by taking into account their inadequate undergraduate education in the giving of grades. The one group that had to be reprimanded were the black employees of the Perkins cafeteria who resented their presence among the students.[32]

Discussions with the Dean (at first) and later with Lamar Cooper, Counselor to Students, covered a wide variety of subjects: what part of the streetcar they should occupy, recreational swimming, attendance at football games in the Cotton Bowl, shopping, getting a haircut, attendance at white churches, and the like. Sometimes decisions were to participate immediately (attendance at football games); sometimes it was delayed (swimming). Dean Cuninggim followed what he called "cautious advance" in his discussions with the students: advance as far and as fast as possible but cautiously, with a consideration of the milieu in which the advance was occurring.[33]

Cuninggim provides an example of how advances made first with caution sometimes led to problems which a somewhat bolder approach avoided. Would the black students play intramural sports on Perkins teams? A white student leader made an unauthorized call on the Director of Athletics, Lloyd Messersmith, to demand that black students be allowed to play on Perkins teams. The director's response was, "Since you're raising the question about it, perhaps I should take it up with the faculty senate."[34] The question went to the Senate, where it turned out that everyone favored their participation, but since the question had been raised, perhaps they ought to consult the administration.[35]

The Perkins representative to the Senate immediately notified the Dean, who called Lloyd Messersmith and simply told him that the black students would be participating in intramurals and he needed to know this in order to head off any surprises. Messersmith's response was: "Oh, I'm so glad you are treating it normally; no point of making a big scene, is there?" (They actually avoided touch football the first year because of the amount of contact in the game.) The Dean concludes his account of this incident with the comment: "Incidentally, the Senate motion, so far as I know, is still on the table."[36]

The first semester moved along with surprisingly few difficulties. But then the enterprise was almost derailed. As Director of Men's Housing, I was informed by a white student that he would like to have a black student as a roommate. So I went to someone I thought might be interested and asked him about the possibility. He readily agreed, and so we came to have two black students with white roommates during the spring semester.

When word got out in the early spring of 1953 that the black students were not only living in the dormitory but that two of them had white roommates, the opposition outside the school coalesced and began to bring pressure on the Board of Trustees, including Mr. Perkins. The situation grew in intensity, aggravated by a female student who wrote to her parents about sitting at the same table with one of the black students at Sunday dinner. (The Perkins cafeteria was not open on Sunday.) It became increasingly clear that the matter would be raised at the May 1953 Board of Trustees meeting.[37]

On the day prior to the Board meeting, the School of Theology Trustee Committee met at the request of Bishop A. Frank Smith, chairman of the Board. The committee decided to try to keep the question from coming to the full Board of Trustees by agreeing that they (the committee) would handle it. The committee's action was to support things as they were[38] and therefore the matter did not come before the Board of Trustees.

Several of the key people in handling the situation were not available. Bishop Paul Martin, chair of the School of Theology Committee and confidante of the Perkins family, was on an extended overseas episcopal visit. President Lee was out with a heart attack, and Tate and Hosford were carrying on the responsibilities of the President. Mrs. Smith had suffered a heart attack, and Bishop Smith stayed in Houston as much as possible.[39] Dean Cuninggim lacked the close relationship with the persons involved which Martin, Smith, and Lee had. (When Tate assumed the presidency of the University in 1954, he became active behind the scenes and helped bring the matter to a close.)

Then in the summer of 1953, Mr. Perkins, at the insistence of the unnamed group demanding the black students' removal at least from the dormitory, did something he had never done before and which neither he nor Mrs. Perkins did later: He wrote a letter to Bishop William C. Martin (presiding bishop of the Dallas-Fort Worth area of the Methodist Church) and sent a copy to the Dean (as well as to other people). When no action occurred, Mr. Perkins wrote directly to the Dean.

The Dean was out of the city, and in his absence well-meaning people tried to get Mrs. Cuninggim to use her influence in having the black students removed from the dormitory. One of the cleverest ploys they used was to warn her that if he did not do so, it would bring on the demise of Mr. Perkins, who was now an old man.[40] Informed of what was going on, Cuninggim wrote out a statement while he was still out of town to use on his return to Dallas.

When he returned, he would show or read the statement he had written to officials of both church and University. (It had been written, he says, in Pennsylvania, not far from the Gettysburg battlefield.) The statement in part read as follows:

Why [then] take the Negroes out of the dormitory? Or why do anything else that would be authoritarian and regulatory?

Because their being in the dormitory has aroused the opposition of those in contact with them? No. Because they themselves have misused the privileges they have possessed? No. Because the University has received unfavorable publicity about it? No. Because the University officials were not aware of what was going on and the thing was done in secret? No. Because it was never intended to consider them as regular students and somehow advantage had been taken of the Board's original action? No. ... Because we are moving too far ahead of the general provision, and our constituency would not support us? No. ... Because the policy of mutual consultation between them and me, on the basis of which they have guided their actions, has failed? No. Because either the things done or the methods followed are out of harmony with the basic character and purpose of the University or the Church? No. None of these reasons is available for our defense, for none of them is sound.

Then why?

There is no reasonable explanation at all; and the explanations based on personal taste will not be sufficient to save us from disaster.

But these dire imaginings are altogether vain, for I am convinced that the Board of Trustees, fully informed as to the situation and to the consequences of the restrictive action, would not take any such step. Yet this does not throw us inevitably into the other disaster. Surely there is a constructive way out of the situation, a way that calls for the painstaking education of those who are disturbed. This education would need to consist of information on both the status of the Negroes in the School and the devastating results of any such change in that status as would inevitably represent a backward step in their treatment as regular students. It will not be easy, but I believe it can be accomplished. For this way of education is the direct and honorable way. It is the way of love as well as of firmness; the only way that can bind the wounds of those who have been hurt, the only way we can testify to the continual working of God's grace among us, the only way that any of us could take.[41]

Hosford and especially Tate were working quietly behind the scenes, handicapped because of their "acting" status. But at one time they said to Cuninggim, "Merrimon, we are with you."[42]

At the first retreat of the faculty in September 1953, the situation was tense. Cuninggim said unequivocally that if the Board required him to take the black students out of the dormitory he would resign. Many of the rest of us were deeply disturbed, both about the situation and our unwillingness to take a similar vow. So each of us in his own way wrestled with his conscience and hoped for the best.

The only change that occurred was that the black students voluntarily withdrew from having white roommates. As I look back on the situation, I believe that placing the black and white students together was probably unwise at the time. I can now see that I might have been more concerned with "advance" than "caution."

Surprisingly nothing happened at the fall Board meeting. Then Bishop Paul Martin returned in November, and he and his wife Mildred spent part of their Christmas vacation with the Perkins in Wichita Falls. He writes:

> One evening, Mr. Perkins in the direct fashion that always characterized him asked me, "Do you believe if this matter is not settled in an amicable manner, it will hurt the University?" I replied in the affirmative. Then he simply but sincerely said, "This is the only consideration. The University must rise above any hurt feelings that can develop. The School of Theology is our first love."[43]

The end of the matter came at the Theology Board of Trustees Committee in January 1954. Bishop Smith described the event in these words:

> When the Committee met in Dallas, Mrs. Perkins very tactfully yet very definitely expressed herself, and that was the end of it. We told Mr. ____ (the leader of the dissenters) that the Board committee had refused to take any action, and he didn't press any further.[44]

Dean Cuninggim commented, "Lois Perkins was indeed a heroine of this story . . ." Her social conscience, he added, came especially from her participation in the women's study program of the church.[45] He also highly praised Bishop William C. Martin, "the only man fully privy to the ongoing push-and-shove who never once sought to change or weaken our policy."[46] Bishop Paul Martin's conversation with Mr. and Mrs. Perkins provided the final impetus. Others in the Dallas community and from around the country were also supportive, clergy and laity alike. The faculty and the student body mostly remained constant in their intention, and thus Cuninggim could rightly conclude, "Lots of folks have said it was a great time in the life of the School, and I think we all knew it and cherished it."[47]

Was Perkins School of Theology integrated or merely desegregated in this struggle? The answer to this question is far more difficult than I once believed. Many years after his student days, I saw Cecil Williams who, by this time, strongly claimed his black heritage and was well known as the pastor of the Glide Memorial Methodist Church in San Francisco where he developed a radically oriented approach to ministry. "Cecil," I said, "I think I refused to accept your blackness when you were at Perkins. My way of dealing with you was to deny that you were any different from me." And then he admitted that

he too had not really accepted his blackness in those days, and how liberating
it had been when he finally did. In the years during which black students both
proclaimed and celebrated their color of skin, I came to realize that most of us
were not fully capable of integration, perhaps because we really did not know
what it meant.

One incident indicates that the students made more progress in integration
than faculty probably did. It happened at one of the student spring entertain-
ments, Panorama, which later became primarily a faculty take-off. Cecil
Williams was about to sing—he had a marvelous voice—and word was passed
from row to row so quickly that it reached the audience of some 300 students,
faculty, and spouses. "Don't applaud when Cecil finishes," ran the injunction.
At the conclusion of his number, the audience was so quiet that the silence was
deafening. At first he looked bewildered, but it took him only a moment to
recover. "Aw, come on," he said, "you know you loved it!" And the applause
that followed was not only for a song well sung but also for a person loved and
cherished.

Other Controversies

The integration crisis was not the only problem that SMU and Perkins faced
during this period. Another, which affected the entire University but in which
Perkins was involved, concerned a professor of English, John O. Beaty, a long-
time member of the faculty and a widely recognized scholar.[48] Beaty published
privately in 1951 a book entitled *The Iron Curtain over America.* The thesis of
the book was that Jews were behind the "Communist conspiracy" and other ills
of the world. It was blatantly anti-Semitic, but the University administration
chose to ignore it. Its circulation was fairly widespread, one estimate being that
it sold more than 45,000 copies.[49] Ralph Lord Roy, a Methodist clergyman,
devoted eight pages to Beaty's book in his book on the hate movements,
Apostles of Discord, and Roy's book was reviewed in the *Southwest Review*
(SMU's literary publication) with due reference to Beaty's book. President Lee
and the remainder of the University still remained silent, however. But Beaty
would not let up, and other people joined with Beaty in espousing the view of
his book. Mrs. Lee believed that this entire process contributed to the President's
declining health and his eventual resignation as President.[50]

Finally, in 1954, Beaty wrote and distributed a pamphlet "How to Capture a
University," accusing SMU of capitulating to Jewish influence and the entire
University of giving in to Communism. Part of his criticism was aimed directly
at Perkins, which he criticized for the awards which B'nai B'rith made to
students at Perkins in the field of social action; the course offered in Contemporary Judaism first by Rabbi Lefkowitz and later by Rabbi Olan, both from

Temple Emanu-El; and the gifts to Bridwell Library setting up a section on Judaism honoring David and Sadie Lefkowitz.[51]

Although the administration had chosen to ignore the book, eventually the *SMU Campus*, in the fall of 1953, decided to open the subject for discussion. The writer in the paper recognized that Beaty had demonstrated scholarly competence in his own field of English literature, but called *The Iron Curtain over America* "the most extensive piece of anti-Semitic literature in the history of America's racist movement."[52]

When the pamphlet directly attacking SMU was printed and distributed, in 1954, it no longer was possible for Beaty to be ignored. The University faculty met on 16 February 1954, and repudiated the publication.[53] The Perkins faculty authorized letters to be sent to Temple Emanu-El and to B'nai B'rith at its 19 February 1954 meeting.[54] The spring issue of the *Perkins School of Theology Journal* contained an editorial strongly condemning Professor Beaty's publications.[55] The administration decided that it could no longer ignore what he had done, and a committee was appointed from the Board of Trustees on March 30 to deal with the allegations in the pamphlet.[56] The committee reported at the May Board meeting that the facts "do not bear out the allegations made by Dr. Beaty in his pamphlets."[57]

Beaty did not resign as the committee had inferred that anyone out of line with the University's policies ought. After Willis Tate became President, he let Beaty know what Beaty had not previously accepted, that the committee's statement about resignation was directed toward him. Dr. Beaty continued to teach until retirement, however, but made no more public broadsides against the University.[58]

The School and Criticism by the Church

The Cuninggim deanship was not without its problems in dealing with the church in the region. There had always existed such criticism, as J. T. Carlyon reminded the faculty in a discussion of the subject.[59] Cuninggim's leadership was primarily academic, and his directness and honesty sometimes seemed harsh to church people. Though Cuninggim was not well integrated into church politics, his positions need to be viewed as he viewed them, prophetic steps by which the churches could measure their own attitude and life and be challenged by prophetic change. In spite of all the efforts of the faculty and the Dean to improve field education, both its quantity and its quality, many church leaders felt that Cuninggim was leading the School away from the close association it had previously had with its immediate constituency.

There were always some theological questions about the School. Strangely enough, some of the earlier Perkins graduates complained during these years that the School was leaning too much toward the new orthodoxy, represented by such theologians as Reinhold Niebuhr and Karl Barth. Others continued to have questions about its "liberal" theology or about its leftist leanings in political and social questions. (In actuality Perkins was probably more conservative on social problems than most of the main-line seminaries.)

This is not to suggest that the administration did not make an attempt to reach out to both the total University and the church. We have already noted the continuing effort to improve the "practical training" of students through field education, never completely successful but at least attempted.

The new Dean, in an article called "The State of the School" and published in the *Perkins School of Theology Journal* for Spring 1952, considered both of the issues stated above. Concerning the relationship of Perkins to the church, he wrote: "[T]he faculty is of one mind that the primary responsibility of the School is to furnish first-class training for the parish ministry."[60] He further stated, "Perkins must come to play its full part in the life and philosophy of the whole institution [SMU]."[61]

Earlier he had stated in the *Journal*, "[I]t is the Faculty, not I, who will do the changing. Or better still, it will be all of us working together."[62] There is no question but that he gave both faculty and students more opportunity to participate in the life of the school, including decision making. Yet the Dean had to take both credit and blame for what happened. Further, Cuninggim was a strong personality who partly by reason of office and partly because of his strong leadership had great influence on the way the school developed during his deanship.

Bridwell Library

Along with other advances which we have noted, the growth and quality of Bridwell Library was also notable. Moving the library into its own building, provided by the Bridwells, was a great step in its development. The coming of Decherd Turner as the librarian was another step in its advancement. Although Turner was quite young when he became librarian in 1950, he already had considerable knowledge of bibliography and he developed that knowledge extensively during his early years as head librarian. He was also both a savant and an entrepreneur, which meant that he either knew or learned how to build a library, and was aggressive in pursuing the steps that led to its greatness.

Mrs. John (Kate) Warnick remained as reference librarian. As she completed thirty-five years of service in 1953, Turner said: "She knows the book stacks of Bridwell Library (about 50,000 volumes) intimately, and with an almost intuitive sense can ferret out the most obscure fact."[63] Her persistence often led to results which could have been attained in no other way, he might have added.

Turner not only began buying individual books, both current and those published in former years. He also had an uncanny ability to find collections and somehow finance them, often outside his budget, or else secure them as gifts. The first major gift occurred at the beginning of his second year, in the establishing of the Sadie and David Lefkowitz collection of Judaica by Temple Emanu-El where Lefkowitz was chief Rabbi for many years. The collection continued to grow over the years.[64]

About the same time Turner made his first "exotic" purchase—a facsimile copy of the Book of Kells, "the richest and handsomest of all Irish manuscripts."[65]

The first collection which he bought was the Steindorff Collection of Egyptology, in the fall of 1952. He called it "one of the most famous private collections in the field of Egyptology in the world." Steindorff had held the professorship in Egyptology for over forty years at the University of Leipzig, but because of his Jewish birth was forced to flee Germany at the beginning of the Nazi Jewish purge. The collection contained more than 1,700 books and 2,000 reprints and pamphlets. The daughters of A. V. Lane, who had been responsible for bringing the Lane Museum (containing, among other things, Egyptian artifacts), helped in the purchase.[66]

The year 1956 was an especially fruitful year, with the gift by Bishop Frederick Leete of his collection called the "Methodist Historical Library, Inc." and consisting of books and manuscripts on the Wesleys and the history of Methodism. Included were several original John Wesley letters which had never been published.[67]

In the fall of the same year the Dan Ferguson Collection came to Bridwell Library. Composed of Texas history and U. S. government documents, the collection was given to Bridwell (in spite of the fact that many of its items did not really fit in a theological library) because of Turner's friendship with Ferguson. The collection also contains signed letters from virtually every U. S. President to that time.[68]

Financing the School

The large gift for which fund raisers of the School of Theology had hoped for many years materialized in the Perkins family's magnificent gifts whose value increased over the years as oil runs were exploited. Without this gift, the school would have continued to struggle to maintain itself. What this gift also did, however, was to convince some people that there was no need for further support, and this had to be changed as quickly as possible.

Dean Hawk had secured many small to medium-sized scholarships. The Crosby and Nicholson bequests were not yet available to the School,[69] nor was

Mrs. Hughey's gift which was directed to the library. Although minimum tuition was now charged, many students received tuition scholarships and therefore paid only the minimum fees.[70] With the rapid rate of faculty addition and the necessity of increasing salaries to secure desirable additions, the School's finances were still inadequate to meet the needs of Cuninggim's rapidly expanding budget.[71]

The John M. Moore Fellowship was presented to Perkins in 1946 by the Bishop, for graduate study beyond the B.D. degree, but it was 1952 before the first fellowship was granted, to Edwin R. Spann.[72]

Mr. and Mrs. Sol McCreless of San Angelo provided yearly support for a Chair in Evangelism, and it was filled for the first time, by George Baker, in 1955.[73] An unexpected bonus came to the Field Work program in 1953 in the form of $50,000 for scholarships presented by Frank Sharp of Houston.[74]

It was also encouraging that the Methodist Church began to provide major support to all its schools of theology. The South Central Jurisdiction pledged $6,250 annually for the 1954–57 quadrennium,[75] and the World Service Fund of the Methodist Church provided $116,250.00 for the budget in 1956–57.[76] Individual conferences also made contributions to the budget.[77]

The cost of education continued to rise, however, at a rate far above the rate of inflation. Therefore the School continued to have budget problems and to seek both new contributions and ways of cutting the budget.[78]

Student Life

One of the most difficult aspects of the life of Perkins School of Theology to describe concerns its students. History, including church history, tends to center on leadership and on principal events rather than on the people who helped to make history through their daily life and contributed immeasurably to the church by their faithfulness. So this history of Perkins School of Theology has been too much concerned with administrative leadership rather than with the students who also made history. Records are sparse, not always clear, often difficult to interpret. We have lists of students in the catalogs, of course, and my own memory of many students over thirty-three years would fill a book. Even so, how many I have forgotten! Any list of graduates I read reminds me of individuals whom I have not seen since their student days and whose names on paper conjure recollections that are buried in my memory.

We have already noted that students were brought into the life of the School such as they never had been previously. Cuninggim called them into session on 16 October 1951.[79] His consultations with the black students were more frequent and more intimate than with the remainder of the student body, of course, but indicative of his openness to all.

Many student activities were continued from the past: for example, the student council, the annual spring banquet, intramural athletics, active work in the planning of daily worship.[80] I cannot determine with certainty when the first student talent show was held—the first recorded is for 20 March 1952,[81] prior to the existence of Lois Perkins Auditorium and thus held in the so-called "AV Room" on the lower floor of Kirby Hall. According to the *SMU Campus* this show was held in connection with the Campus Chest, an all-student effort to raise money for "Little SMU" in Brazil and other causes.[82] This spring entertainment later became a faculty take-off with some wonderful shows developing over the years.

The Seminary Singers, under the direction first of Fred Gealy and later Lloyd Pfautsch, continued to be a primary source of community for its members. No other Perkins organization has been as meaningful to generations of Perkins students.

The Log, a student publication, was first published in the fall of 1952 with Hobert Hildyard as the first editor.[83] A Woman's Society of Christian Service circle had been organized for student wives by Mrs. A. W. Martin about 1948. By 1953–54 it had a membership of almost ninety.[84] Under the nurturing hand of Whitty Cuninggim courses taught by Perkins professors were also conducted, and other activities for student wives were held. Mrs. Paul Quillian, director of married students housing, was responsible for beginning a day nursery in Hawk Hall in 1951–52.[85]

Some Perkins students also participated in the activities of the University, and on at least one occasion a Perkins student, Richard Deats, was elected President of the SMU Student Association, in 1955.[86]

The student body gradually became more diverse. The most dramatic change, of course, was its ethnic diversity, at first with blacks and later more Hispanic students than previously. It had always had a sprinkling of international students, and only a lack of scholarship funding kept this from expanding even more rapidly. The geographic distribution of students increased, but the Perkins student body remained still predominantly from its own constituency, as is natural that it should. The adding of other degrees, such as the Master of Sacred Music, drew from an increasingly wide group of applicants.

All in all the Perkins quadrangle was an active place, aided by the fact that now almost one-half of the student body lived on campus. Yet even these students, some of whom were pastors of churches (for the number of students holding charges remained high), and almost all of whom had some kind of paying job, were divided in their loyalties. Unfortunately many, especially those who commuted daily to their parishes, had little or no contact with the School outside the classroom.

Perkins Reaches Out

If the impression has been given that Dean Cuninggim was uninterested in the relationship of school and church, I have failed in my interpretation. He did a great deal to contribute to the tradition of the School's service to its immediate constituency. Some of the School's outreach was a continuation from the past. The Course of Study School for those unable to secure a seminary education, begun by A. W. Martin, had continued for some years. Its largest enrollment up to this time occurred in 1953 with 114 enrolled in the second of two summer terms.[87] This school, without offering seminary credit, has been of immeasurable benefit, mostly to the South Central Jurisdiction of Methodism, and has developed the kind of student loyalty scarcely matched by degree students.

Ministers' Week continued to draw more than one thousand pastors to many of its sessions. The first alumni/ae luncheon was held in 1950[88] and continued until many years later its name was changed to "Ministers' Week Luncheon" so that non-Perkins graduates would feel free to attend.

A week in which students and faculty spent time with student pastors in the field began under A. W. Martin's leadership prior to Cuninggim's deanship. It was continued for a number of years with quite mixed results in the various parishes. A much more ambitious field education program came into being, also with mixed results, until some years later when the Intern Program replaced it.

The *Perkins School of Theology Journal* had been initiated in the fall of 1947 with the distinct purpose of keeping in touch with graduates of the School.[89] Under the editorship of Thomas H. Marsh for its first six years, the *Journal* was edited by Howard Grimes beginning in 1953. It still carried alumni/ae news and campus happenings until in 1957 a news bulletin came into being and the *Journal* was free to carry more serious articles (but still aimed toward the practicing pastor).[90]

George Baker became director of Perkins Outreach after taking over the McCreless Chair of Evangelism and planned various ways in which Perkins faculty could reach out into the church. Continuing Education, as an organized Perkins activity, came some years after Cuninggim's deanship. But the activity of the faculty in local churches served some of the purposes included in the organized activity of a later period.

Conclusion

Dean Cuninggim arrived at Perkins when it was on the threshold of change. His leadership, as we have seen in two chapters, shaped the character of that change and led the School to the place where the theological and the church worlds recognized it as a leading school of theology. Much remained still to be done, and Joseph D. Quillian, as Cuninggim's successor, built on the achievements of those nine years and broadened their base. Many years later, Dean Quillian, speaking of Cuninggim, wrote, "It is not excessive to say that he might have been the best 'inside dean' that any seminary ever had."[91] In his own quite different way, Quillian both sustained and strengthened "the School that Merrimon built" and launched it into new paths that moved it forward.

To close the Cuninggim part of the Perkins story, I want to quote from his commencement address to the Perkins graduates of 1953 (without changing its masculine language). "Who is the ideal student?" Cuninggim asked, and replied:

> . . . he is the one who respects his mind and will continue to develop its powers, who is not afraid to enter dissent, even to engage in controversy if necessary, against the evils of his day, and who, most of all, is aflame with the transforming fire of the love of Christ in his heart, a fire that will light up the hearts and lives of others.[92]

R. Harper Kirby, ca. 1924

Annie Kirby, ca. 1924

Dean Eugene B. Hawk, ca. 1948

Prof. John H. Hicks, ca. 1949

Groundbreaking for Perkins Chapel, 1949. *From left:* President Umphrey Lee, J. S. Bridwell, Mrs. J. J. Perkins, J. J. Perkins, Dean Eugene B. Hawk, and Bishop A. Frank Smith (*Courtesy of SMU Archives*)

Dean Merrimon Cuninggim, ca. 1952

Dean Joseph D. Quillian and Prof. Albert C. Outler, 1964

Perkins School of Theology Committee, SMU Board of Trustees, 1968. *From left, seated:* Prof. Betty Maynard (Sociology), Bishop Don Holter, Dean Joseph D. Quillian, Jr., Chancellor Willis Tate, Mrs. Charles (Elizabeth) Prothro, Bishop W. McFerrin Stowe. *Standing:* Bishop Finis Crutchfield, Mr. Leo Baker, Dr. Wayne McCleskey, Prof. Ronald E. Sleeth, Mr. James E. Redman, Mr. Jack Butler, Prof. James M. Ward

From left: Dean Joseph D. Quillian, Jr., Mrs. J. J. (Lois) Perkins, Mr. Joseph S. Bridwell, and Dr. Decherd H. Turner, after SMU awarded honorary doctorates to Mrs. Perkins and Mr. Bridwell, May 1965

Entering class, 1969, on steps of Perkins Chapel

Prof. Nathaniel L. Lacy, Jr., ca. 1970

Groundbreaking for annex to Bridwell Library, 1972. *From left:*
Dr. Decherd Turner, Mrs. Kate Warnick, Mr. Page A. Thomas,
Dean Joseph D. Quillian, Mr. Horace Dryden, Mrs. Jerene Sim-
mons, Prof. Howard Grimes

Chicano Seminarians award, 1973. *From left:* Dr. Alfredo
Nañez (recipient), Rev. Jose Salas, Rev. Rodolfo Barrera

Prof. Phyllis Bird, ca. 1976

Dean James E. Kirby, Jr., and Mrs. Howard (Johnnie Marie)
Grimes, 1991 *(Courtesy of Johnnie Marie Grimes)*

10

The Quillian Years: 1960–69

Southern Methodist University began to come of age academically during the presidency of Umphrey Lee. The granting of a Phi Beta Kappa chapter in 1950 is both a symbolic and substantive indication of this progress. The effort to improve the academic quality of the school continued during Willis Tate's administration even though some people saw him more as an administrator than an academic man. One of his strengths was the appointment of the right people to key positions, and one of these appointments was making Albert Outler chair in 1962 of the committee to develop the Master Plan, the purpose of which was to restructure the academic life of the University. This committee, assisted by the Council of Deans, a student committee, and a committee of fifty people from outside the SMU community, was in part a response to the increasing pressure from certain leaders of Dallas to make SMU a technical/technological institution.[1]

The result of the Master Plan was the University College, a common body of courses which all SMU undergraduates were required to take.[2] The work of the Committee followed Tate's message to the Board of Trustees in 1961. At the November meeting he reported:

> Our University is in a period of transition, and in order to make it, we have to rethink our purposes and our role as a University. We are making a transition from an undergraduate school, with professional schools, to a University giving a terminal education degree; from the role of teaching to the role of teaching and research; from a role of merely transmitting our culture to an originator of leadership during a period of rapid change; and from a local institution to a regional University with a growing role of pioneering academic leadership for our section.[3]

The University continued to grow, from a full-time faculty of 248 in 1959–60 to 379 in 1967–68; from 500,376 volumes in all libraries in 1959–60 to 974,686 in 1967–68; and from a budget of $7,773,000 in 1959–60 to $20,169,000 in 1967–68. Annual gifts varied from under $2,000 in 1959–60 to almost $8 million in 1965–66, and endowment increased from $11,293,000 in 1959–60 to $23,700,000 in 1967–68.[4] Even so, the endowment was far too

125

low for a university, and SMU continued to have financial problems and often ran on deficit financing. The "Fund for the Future," an effort to raise $100,000,000 for endowment, begun in 1962,[5] proved only partly successful, and the new trustees in 1964 were told that SMU's greatest need was for endowment. At the same meeting, Mr. Eugene McElvaney, who had become chair of the Board of Trustees in 1960, said: "The University is devoted to the ideals of Christianity, and its purpose is founded upon the principle that the free search for truth by competent scholars will produce a growing understanding of the work of the Creator."[6] What he thus envisioned for SMU would require financial undergirding, and much of the work of the Presidents of the 1970s and 1980s was devoted to the raising of these funds.

Joseph D. Quillian, Jr.

Merrimon Cuninggim resigned as Dean of Perkins School of Theology in January 1960. Soon after Cuninggim's resignation, area clergy began to write to Tate requesting, even imploring for, a dean who would be more attentive, in their view, to the churches of the area. One even went so far as to say, "The resignation may be Providential for our Methodism." Another, typically, described the person needed as someone "to help mould the young men of our Methodist ministry into loyal workmen in the church." A telegram asked for "someone who is basically loyal to evangelical traditions and the heritage of Methodism and is not ashamed of them."[7]

President Tate convened the Trustee Committee for the School of Theology which authorized him to proceed with a search for a new dean.[8] Herndon Wagers of the Perkins faculty was asked to be the faculty person responsible for consulting with the President, to chair the faculty search committee, and to secure recommendations from other faculty.[9]

A total of forty-five names were submitted to the Trustee Committee. These included the faculty committee's first choice, Joseph D. Quillian, Jr. The forty-five were narrowed to five—three from the faculty (including Quillian) and two from the outside. President Tate, who made the final choice to recommend to the Board of Trustees, selected Quillian, and the Board of Trustees in turn formalized the election.[10]

Who was Joseph Dillard Quillian, Jr.? One way to put it for many Methodists is to say that he was one of the Georgia Quillians, a Methodist family that produced a long line of clergy, educators, attorneys, and judges (including Paul W. Quillian, who had been due to come to Perkins after a long pastorate at First Methodist in Houston but had died of a heart attack before his appointment began). Joseph D. Quillian, Jr., is among the eight Quillians listed in the 1952 edition of *Who's Who in Methodism*.[11]

Joseph D. Quillian, Jr. (commonly known as "Joe") was born in Buford, Georgia, in January 1917, the son of Justice Joseph D. Quillian of the Supreme Court of Georgia and Jeannette Evans Quillian. He earned the B.A. degree from Piedmont College (1938), the B.D. from Vanderbilt (1941), and the Ph.D. from Yale (1951). In December 1944, he was married to Elizabeth Mary Sampson; their children are Suzanne Elizabeth, Alma Jeannette, Mary Shannon, Joseph Dillard III, and Ellen Evans. Quillian was a pastor in Tennessee (1938–42) and Connecticut (1946–50) and a chaplain in the U. S. Naval Reserve (1942–46). After completing his graduate work, he served as President of Martin College in Pulaski, Tennessee, from 1950 to 1954. In fall 1954, he became Professor at Preaching and Worship at Perkins School of Theology.[12]

President Tate, in a letter to the ministers of the South Central Jurisdiction of the Methodist Church, described him as being "effectively practical in his philosophy and attitude toward the pastoral ministry," "attractive to scholar, layman, minister, and student, showing a sensitivity to direction, yet firmness in administration."[13] Reflecting on his beginning as Dean many years later, Quillian concluded that his two predecessors had brought different strengths to the office. Eugene Hawk had emphasized the relationship of the School to the church; Merrimon Cuninggim had been largely an "inside Dean, developing the school as an academic institution." "I knew," he writes, "that I had to try to hold all of the notable inside gains that had been made during Dean Cuninggim's tenure, and to maintain the momentum. I also knew that I had to work at restoring our relationship with the Church and to make major gains in financial development. It was a presumptuous undertaking, but a necessary one, to try to do both kinds of work in which my two immediate predecessors had excelled."[14]

The State of Perkins School of Theology

When Dean Quillian reflected on his more than twenty years as Dean, not long before retirement, he concluded that he had "succeeded fairly well in doing what I had set out to do—but only fairly well."[15] He gave two reasons for his success, the first of which was a tribute to his predecessor's building of the faculty. When he became Dean, Quillian observed, "I probably had fewer inside problems on basic matters than any other long-term dean of a major seminary. If I had been serving a Faculty of sub-par quality, and with a disposition to cabals and contentions, etc., I simply could not have lasted."[16] The other reason he gave was "the understanding, sensitive and superb support of Mrs. Perkins and the growing understanding and support of officials, ministers, and laypersons in the church and of benefactors that I inherited from Dean Hawk and quite a few new ones that I came to know."[17]

We have already seen how the church in the area had been growing in its suspicions of Perkins, and the new Dean faced not only an immediate problem but one that would occupy much of his attention throughout his twenty-one years as Dean. Another problem the school faced was that its endowment had not increased substantially beyond the original and subsequent gifts of Mr. and Mrs. Perkins.[18] A third problem was a declining number of students. The number of students enrolled in the fall semester was 415 in 1958. The decline then set in so that by 1963 the number had fallen to 353.[19] The largest number of B.D. graduates occurred in May 1955, with a total of 92,[20] and then the number decreased.

Part of this decline after 1959 can be attributed to the opening of St. Paul School of Theology (United Methodist) in 1959 in Kansas City. There is no question that this new seminary siphoned off some potential students from Kansas and Nebraska. The enrollment of St. Paul increased from 51 in its opening year to 164 in 1963.[21] In the Dean's statement to the faculty at the opening on 21 September 1961, he envisioned a B.D. enrollment at Perkins of 340 to 360 each year.[22] The actual number of B.D. students in 1961 was 302.[23]

From the beginning, as we have seen, Quillian was much aware of the peculiar responsibility Perkins had to its constituent church, the Methodist Church, later United Methodist. He said in his first public statement, a short time before actually assuming the deanship, the following:

> One way to speak of the great inclusive hopes of the Methodist Church in the South Central Jurisdiction is in terms of EVANGELICAL EFFEC-TIVENESS. This means no other than the expectation and desire that the Gospel of Jesus Christ, the Evangel, transform and sustain us, that we may be thankful and faithful members of His Church, the community of redeemed and obedient servants of God.[24]

In a somewhat later statement he made it clear to the faculty that he understood a seminary to be *more than* an academic institution. A great seminary, he said,

> is a community of devout teaching, learning, worship, and fellowship in which those who are there build each other up in Christian being and living. A great seminary is a community where *some*, for the first time, come into life in Christ in conscious awareness, and where *all* are increased in life in Christ.[25]

Joe Quillian was neither naive nor unrealistic, but it is perhaps just as well that he could not envision all the problems that would arise during the following twenty-one years. He knew that the job of Dean was a formidable one, but fortunately he had no crystal ball to see all the problems that would emerge. We shall look at some of these in the pages that follow; but first we need to examine the faculty and staff changes that occurred during the 1960s.

The Faculty

One of the legacies which Dean Cuninggim left for his successor was a superior and relatively stable faculty. The Board of Trustees was told in 1964 that this was one of the accomplishments of Perkins School of Theology—the faculty had stayed together and had not been "raided" by other schools.[26] It was a white, male faculty, however, and remained that way at the end of the decade (1969). Over the years, a few women had taught on a visiting basis, and there had been women on the library staff—the first theology librarian, in fact, from 1924 to 1950, was Mrs. Kate Warnick. The support staff—secretaries and administrative assistants—were also women and often were the ones who carried on the work of an office while the male head was either teaching or otherwise engaged in the work of outreach. By the end of the decade, pressure was mounting to secure minority and women faculty, but the first response did not occur until 1970.

1960–61. Faculty appointments for Quillian's first year were due to Cuninggim searches. One retirement occurred in June 1961: Mrs. John H. (Kate) Warnick who came to the University library in 1919 and to the theology library in 1924. After her retirement, she stayed on until 1979 as curator of the Methodist Collection.[27] The new faculty were Frederick S. Carney in Ethics, Franklin Littell in Church History, W. J. A. (Bill) Power in Old Testament, William C. Robinson in New Testament, and James M. Ward, also in Old Testament. Robert Anderson came also in 1960 with his appointment being in the School of the Arts but as organist for Perkins Chapel.

Unofficially Quillian asked former Dean Hawk, who had no relationship to the School during Cuninggim's tenure, much to the latter's concern, to return as advisor to the Dean. He did so and regularly came to his office until his death in 1963.[28]

1961–62. Quillian's first appointments were for 1961–62, including a replacement for himself in the field of Worship and Preaching, James F. White. Thompson Shannon, formerly pastor of First Community Church of Dallas, was an addition in· the field of Pastoral Theology (Counseling). Two staff positions, the former with faculty status, were also filled. Edmund B. Deane came as Assistant Director of Field Education, and Elizabeth Twitchell became Assistant Bridwell Librarian.[29]

James Phillip Hyatt and James W. May were added summer school visitors.[30] Albert Outler was elected a member of the SMU Faculty Senate, and became the first of many Perkins faculty members to hold this University office.[31]

1962–63. Floyd Curl resigned from Perkins in 1962 as Director of Field Education, and Marvin Judy took the position temporarily with Edmund Deane continuing as assistant. Klaus Penzel, in Church History, was the only full-time faculty addition. Luís Martín of the SMU history faculty, Kenneth F. Thompson, and John W. Wevers taught during the summer.[32]

Tom Marsh, Professor of Speech for more than fifteen years, became the third faculty member to die in office, in March 1962.[33] (The other two were Frank Seay and Paul Root.)

1963–64. For the first time in many years, there were no new faculty appointments for 1963–64. Heinz-Dieter Knigge was a visiting lecturer in New Testament, and during the year Charles Johnson resigned and Lloyd Pfautsch became full-time in the Division of Music of the Meadows School of the Arts. New summer visitors included H. Jackson Forstman and Niels C. Nielsen.[34]

1964–65. Bishop W. C. Martin assumed the position of "Bishop in Residence" (though the term was not used officially until several years later) after his retirement from the Fort Worth-Dallas area of the Methodist Church. The duties of the Bishop were to be the advisor to students on their conference relationships and advisor to the Dean, and on occasion, to teach one or more courses.[35]

New faculty included Ronald E. Sleeth, generally recognized then as a truly outstanding Professor of Preaching, and Carlton R. (Sam) Young as Director of the Church Music Program and the Seminary Singers.[36] Young was editor of *The Methodist Hymnal* (1964) and would later also edit the 1989 edition.[37]

A large number of visiting faculty supplemented the regular faculty: Jesse Paul Ephraim, Bryan Forrester, James Hares, Raymond J. O'Keefe (summer), George Stricker, David Switzer (summer), Joseph B. Tyson, Bishop Edwin E. Voigt, Howard W. Washburn, and the University Chaplain, J. Claude Evans.

Dean Eugene B. Hawk's life ended in the fall of 1963. At the time he was working on organizing his papers and getting historical material together. Hawk, who had served longer than any other dean to that time, died suddenly at home after having attended a dinner party at the home of Jackie Selecman (Bishop Selecman's widow). He had gone home early and was found the next day lying across the bed with the radio still on the station that had broadcast the marvelous SMU-Navy football game, a game which SMU won, even though Roger Staubach was the star quarterback of the Navy team. (Mrs. Hawk was away visiting a son at the time of Dean Hawk's death.)[38]

A. W. Wasson, whose long association with the School of Theology began in the School's very early days, died during the same year.

Herndon Wagers became the first Associate Dean in 1964. Alsie Carleton, later Bishop, was selected as the Director of Field Education.[39] Marvin Judy was made Director of the Center for Research and Planning.

1965–66. New appointments for 1965–66 included Joe R. Jones in Philosophical Theology and H. Edward Everding as visiting Lecturer in New Testament. Travis Jordan became Assistant Librarian with faculty rank, and Kenneth Pepper went to the Institute of Religion in Houston, with which Perkins was affiliated.[40] Additional summer school faculty included Thomas T. Love and D. Moody Smith, Jr. The long-time secretary and Administrative Assistant to the Dean, Warrene Nettles, retired in 1966 but stayed on as Eunice Baab's successor as Director of Housing.

1966–67. Richard T. Murray was appointed to the faculty in Christian Education and as Director of Continuing Education in 1966 but was on leave for the year to do further graduate study. David Robertson began a teaching stint in Old Testament, and Frederick Streng came on a joint appointment with the University in History of Religions. Visiting faculty included Viktor E. Frankl, Friedrich Gogarten, and Charles Hartshorne.[41]

Changes occurred in administration: Herndon Wagers became Director of the Graduate Program in Religious Studies, and H. Neill McFarland assumed the post of Associate Dean. A few months later, however, President Tate asked McFarland to become acting Provost (later Provost); David Switzer followed him in the Associate Dean's office in the fall of 1967.

Roger Ortmayer resigned effective 31 August 1966. An unusually large number of deaths occurred among former faculty: Robert W. Goodloe on 22 September 1966; J. S. Seneker on 2 April 1967; and Ivan Lee Holt, a member of the first School of Theology faculty, on 12 January 1967.[42]

1967–68. Richard (Dick) Murray began his work in the fall of 1967, both in teaching and in developing a program in Continuing Education. William S. Babcock assumed a post in Church History. In the meantime Thompson Shannon resigned to become President of the Institute of Religion in Houston. Visiting faculty included Robert O. Cooper, William Paul McLean, and Charles A. Rogers. An additional clinical supervisor was added, Andrew G. McDonald of Parkland Hospital.[43]

1968–69. Bishop Paul E. Martin succeeded Bishop William C. Martin as Professor of Practical Theology and, using a later designation, Bishop in Residence (at that time Counselor to Students on Conference Relations). James B. McGrath was now listed as a regular member of the faculty (though his primary teaching was in the Meadows School of the Arts). Claudia Robinson taught a course in drama. She had been a teacher of drama and a director in the prestigious Northwestern University School of Speech and Drama.

Bishop William C. Martin was no longer an active member of the faculty. Van Harvey resigned on 30 June 1968, and Schubert Ogden went to the

University of Chicago as University Professor, a prestigious appointment, at the end of the year. (He returned to the Perkins faculty at the beginning of the 1972–73 academic year, expressing his desire to be more fully involved in preparing leaders for the church.) And finally a staff member, Elsa Cook, who had made a deep impression on students because of her work with them in the office of the Counselor to Students' office, retired in 1967.[44]

Alsie Carleton was elected bishop in 1968 by the South Central Jurisdiction, and therefore a change in leadership for field education had to be made.

1969–70. The final year of the 1960s resulted in several additions. Claus Rohlfs succeeded Carleton as Director of Field Education. David Robertson resigned, but three additional faculty members helped fill in the gaps: Harville Hendrix in Pastoral Counseling, Leroy T. Howe in Philosophical Theology, and William M. Longsworth in Christian Ethics.[45]

At the 27 September 1969 faculty conference, Albert Outler reported as Chair of the Theological Study Commission of the United Methodist Church, a report made to the 1972 General Conference.[46]

Curriculum

In his report to the faculty for 1961, Dean Quillian said: "The time has come for a 'from-the-grass-roots up' re-examination of our purpose as a seminary, against the background of which we may set about whatever restructuring of the curriculum and re-order of our procedures that may seem to us to be advisable."[47] At the meeting at which the Dean's report was made, Joseph Allen proposed that such a move be made, and set up six meetings throughout the year for these purposes.[48]

The discussion took two related directions, in addition to the general discussion of the nature and purpose of Perkins: the course of study (what courses ought to be required) and Field Education (how students would get their practical experience). The report was almost completed by the faculty meeting of 9 November 1962,[49] and Allen made the formal report on 7 December 1962.

One of the problems the committee had addressed was the excessive number of required courses, two-thirds of the total to be taken for the B.D. degree. Their solution was to drop all required courses and substitute a series of comprehensive examinations in the previously required area of study. Syllabi, bibliographies, and sample exams were to be provided for students' study, with 92 semester hours of course work, to be arranged in whatever way the student might want. (Courses on Methodism were required for Methodist students.)[50]

Additional requirements added later included a biblical exegesis paper[51] and an oral preaching exam.[52] The new curriculum was made mandatory in 1964.[53]

What began to happen immediately was that students with the fearful prospect of comprehensive examinations three years ahead almost invariably took the old graduate requirement courses which gave them preparation for a particular examination. The students feared the exams; the faculty looked with horror on having to read them; and therefore no one accepted them with any enthusiasm.

In any case, one of those strange but common events occurred at the fall faculty conference in 1965 (the second year of the new course of study). The faculty had spent hours discussing some topic. The matter of the examinations came up for discussion, and after a brief time, Van Harvey moved that the exams no longer be required. With almost no further discussion the faculty voted by a large majority, if not unanimously, in favor of the motion.[54]

This is not quite the end of the matter, for on 10 May 1966 the faculty voted to substitute a "Senior Colloquy" for the comprehensives and adopted the first topic for 1967, "Studies in Vatican Two."[55] The colloquy would employ a number of lecturers, as well as discussion, and would draw heavily on Albert Outler's participation in the Second Vatican Council of the Roman Catholic Church. The written requirement was a project paper, from twenty-five to thirty-five pages in length.[56]

Nor is this quite the end of the matter. A few months later the faculty also voted out the preaching exam since most students took a course in which practice preaching was involved.[57] In addition to the senior colloquy, which was held for several years, there had been a provision for a "senior seminar." This too was dropped, and a senior retreat took its place. Held first on 11–12 May 1967, its purpose was to provide a culminating experience for the student's three years of study. This too was dropped after being held for several years.[58]

If this account seems somewhat opportunistic, it should be noted that the faculty, or at least part of it, was aware of this fact. At a faculty meeting in early September 1966, the minutes contain this terse analysis: "Mr. McFarland presented a paper on the rationale for the present curriculum, or the lack of such a rationale. Various problems were discussed by the faculty."[59]

Field Education

Organized "field work" (later "field education") had begun under A. W. Martin in the 1940s. No aspect of the Perkins curriculum has had a more checkered career. Everyone seemed to agree that students needed to be exposed to the work of the local church and social agencies. But how? As we saw in Chapter 10, the faculty spent an incredible amount of time during the 1950s trying to come up with a viable program. By 1959 an elaborate system was in place and actually remained until 1963. As the *Perkins Catalog* described the program, the first year consisted of an orientation "course" with various lectures and panel discussions, and consultations between faculty advisors and student advisees. The entire faculty was involved, and part of its outcome depended on how seriously a particular faculty member considered this drain on time.

Advanced field education consisted of projects chosen by the student and approved by the Field Education office. There was both a junior convocation on the ministry, meeting for one hour per week with the Dean in charge, and a senior seminar also on the ministry.[60]

For reasons which are hazy to me, the required participation was dropped in 1963 and the catalog now stated that students were expected to participate in a local church but did not specify how. There was also a planned program of visitation to synagogues, Catholic and Orthodox churches, and social agencies.[61] The seminar remained the same until 1965.[62]

In 1965 the requirement was again changed. "Every Methodist student who is a candidate for the B.D. degree will be required to work for at least one semester in a church-related position before receiving his degree."[63] The one exception was working for a social agency instead of a local church. Students not fulfilling the requirement before the beginning of the senior year would be assigned to a "pastoral training group" in a Dallas church. A two-semester-hour course on the parish ministry accompanied the doing of the local church stint. Faculty were asked to visit student pastors, and a seminar accompanied both the fall semester of the junior year and the fall semester of the senior year.[64]

The requirement was increased to five units of credit in 1966, including visits to local church and social agencies; the senior seminar was moved to the spring semester.[65] Later, this senior seminar became a weekend retreat.[66] The intern program was projected by the self-study Curriculum Committee in 1968–69, and we will consider that major change in connection with the self-study.

Degrees

All that has been said about curriculum pertains directly to the B.D. (later M.Th., then M.Div.) degree. The M.R.E. degree has always paralleled the basic degree, and modifications in one often brought changes in the other. The interest of the total faculty has always been in the B.D.-M.Th.-M.Div. degree, and its development has occupied a major part of faculty time and attention.

Almost from the beginning of the school, a joint B.D.-M.A. program was available and was continued for many years. As we have seen, at one time there was a Master of Church Administration (M.C.A.) degree for persons not expecting to be ordained, and for a few years a stopgap Bachelor of Religious Education existed. This was followed by the M.R.E. in 1950. Six years later, in 1956, the S.T.M. (Master of Sacred Theology), a post-B.D. degree, came into being and persisted until after the Doctor of Ministry (D.Min.) degree was adopted in 1973.

The Master of Sacred Music degree (M.S.M.) was inaugurated during Cuninggim's deanship, with its first students entering in 1960. It was under the direction of Lloyd Pfautsch, who later went to the Division of Music and was succeeded by Carlton R. Young.

A joint degree with the Meadows School of the Arts, the M.S.M. program has trained church musicians of various denominations for almost thirty years and is one of the few such programs of study remaining. The presence of the music students in the Perkins student body has been genuinely enriching, and the further extension of this program requires only more endowment and more adequate facilities for its housing.

Another degree located in the SMU Graduate School but developed with a great deal of effort by the Perkins faculty is the Ph.D. in Religion (later Religious Studies), begun in 1965 largely through the efforts at the beginning of Dean Quillian.[67] It had been talked about for a decade, and the first graduation took place in 1970.[68]

Bridwell Library

Dean Hawk brought the young Decherd Turner to be Bridwell Librarian in 1950. At that time the library had a collection of fewer than 40,000 volumes and spent under $12,000 for the academic year 1950–51.[69] By 1970 the number of volumes had increased to 131,242, with an annual expenditure of $31,976 for books only.[70] By 1977 the number of volumes had reached 172,979, and the annual expenditure for books, periodicals, and binding was $509,954.[71]

Decherd Turner's genius consisted of more than building a working library. He also believed that a library was a repository of the records of civilization and that in the long run this was the more important function.[72] We have noted in earlier chapters the acquisitions of certain collections, but all of these were dwarfed in 1962 by the acquisition of the Bridwell-DeBellis collection of Incunabula (fifteenth-century books printed with movable type).

The story of the acquisition of this collection is worth telling in some detail.[73] Mr. Eugene McElvaney, chair of the Board of Trustees, received word that a collection of fifteenth-century printing was available from a Mr. Frank V. DeBellis in California. He called Dean Quillian about it, who in turn called Turner. Turner, not really believing that a collection of any value existed, went with some skepticism to McElvaney's office and began going through the list. After a short time, he called the Dean and in his intense excitement said, "It's either the cleverest con job I've ever seen, or the most wonderful collection of incunabula I can imagine."

Convinced that it was worth looking into, Turner then went to California to see the collection. He telephoned back to the Dean and again with the excitement that only he could express over books said, "It's unbelievable—but it's real."

DeBellis, it turned out, was an Italian immigrant who had made a fortune in real estate. He had begun his collection many years earlier, and now it was estimated to be worth two million dollars. He needed cash, however, and in order to keep the collection intact was willing to sell it for $100,000.

After Turner returned from California, the Dean called a high level meeting with J. S. Bridwell, President Tate, former Dean Hawk, Earl Hoggard, Sterling Wheeler, Dean Quillian, Eugene McElvaney, and Turner. "We don't know where we'll get the money," McElvaney observed. "I'm able to contribute some, and Mr. Turner has promised several thousand dollars out of his meager salary." Immediately, Quillian turned to Mr. Bridwell and said: "We ought to give Mr. Bridwell the first chance to help us." Whereupon Bridwell, who was acquiring a taste for rare books, observed, "Yes, I think I can manage that. I'll give $50,000 immediately and a similar amount a short time later."

Bridwell then said, "Let's get that man [DeBellis] on the telephone right now and strike the deal. He might drop dead of a heart attack." Turner placed the call and introduced DeBellis and Bridwell, who soon agreed to the terms of the collection's sale.

Bridwell then turned to Turner and asked, "Decherd, how are you going to move the books?" Turner replied, "We'll have to break up the collection and bring them to Dallas in various ways. We can't afford to endanger these foundation stones of Western civilization." Quillian thought that Turner was saying this for Bridwell's benefit, and since the two often shared moments of humor, Quillian looked toward Turner for such a moment now. When he looked at Turner, however, the Dean realized there was absolutely no humor in his remark. "This was," Quillian concluded, "an utterly sacred moment for Decherd."

The original DeBellis collection consisted of 208 titles.[74] The idea of great books printed in the fifteenth-century caught the imagination of a West Texas rancher turned bibliophile, and he continued to add to the collection. After his death the Bridwell Foundation provided one million dollars for Turner to spend on rare books, and other gifts followed. Eventually the collection was tripled in size, and according to experts is one of the very finest collections of fifteenth-century printing between the East and West coasts.

Collections tend to draw other collections, and this is what occurred at Bridwell Library. As Roger Ortmayer, editor of the *Perkins School of Theology Journal,* put it: "We have asked much from him [Decherd Turner] and received even more. We were not quite prepared, however sanguine our expectations, for the bibliographical eruption we have witnessed this year."[75]

Mr. Everett L. DeGolyer, Jr., followed the Bridwell-DeBellis collection with a copy of the Nuremberg Chronicle (1493).[76] And, as Mr. Ortmayer continued, "We had scarcely recovered our balance when along came the Levi A. Olan Collection."[77] The books, presented on the occasion of Rabbi Olan's sixtieth birthday, consisted of fifty-five volumes representing ten titles of rare books from the fifteenth, sixteenth, seventeenth, and eighteenth centuries, with one special edition from the 1960s.[78] To these were added the Aldine Dante, given by Mr. and Mrs. Paul P. Steed, Jr. Published in 1502 in Venice, the book consisted of a collection of "Le Terze Rime di Dante."[79] The final acquisition during the academic year 1962–63 was a copy of the 1602 Bishops' Bible, given by the library itself in honor of Dean Emeritus Eugene B. Hawk[80] and presented at the Alumni Luncheon during Ministers' Week.

Other special collections soon followed, including (in 1964) the Harrison Bible Collection brought together by Thomas J. Harrison of Pryor, Oklahoma. In 1971, Turner was able to acquire thirty-one consecutive leaves from the Gutenberg Bible (ca. 1454), from the book of Jeremiah, through the generosity of Mr. and Mrs. Carr P. Collins, Jr., their friends and family.[81] By 1980, the Board of Trustees established a policy requiring a two-thirds vote of the Board to permit the deaccessioning of any rare book in Bridwell Library. Nineteen special collections are listed. Books from forty special presses are also included in the Trustees' policy.[82]

But to focus solely on the library's special collections is to miss the crucial role played by Turner and the library in fulfilling the research and study needs of faculty and students. Turner put it thus:

> These are some of the facets of Bridwell Library. Not all of its treasures are seen in the colorful rows of volumes in the "W. R. Nicholson Reading Room" nor between the bright covers of the items in the "Annie Young Hughey Periodical Room." Some are under lock and key in the Rare Book Room. Yet its greatest treasures have a far less grandiose setting—when someone seeks information, and the staff is able to match the right book with the right person at the right time, the result is the greatest treasure of all.[83]

The 1960s: A Summary

The 1960s were years of consolidation for Perkins School of Theology. The revolution under Merrimon Cuninggim necessitated a time of assimilation and maturing. Quillian knew that his first task was to begin to solidify relationships with the church, and he went about doing just that. His style of operation was a kind of benevolent paternalism, nudging, sometimes being more assertive, always standing by ready to pick up the pieces which he had to do on many occasions in the following decade.

Student unrest was by and large still to come at SMU, though it had begun in the mid-1960s elsewhere.[84] It did not reach its heights in Dallas until 1972,[85] matters which we shall examine in the following chapter.

The assassination of President Kennedy in Dallas on 22 November 1963 brought a rare collective response to public events from the Perkins faculty. The faculty responded to Mayor Earl Cabell's call to community concern by adopting a statement containing these words: "We pray that Dallas will be remembered not simply as the scene of President Kennedy's death, but that his death will be recalled as an event in which the city began a new and more authentic life."[86]

President Tate responded for the University by asking the Law and Theology faculties and selected faculty from other schools to sponsor public dialogues on the problems the city faced. Douglas Jackson of the Theology faculty, Johnnie Marie Grimes, and Jo Fay Godby formed the committee.[87] Growing out of this temporary project was a new concern by the University for the Dallas community under the continuing leadership of Mrs. Godby.

Externally, Dean Quillian's positive and knowledgeable interaction with the churches re-solidified a somewhat weakened relationship with congregations in the South Central Jurisdiction during the 1960s. The decade was not a time of great internal change for Perkins, however. The next revolution occurred only when there was a complete restudy of governance, curriculum, and student life in 1968–69, a study which propelled the School into new life and new patterns of endeavor.

11

The Quillian Years: 1969–81

In the U. S. civil rights movement of the 1950s, truly a remarkable period of American history, the non-violent tactics of Martin Luther King, Jr., by and large prevailed. In the 1960s, however, both the cities and the campuses erupted in violence. In the cities the slowness of or the failure to carry out reform led to minority frustration, and actions on the campuses were triggered partly by these same frustrations but much more by the fact that the Vietnam War dragged on and on.

The years from 1966 to 1970 were especially difficult, leading one commentator to write of 1970: "American society became increasingly fragmented into mutually hostile groups, based on such facts as class status, age, race, and ideology."[1]

The violence affected some of the most prestigious universities in the country: Harvard, Cornell, Dartmouth, Columbia, Stanford, Indiana University, Ohio State University—and eventually Kent State University, on 4 May 1970. Schools in Texas remained remarkably calm, although Rice University students refused to accept a new President in 1969, leading to his resignation.[2]

SMU had few protests during the early years of student unrest and they remained non-violent.[3] The first open protest, so far as I can determine, occurred in April 1969, and was a sit-in in a temporary girls' dormitory, Tower Hall, protesting the lack of visitation rights by male students in female-occupied rooms. The students were judged guilty by the Student Judiciary but given no penalty.[4]

About the same time a more serious incident occurred. The BLAACS organization (Black League of Afro-American and African College Students) presented eight "demands" to the University on 23 April 1969. The demands dealt with such matters as the request that Afro-American students be employed to recruit students, that more financial aid be made available, that the liberal studies program include courses dealing with the accomplishments of black people, that a program of Afro-American studies be developed, and so on. President Tate took the requests quite seriously, consulted broadly concerning the list, and instigated plans for implementing as many as possible.[5]

One year later, on 30 April 1970, the United States invaded Cambodia, and there followed the most intense series of protests yet mounted on U.S. campuses. At Kent State University, in Kent, Ohio, students made a window-smashing march into the town and burned the campus ROTC building. On May 4, National Guardsmen were called to disperse a noon rally of 2,000 anti-war demonstrators, leading to the deaths of four students and the wounding of nine others. As a result of what happened at Kent State, it is estimated that 760 campuses experienced strikes or demonstrations, many accompanied by violence.[6]

Included in the protests was the largest yet held on the SMU campus, non-violent but involving deep feeling.[7] The *Dallas Morning News* described the ceremony as follows:

> Students bearing four black cardboard coffins, draped with the American flag and representing the four students killed in the Monday confrontation between Kent State demonstrators and National Guardsmen, marched into the crowd and placed the coffins in front of the building [Dallas Hall]. Then listened to speeches.[8]

President Tate spoke at the flagpole after the student-planned service in Perkins Chapel on May 6. In in his remarks, he said:

> I know you want to do something. I know you need to express how you feel. I am here to protect you against any intimidation in your right to express your deep feelings. I am sure you know that violence will damage the structure of this academic community. Each of you, however, will be protected from other students or outsiders as you express in a nonviolent way, your hurt over this terrible tragedy.[9]

One additional demonstration occurred, without violence but one that could easily have led to open confrontation. On 9 May 1972, twenty-two students occupied Perkins Administration Building, protesting the continued escalation of the Vietnam War. Beginning in the late afternoon, they remained for ten and one-half hours, well into the early morning. President Tate remained in his office suite throughout the sit-in, and finally requested security guards to carry the students from the building.[10] His basis for doing this was that they "were disrupting the University."[11] Demonstrations that are not disrupting, he explained, were allowed. But soon the protests had run their course, as the de-escalation of the Vietnam War began.

Why was SMU spared the violence that occurred on so many campuses? One reason is that SMU students generally have constituted a conservative group. Most Perkins students were too busy earning a living and going to school to spend much time in protest (there were exceptions, of course). President Tate deserves a great deal of credit for the handling of the situations. He was student-oriented, and students knew it. He was open to their presence and would listen both to what they said and how they felt. We have already quoted his statement to students around the flagpole, and this was typical.

What is perhaps just as significant is the fact that Tate had already begun opening the University's decision-making process to students, and newly elected members of shared governance met on 9–10 October 1970 to begin their work.[12] Out of this process came radical changes in governance, especially in the case of Perkins School of Theology.

Shared Governance at Perkins

Dean Quillian had anticipated the President's action concerning shared governance, and the process of discussion occurred during 1968–69 at Perkins. As early as 8 December 1967, the Dean projected a major self-study to accompany the University's self-study for the Southern Association and to prepare for the Association of Theological Schools' visit to Perkins in the early 1970s.[13] Four months later a tentative structure was presented with four committees: steering, curriculum, academic life, and administration.[14] (The final names were Curriculum and Degrees, Academic Life and Work, and Organization and Administration, or Governance.)[15]

The three working committees were chaired by faculty: John Deschner for Governance; Fred Carney for Curriculum; and Ronald Sleeth for Life and Work (which became Community Life). The Steering Committee consisted of the three chairs and an additional member from each committee, chaired by the Dean.[16] All committees consisted of both faculty and student members.

The committees went to work very quickly, and worked with diligence for almost a year. Although attempts were made to keep the community informed, both students and faculty not on the committees often felt left out. There was enough information provided, however, that the results did not come as a complete surprise to those not on the committees.

Reports were made to the faculty on April 18, and student hearings and votes were set for April 29 and May 1.[17]

The Governance Committee's chief work was the creation of a Student-Faculty Senate to be the chief governing body of Perkins School of Theology. It was approved by the students on 1 May 1969 and adopted by the faculty on May 9.[18] I wonder now how we who composed the committee dared to propose such a radical step—a form of governance in which most of the decision-making became a joint student-faculty matter. The Dean, of course, remained for administrative purposes the link of authority between school, administration, and Board of Trustees. But the principal shared governance plan became such an ingrained practice in the school that only on a few occasions did he exercise this authority. The governance plan was put into effect immediately after the first Senate meeting held on 16 May 1969. Four student senators were already elected: Rex Shepperd, Mel Morgan, Mike Harper, and John Bengel. Roger Loyd had already been elected as a student member of the Committee on Curriculum.[19]

The governance plan was set forth in a document called "Articles of Operation and By-Laws of the Perkins School of Theology." The principal writer was the chair of the committee, John Deschner, and it was a masterfully written document.[20] Article II clearly states: "The Senate shall be the primary governing body of the Perkins School of Theology."[21] Article VII lists items reserved for faculty action: admission of students to degree candidacy and approval of the granting of degrees, election of faculty to the Rank and Tenure Committee, and application of academic policy decisions regarding individual students. Under the control of the Student Association Council (Article VII: 5) the gray areas that soon developed pertained mostly to the independence of Student Council committees to act without Senate supervision.

"The Senate shall do its business," Article VII:1 states, "with a lively regard for the Perkins tradition that sizeable differences in judgment should be thoroughly discussed . . ." There was also a recognition that the Constitution and By-Laws of the University might supersede or restrict the actions of the Senate.

The work of the Senate was carried out by seven "standing committees" composed of faculty, administrators, students, alumni/ae, and a member of the Perkins Trustee Committee, who also became a member of the Senate.[22] The committees were Academic Procedures, Community Life, Curriculum, Faculty, Long Range Planning, Recruitment and Admissions, and School Relations. Other committees were the Advisory Council, Faculty Committee on Rank and Tenure, Nominations, and a Student Committee on Faculty Evaluation.[23]

In addition, there were also Student Council Committees, some of them completely independent, others responsible to the various Senate Standing committees. For example, the Worship Committee, a student committee with faculty members, was assigned to the Community Life Committee, of which I was chair.[24] It was my strong opinion that this committee had become almost completely independent over the years. I am still not sure of my motives in taking on the task of making this committee more responsible to the total community through Community Life. Perhaps it was due to the long years of suffering through worship that was either almost Anglo-Catholic or wildly experimental.

Students willing to give time to planning and carry out worship—and it required a great deal—were often quite "high church" in their understanding of worship. And even though I like liturgy—even ancient liturgy—I at times felt we moved beyond the Methodist tradition, especially as it existed in the South. So, encouraged by the President of the student body, I decided to insist that the Worship Committee develop its by-laws (mandated by the Senate) and include a clear recognition of its responsibility to the Senate and the Perkins community through the Community Life Committee.

The result was that the chair and several members resigned, and for a long time I wasn't sure but that I would have to take over the work myself. Fortunately, a member of the Committee volunteered to become chair, and with the members remaining and some new people, the committee carried on. I really did not win the war, and I am not even sure I won the battle. It is true, however, that the committee did become more responsive to the entire community.

A second incident that occurred during the second year of the operation of the Community Life Committee indicates how many students did not trust faculty. The committee was quite large and we set up an Executive Committee one of whose responsibilities was to set the agenda for the large group. Early in the year the vice-chair of the group, who was also a personal friend, came to me—rather embarrassed—and said, "Would you mind if I made out the agenda? [Name] is afraid you won't follow the executive committee's wishes in making it out." I found this highly amusing at the time, and even more so a few years later when I turned up as a member of the suspicious student's Doctor of Ministry committee!

The shared governance plan worked remarkably well during its first years. Although occasionally students and faculty lined up against one another, it was much more common for opposing sides to be a mixture of both. Most students took their assignments quite seriously and often brought a dimension of depth to the discussion. Either because they lost some of their enthusiasm or because they still felt overcome by faculty authority, the interest level seemed to lessen as the decade of the 1970s neared its end. The amount of student participation decreased, and in the early 1980s, the structure was modified.

One of the problems for the faculty was that it had no opportunity for a discussion in decision making. Guild meetings were held regularly, and lunches and other faculty occasions at times, but many did not believe these were sufficient. In an evaluation of the process in 1981, Joe Allen pointed to factors which had radically changed the Perkins situation—not the process of decision making, which had been participatory in nature since the 1950s. What had changed were the *structures* of participation.

Three factors were responsible, he wrote: the increase of the number of administrators, from seven or eight to more than twenty.[25] A second factor was the changes in faculty, so that only a dozen or so of the core faculty remained.[26] And the third factor was the nature of the Senate, a body of some sixty faculty, administrators, alumni/ae, students, and the chair of the Perkins Board of Trustees Committee, almost doubling the deliberative body of the 1960s.[27] Allen concluded by admitting that this matter had never been a matter of serious faculty or Senate examination, and had only occasionally come out in informal faculty discussion.[28]

A New Curriculum

A second committee which worked through 1968–69 was concerned with curriculum. The results of the study were weighted heavily toward required courses in Biblical and Theological Studies, with eight semester hours each in Old and New Testaments; eight in History of Christianity; sixteen in Theology (Method, Moral, and Systematic); and four in History of Religion: a total of ninety-six required hours in course work, with a required internship in addition.[29]

Two unique features were introduced: first, a twenty-semester-hour sequence in "practical studies." An eight-semester-hour course called "Church and World" was required for the first year, described as "a critical psycho-social analysis of the physical and cultural environment, its influence upon developing personalities and institution of ministry."[30]

The student's middler year included a new course called "Practical Theology" taken concurrently with the first semester of "The Ministry of the Church." The committee failed to develop much about what either of these courses should include. As described in the *Perkins Catalog*, "Practical Theology" was "an historical and theological analysis of the church, its mission and ministry, with special consideration of what it means to be a professional church leader in the late twentieth century."[31] "The Ministry of the Church" was a two-semester sequence "involving a critical analysis of the Church as a functioning community in which and from which ministry occurs."[32]

As the ministry course developed, it consisted of limited lectures and the practice of ministry in workshops and seminars. An attempt was made—impossible though it proved to be—to provide at least minimal understandings and skills in the total range of ministerial practice with specialists from the various fields leading seminars and workshops. The managing of the course was a massive administrative job and required the full time of one faculty member and limited time from many others. These courses were offered first in 1971–72.

Students reacted to the omnibus course almost entirely negatively. Faculty reaction was not much better. Most faculty preferred to teach in their own specialized fields. Students were not accustomed to such courses and did not quite know what to do with them.

"Church and World" lasted two years. "Practical Theology" and "Ministry of the Church" persisted for only one. I am still not certain that the decision to abandon them was correct. It seemed to me that we were just emerging with something that was innovative and possibly important in seminary education. But the changes were made in 1972, and they were at best makeshift.

Six areas of ministry were defined: Preaching, Worship, Pastoral Care, Church Education, Church and Society, and Church Organizational Behavior. Each student selected four of these areas, which meant that unless he or she opted to take other ministry courses as electives, two areas of ministry were missed altogether.[33] A year later a seventh option was added, Evangelism, which meant that three areas were not required. This year also the graduation requirements were reduced to 72 semester-hours, with all four-semester-hour courses being changed to three.[34] Other changes occurred during the next few years, and we will examine these later.

A second innovation fared better. This was the intern program, a requirement for each M.Th. student.[35] The first version required a minimum of ten weeks of work in a local church or in special instances some other setting. The purpose was understood as being

> to provide the student with the practical experience and instruction which is not available in the classroom, in order to help him gain insight, confidence, and poise in his role and function as a minister.[36]

The principal supervision was provided by a local church person (usually the pastor) and a lay committee. Students in the same area met regularly with a psychological consultant and for occasional seminars with faculty members. The Perkins intern staff made the appointments, met regularly with students, and visited the field units. Claus Rohlfs did a masterful job of working out the details of a plan only partially formed by the committee.

The ten-week period proved too brief, and within a few years such internships were eliminated. More and more students, in fact, opted for nine months (or even twelve) so that for an increasing number of students the Perkins M.Th. program became four years long.[37]

The program is an expensive one, and Dean Quillian was required to raise special money for its support each year. As James Ward says in the special edition of the *Journal* honoring Quillian, "It takes a courageous dean to attempt such an enterprise. . . . However, Dean Quillian has never considered turning back …"[38]

Academic Life and Work (and Community Life)

A third committee for the 1968–69 seminary review was given a much more nebulous mandate. Much of what it considered overlapped one of the other committees, and its major contribution became its concern for the non-academic life of the Perkins community.

Unlike many educational institutions, Perkins has always considered itself more than an academic center. Prior to its growth in size, much of this function was fulfilled by the free association of students both in the classroom and in other places. Although many students lived off campus and some had student charges, the quality of academic life was a natural outgrowth of common interests and concerns.

When the School moved into its own quadrangle in 1950–51, the conditions seemed to exist for a deeper experience of community. With half the students living in its own dormitories or apartment houses, we all rejoiced in the nearness to one another and hoped it would lead to genuine *koinonia*. During the early years of the new buildings, this seemed to work fairly well. Even so, many students lived off campus and some lived at their churches and commuted daily. Most students on campus had outside jobs, and spouses either worked off campus or cared for children. It was to deal with the separation, increased by the growing diversity of the student body, that the third committee directed its efforts.

One of their resolutions was "that the student be a full partner in the academic enterprise at Perkins."[39] Serving on the Senate or on a committee helped in the realization of this goal but did not solve all the problems of the Perkins community.

Other recommendations, referred to the new Community Life Committee, asked that Kirby Lounge be used as a commons room, that there be a weekly noon meal in Lois Perkins Auditorium, that there be monthly evening meals, that the kitchen of Selecman Lounge be remodeled to make such meals possible, and that a shared community day for work and play be planned.[40] Community lunch had in fact been initiated the year before by James and Marilyn White and became (and remains) an important occasion for fellowship and for learning what is happening at Perkins.

Worship at Perkins fared rather better than it did at many seminaries. Dean Quillian and faculty were frequently asked by people from other schools how this came about.[41] Yet attendance, which was usually quite good at the beginning of the year, tended to decline and often to be embarrassingly low by examination time. Quillian sometimes appealed to the faculty to be more faithful in worship participation, and a sizeable number of faculty were regular in doing so.

Further Curriculum Changes

There is a curious phenomenon among faculty—or at least it has existed at SMU's School of Theology since its earliest days. The search for the perfect curriculum is as intense as the search for the Holy Grail in medieval times. Perhaps over the years the faculty has been looking for a symphony as they have worked on curriculum. Instead, the best that has emerged has been "variations on a theme." That theme was set in the beginning of the school: a classical German theological education consisting of Bible, church history, biblical, historical, systematic, and practical theology.

Over the years various areas have been added, deleted, reclaimed, reshaped, and renamed. The core has held fast, however, and has saved the education of Perkins School of Theology from the aberrations to which some schools have subjected their students from time to time, in my opinion. I suspect that the best a school can do is to provide variations on a theme, with the variations as closely related to specific cultural and church needs as a faculty's ingenuity can devise.

In any case revisions continued during the 1970s. A review began in the fall of 1973, and a number of issues were identified: the General Requirement Courses (GRCs) in ministry, the intern seminar, the location of the internship, the possibility of reducing hours in required courses, more intermediate courses in theology, and theological education for professions not requiring ordination.[42]

The changes, approved in January 1974, were minimal. Two courses in ministry were given three semester hours of credit each and required, Pastoral Care and Preaching. The other six functions were given either one and one-half semester hours, or in the case of Worship two and Church Music one. From this group six additional hours in ministry courses were mandatory, which still left two of the courses as elective. The satisfying of the requirement in the History of Christianity was made more flexible.[43]

The GRCs in ministry were later combined into three-semester-hour courses, with, for example, Education and Evangelism being made a single course of three semester hours.[44] Ways of satisfying the church's Methodist requirement were still a matter of concern, but a revision was not adopted until 1980.[45]

The ministry courses again came under scrutiny in the self-study of the later 1970s in preparation for an Association of Theological Schools review in 1980. The conclusion was that the changes which had been made "have not produced genuine satisfaction."[46] The definition of areas of ministry is a problem, the committee stated, and there is no way of giving "attention to the ministerial office construed as a single office."[47]

A task force was set up in 1978 to deal specifically with the ministry core, and at first an integrative course called "Introduction to Ministry" was proposed.[48]

The objections to such a course, however, proved insurmountable and the final recommendation was that a plan already in existence be continued, namely, that exposure to areas of ministry not carried as courses be given during the internship.[49]

In May 1972, the faculty voted to add the Doctor of Ministry (D.Min.) degree to its curricular offerings. The degree was designed "to enable specially qualified and promising persons to achieve advanced competence in ministry for leadership in the church."[50] Howard Grimes was named the first director of the D.Min. degree program, which required the completion of twenty-four semester hours beyond the first theological degree, including a practicum and a professional project, a written essay containing theological reflection on the practicum.

The 1980 report of the Association of Theological Schools was by and large favorable, but questions were raised again concerning the ministry core, with no specific recommendations offered.[51]

And so again, during Quillian's last year as Dean, another curriculum review committee was established by the Senate, a study to be reported to the Senate during the spring semester of 1982![52]

Changes in Faculty and Administration

Though the faculty remained relatively stable during the 1960s, the 1970s brought a larger number of moves. The full-time faculty remained about the same size: thirty-seven on 1 January 1970, all Anglo males, ages 29 to 65, with an average age of 46.1. On 1 January 1980, there were thirty-five faculty members including thirty-one Anglo males, two African-Americans, one Hispanic, and one female, ages 31 to 64, an average of 50. Six of the thirty-seven listed in 1970 had retired: Baker, Cooper, Judy, Outler, Schoonover, and Wagers. Five had gone to other schools: Jones, Longsworth, Robinson, Sleeth, and Young. Two—Elliott and Hendrix—had entered private counseling practice, and one, McGrath, now taught full-time in the School of the Arts. Eleven were new, and one had returned to the faculty after going to another school.[53]

The intern staff, who were eventually given faculty status, had grown from one (Claus Rohlfs), to five: Rohlfs, Emerick, Gilmore, Gwaltney, and Stewart. One was female and one was African-American.[54] The Bridwell Library staff was still incredibly small—Decherd Turner, Page A. Thomas, John Hooper, J. Mac McPherson, and Kate Warnick (as the curator of the Methodist Collection).[55]

The number of administrators had increased greatly. Seven of the administrators also did some teaching. The total included the Dean, two Associate Deans, the Director of Academic Procedures, the Financial Officer, the Bishop in Residence, the five Directors and Associate Directors of the Intern Program, the principal officers of Bridwell Library, the Director of the M.S.M. program, the Director of Continuing Education, the Director of the Mexican-American Program, the Director of the D.Min. program, the Director of Perkins Relations, the Director of Development, and the Director of Community Life. The Director of the Ph.D. program was also a Perkins professor, and the Director of Black Studies was a temporarily vacant position.[56] There were also sixteen members of the support staff (secretarial and administrative assistants) and a bookstore manager.[57]

1970–71. New faculty included Nathaniel L. Lacy, Jr., Practical Theology and Coordinator of Black Studies; William W. Mount, Jr., New Testament; Alfredo Nañez, Mexican-American Studies; and Edwin E. Sylvest, Jr., History of Christianity. George Baker had retired; Bill Robinson had joined the faculty of Andover-Newton Theological School; and Charles Braden, former faculty member, died in 1970. In addition there were seven clinical instructors working in the field of Pastoral Care, three new: George F. Roberts, Jr., David Erb, and Kenneth Pepper. Richard F. Vieth, Robert E. Ellen, Jr., and Edwin M. Byron taught part-time.[58]

1971–72. J. B. Holt was elected Secretary of the General Conference in 1972.[59] No new faculty were added in 1971–72, and only three visiting faculty were included: Rabbi Levi A. Olan, John N. Flynn, and Lama Govinda. James Gwaltney became Associate Director of the Intern Program, Robert Bell was named Director of Perkins Relations, and Mike Harper served as Coordinator of Community Life. Leroy Howe became Associate Dean on 1 June 1972, and James Ward became acting Dean while Dean Quillian had a year's leave. Floyd Curl had died prior to the beginning of the school year.[60]

1972–73. 1972 was a significant year as Perkins welcomed Phyllis A. Bird, in Old Testament, its first full-time female faculty member. Another important event was the return of theologian Schubert Ogden to the faculty from the University of Chicago.[61]

A third faculty member came under special circumstances. The post in Evangelism, a chair provided annually by Mr. and Mrs. Sol McCreless of San Antonio, had been vacant since the retirement of George Baker two years earlier. For only the second time, Dean Quillian used a special provision of the 23 January 1970 "Guidelines" in dealing with what the Dean considered an emergency situation. The Senate had been unable to agree on an occupant for the chair. Dean Quillian, without benefit of a task force to make recommendations to the Senate, invited George G. Hunter III for an official visit in May 1972. The Senate was still badly split, but the Dean recommended Hunter to the Provost, and he was duly invited to the faculty.[62] In fairness to the Dean, it should be noted that this procedure was not often used.

Bishop W. Kenneth Pope, who had just retired as Presiding Bishop of the Dallas-Fort Worth area, came as Bishop in Residence and Advisor on Conference Relations.[63] Elaine Smith became Coordinator of Community Life.[64] Craig Emerick joined the Intern Staff.[65] In addition there were twelve clinical instructors who dealt with "field units"[66] (groups of interns in geographical proximity) and 62 field instructors in local churches.[67]

Albert Outler, the chair of the General Conference for a new theological statement for the United Methodist Church, led a lengthy discussion on the development of the statement.[68] Alfredo Nañez concluded many years of association with Perkins School of Theology, the final three years as a full-time member of the faculty.[69] Paul Hardin was inaugurated as President of the University on 16 November 1972.[70]

1973–74. Since Dean Quillian had been on leave during 1972–73, no faculty appointments were made for 1973. Brooks Jones came from Scarritt College to be on the SMU Development Staff and was assigned to Perkins.[71] Neill McFarland resigned as Provost of the University and returned to full-time teaching at Perkins.[72]

In May 1974, Dean Quillian issued a "manifesto" concerning future faculty and staff appointments: (1) they must be clearly needed; (2) they must be fully qualified; and (3) we must give ourselves time to search for qualified ethnic minorities and women.[73] The search for women and minorities had been undertaken in earnest some time earlier, but now it was considered to be an even higher priority. Finding such persons was not easy since dozens of other seminaries were also looking for such qualified persons, and the results had been less than had been hoped for.

The year 1974 was one of turmoil for the University. Paul Hardin had become president of the University two years earlier, and with no explanation was forced to resign on 18 June 1974. Former President Tate, now Chancellor, was vacationing in Mexico, and the Board of Governors on the afternoon of June 18 sent an airplane to bring him back to Dallas to become once again the interim President of the University.

Marshall Terry describes this as Tate's "last great contribution to his University," "in the painful position of coming back as president to hold things together while the search for a new president went on again."[74] President Hardin became President of Drew University and continued there until 1989, when he became Chancellor of the University of North Carolina (Chapel Hill).

1974–75. This was the year for two steps ahead in the employment of minorities. Nathaniel Lacy, an African-American, had come on the faculty in 1970 but left to do graduate work after a few years. His successor was Zan W.

Holmes, a well-known African-American preacher who had also been a member of the Texas State Legislature. Although his principal work was as a member of the Intern Staff, he was given faculty status and made responsible for Black Studies. Roy D. Barton, a member of the Rio Grande Conference, became Director of the Mexican-American Program, also with faculty status, teaching Practical Theology. Mike Harper was made Director of Community Life.[75]

Bishop Paul Martin, whose friendship with Mr. and Mrs. Perkins did much to direct their major giving to the School of Theology, died in February 1975, with his funeral at Highland Park United Methodist Church on February 17. Bishop Martin's body lay in state in Perkins Chapel with a walking cortege to the church consisting principally of faculty, staff, and students.[76]

Albert Outler retired at the end of the 1974–75 academic year but was retained as Research Professor of Theology. He taught at least one course each year but gave most of his time to his work on the Wesley sermons, assisted by Wanda Smith, who became something of a Wesley authority herself.[77]

1975–76. James Zumberge, of the University of Nebraska at Lincoln, became President of SMU in the fall of 1975 and attended a part of the Perkins Senate Conference soon afterwards. He later met with the faculty at the October meeting of the Senate.[78]

The largest turnover in the Perkins faculty in many years also occurred. Herndon Wagers and Kermit Schoonover retired; Carlton Young went to Scarritt College; Joe Jones became Dean of the Graduate School of Religion of Phillips University; and William Mount resigned.[79] Wesley Davis, Professor of New Testament from the 1930s to the 1960s, died on 29 October 1975.[80] Roger N. Deschner, Minister of Music at First Methodist in Houston, succeeded Young as Director of the M.S.M. program.[81] Virgil P. Howard became visiting Professor of New Testament. Many of these changes occurred late in the year, and hence replacements were not immediately available.

James Gwaltney became Administrative Director of the Intern Program, and Emma (Trout) Justes was brought to the campus as an Associate Director of the Program.[82] Kenneth Black was assigned to Perkins by the central business office as Financial Officer.[83] Four visiting faculty helped fill the gaps: The Right Rev. Donald Davies, Jane M. Marshall, Rabbi Levi A. Olan, and DeForrest Wiksten.[84]

Although the process of selecting new faculty had been in operation for some time, it was put in writing during the year. The first step in the process was the appointment of a student-faculty committee whose first job was to draw up a job description, which was then approved by the Senate (or modified or even returned to the committee). The committee then canvassed possibilities with as broad a search as possible. The committee discussed possibilities with the Dean and eventually recommended one candidate to him. The Dean visited the candidate personally and formed a judgment whether the person should receive further consideration; the Dean in turn made the recommendation to the Senate and the candidate came for a stated visit. After the visit the Senate took an advisory vote for the Dean, who in turn recommended the person to the Provost who then recommended the person to the Board of Trustees for election.[85]

1976–77. This year was also one of changes for the faculty. Allen Lamar Cooper retired in 1976, and George Hunter became Director of the Section on Evangelism of the United Methodist Church's Board of Discipleship on 1 January 1977. Ronald Sleeth resigned to become President of West Virginia Wesleyan University. Marvin Judy retired in 1977, and Fred Gealy died in December 1976. (He had just completed teaching a course at Perkins.)

New faculty included Charles M. Wood in Theology, O. Eugene Slater as Bishop in Residence, Hans Dieter Betz as visiting professor of New Testament, and Merrill Abbey as visiting Professor of Preaching. Phyllis Bird became a member of the University Senate of the United Methodist Church in 1976.[86]

1977–78. Harold W. Attridge, the first Roman Catholic member of the faculty, joined the New Testament department. Richard P. Heitzenrater, researcher of John Wesley's diaries and later editor of the Wesley Works Project, began teaching in Church History and Methodist Studies, and later became curator of Bridwell's Methodist collection. Virgil Howard was made a regular member of the New Testament faculty, and Martha Gilmore, a recent Perkins graduate, was appointed as a permanent member of the intern staff.

Earl Marlatt died during the year. Bishop Pope became Bishop in Residence emeritus, and in 1978 William Longsworth went to Brite Divinity School in Fort Worth.[87]

1978–79. One new faculty member assumed responsibilities in September 1978: David L. Watson in Evangelism. Both Robert Elliott and Harville Hendrix had gone into private counseling practice, and visiting faculty in Pastoral Care included Charles Steward, Herman Cook, and Heije Faber. Ruth Smith was added to the staff of Bridwell Library.[88] Tony Fadely served as Missionary-in-Residence for the year.

In 1979, Kate Warnick retired for the second time after sixty years and six months of service to the SMU libraries, fifty-five of which had been to the School of Theology.[89] Her first retirement had been in 1961, so she had been curator of the Methodist collection for eighteen years past her sixty-fifth birthday.

Emma Justes left in 1979 to go to Garrett-Evangelical Theological Seminary, and Jim Ward again became Associate Dean.

1979–80. With the departure of Elliott and Hendrix, it was decided that a reorganization of the Pastoral Care staff was in order.[90] Two faculty members already at Perkins became the first two of a three-person staff: David Switzer who had been counseling chaplain, and Leroy Howe who shifted from Philosophical Theology to Theology and Pastoral Care. The report concerning the third position was that "a qualified woman will continue to be sought for the third appointment."[91]

Zan Holmes, who had been on the Intern Staff, was approved for a position in Homiletics, to be on leave during 1979–80 for further study. Richard Stewart was appointed to succeed Holmes on the Intern Staff, and Martha Gilmore, who had held a two-year term on that staff, now became an Associate Director of the program. Bill Matthews, after the departure of Bob Bell, became Director of Perkins Relations and Associate Director of Continuing Education.[92]

Charles B. Thomas (an African-American) was invited to a post in Sociology of Religion, and the Dean expressed his intention of making a Mexican-American appointment to the Intern Staff.[93] John Holbert was visiting Professor of Old Testament.[94] Charles R. Allen became Director of Development, and Barbara Ruth Director of Community Life.

Perhaps the most shocking news of the year was Decherd Turner's announcement that he would be leaving Bridwell Library after thirty years to become Director of the Harry Ransom Humanities Research Center, and University Professor, at the University of Texas at Austin.[95] Turner would now be searching for manuscripts rather than rare books. As the Dean put it, "one can hardly overestimate the work he has done at Bridwell Library"; it "has been with quality and style" and one can hardly "envision [his] being replaceable."[96]

1980–81. After a careful search, however, a replacement was found for Turner, at Iliff School of Theology, in the person of Jerry D. Campbell.[97] Campbell's style was different from that of Turner, and his interests were not identical, but he was an excellent librarian.[98] In August 1980, he was joined by Roger Loyd, a long-time friend and graduate of Perkins, as Associate Librarian.

Ruth T. Barnhouse, a psychiatrist with theological training and an Episcopal priest, became the third member of the Pastoral Care staff.[99] Bishop Slater retired as Bishop in Residence, and Bishop W. McFerrin Stowe took his place.[100] Stowe held the Ph.D. degree and regularly taught courses, especially in Methodist polity, until his death in 1988.

Zan Holmes began his teaching in Homiletics. Father David Balas of the University of Dallas and Rabbi Jack Bemporad of Temple Emmanu-El were visiting faculty.[101] An unsuccessful attempt was made to secure a Hispanic for the Intern Staff. Dale Hensarling began a two-year postgraduate residence as Assistant Director of the Intern Program.[102]

1981–82. Dean Quillian did not officially retire until 1982, but his final year was spent on leave. The new dean was James E. Kirby, Jr., whom we will consider in more detail later. The faculty changes were primarily Quillian's, however, and so will be considered at this point.

James Zumberge had resigned as President to go to the University of Southern California in the same position, and L. Donald Shields was named President of SMU. John Holbert became Director of Continuing Education and of the D.Min. program after Richard Murray left Continuing Education for full-time teaching. Heitzenrater likewise shifted to full-time teaching and the Wesley Works Project. Howard Grimes, Grady Hardin, and J. B. Holt officially retired in 1981 but continued for an additional year. Wanda Smith became a member of the library staff. Hanno W. Kirk was added to the visiting faculty, in Pastoral Care.[103]

Conclusion

Perhaps no other decade in the history of SMU's School of Theology was quite so volatile as the 1970s. Nor has the story been concluded. Some of the more interesting, and the more bothersome, events will be considered in the following chapter—conflicts and criticism, and some of the gains made toward reconciliation, both internally and externally.

12

The Struggle to Become
an Inclusive School

Students of Perkins School of Theology were almost all Anglo males at the end of the 1960s. There were, of course, minority students—African-American, a few Mexican-Americans, internationals, an occasional Native American. The number of women students in the M.Th. program had not increased significantly—there were ten women students in this basic ordination degree program in the fall of 1970.[1]

Only in 1970 did Perkins make its first African-American and Mexican-American appointments to the faculty, and two years later received its first woman faculty member.[2] This may seem almost unbelievable to us today, but the truth is that it took a great deal of effort to change the situation with less success even now than one might have hoped. To say that such faculty persons were hard to come by—and to some extent still are—may suggest something about the Anglo male orientation of the faculty but also about the real problems in academia—especially in graduate schools—one encounters in the process.

Hispanic Developments[3]

The history of Hispanic students at SMU goes back very nearly to the beginning of the University. The earliest record of a Spanish surname is in 1917—Santiago Gomez who received the B.D. degree in 1919.[4] For unexplained reasons he was largely forgotten, and Alfredo Nañez is usually named as the first graduate, in 1932. Eleazar Guerra was graduated in 1926, and later became a bishop in his native Mexico.[5]

Methodist work with Mexican-Americans in Texas began soon after the Anglos became the predominant group—after the independence of Texas in 1836 and the end of the Mexican War in 1848. An annual conference was organized by the M. E. Church, South, in 1882, and somewhat later by the M. E. Church (North). At unification of the three Methodist churches in 1939, the conferences were brought together and eventually became the Rio Grande Conference, presided over by Bishop A. Frank Smith.[6]

Probably the most difficult problems Anglo-Americans face in the process we have described is the failure to remember that both European culture and

Christianity came into the Southwest by way of Hispanic exploration and settlement, almost two centuries prior to the coming to the Southwest of the Anglos from the North. History books either ignore or play down these facts, or at least they have in the past. I had to go to Alistair Cooke's *America* to find some of the facts I wanted![7]

At first,Mexican-American clergy were trained in Mexico. After Frank S. Onderdonk, an Anglo, was forced to return to Texas after the Mexican Revolution in 1914, this was no longer possible. In 1917 the Wesleyan Institute in San Antonio was organized, and subsequently this school along with Lydia Patterson Institute in El Paso provided training for Spanish-speaking clergy.[8]

In 1948, a meeting was called to discuss the training of Hispanic clergy at SMU and the School of Theology. Representatives from the School, the Methodist Church in Mexico, the predecessor of the Rio Grande Conference, and the Latin American Provisional Conference in California met to discuss the matter.[9] The first step was the bringing of the Rev. Ben O. Hill to Perkins by the Department of the Ministry of the former Board of Education, now the Board of Higher Education and Ministry. Hill, an Anglo, was a member of the Rio Grande Conference and had served for many years in Cuba, beginning in 1907.[10]

The number of candidates eligible for admission to the seminary has never been large, and the problem of language has also been a barrier. Therefore, the Rio Grande Conference and the former Board of Education in Nashville initiated a Spanish-speaking "Course of Study" school at Lydia Patterson Institute in 1949. In 1951 the program was moved to Perkins, and since that time there has been a Spanish-language four-week school at Perkins.[11]

For those students with college degrees, Perkins has also attempted to provide a seminary education. Dean Quillian had as one of his highest priorities the broadening and deepening of the School's emphasis on Hispanic studies. In 1969 a special task force was set up under the leadership of Richey Hogg to consider the problem. The first step in implementing such a program was the bringing to the faculty in 1970 of Alfredo Nañez. He was the acknowledged leader of the Rio Grande Conference, and his task at Perkins was to prepare the foundation for a more extensive program at his retirement, which occurred three years later.[12]

At his retirement, in January 1974, Roy Barton, a graduate of Perkins and a leader in the Rio Grande Conference, replaced Nañez, and in October of that year he prepared a program that would have two foci: to enable Hispanic students to know and function in their own context, and to help other students and faculty understand the Mexican-American context and to work out better relationships with that context and its people.[13] Subsequently, guidelines for courses and other experiences have been worked out and modified on three occasions.[14] One of the assets of this program is the teaching of Edwin E. Sylvest, Jr., an Anglo who has identified himself with the Hispanic culture and belongs to the Rio Grande Conference. His teaching field is Church History with special expertise in the history of Hispanic Christianity.

Barton's work was understood as reaching beyond the degree program and the Course of Study School to include work with the Rio Grande Conference and other Hispanic groups throughout the United States and Latin America. One important aspect of this larger ministry was the organizing of the Hispanic Instructor Development Program whose purpose is "to identify and develop further the experience of Hispanic practitioners who have a basic seminary or undergraduate degree and offer their services to seminaries for their degree, continuing education, and course of studies programs and to do lay training in their annual conferences."[15] The first session was held in January 1976. The program also sponsors special symposia, a recent one having been concerned with preparation for the 1992 quincentenary of the arrival of Christopher Columbus in the Western hemisphere.[16]

Another program with far-reaching possibilities is the Lay Administrator Program. Funded by a grant from the General Commission on Religion and Race, the first step was taken in 1980. Subsequent grants, in 1983 from the General Council on Ministries and in 1985 from the General Board of Discipleship, have enabled two additional sessions. The program brings to the campus thirty lay persons for five weekend sessions over a three-year period, with an additional session being held at the Harwood Training Center in Albuquerque, New Mexico. Instruction is provided by the Hispanic Instructor Project. On 16 April 1988, the three groups from the three sessions met together for a weekend celebration.[17]

The program also launched a quarterly journal, *Apuntes,* in 1981. It is a bilingual journal, published by the Perkins Mexican-American Program and the United Methodist Publishing House, designed to develop significant statements on theological, biblical, cultural, and other themes related to Hispanic Christianity in the United States.[18]

For more than forty years, Perkins has sought to be a center for the development of Hispanic Christianity, drawing its strategic vision from Frank Onderdonk, Bishop A. Frank Smith, Ben O. Hill, Dean Quillian, and Alfredo Nañez, and more recently Edwin Sylvest and Roy Barton.

African-American Developments

We have seen in previous chapters how efforts were made by SMU's School of Theology as early as the 1930s to circumvent segregation laws and practices in order to provide at least a minimum education for African-American students (then most commonly designated as Negroes).[19] In 1950, by Board of Trustees action, African-Americans became eligible for admission to the degree programs,[20] with the first permanent students entering in 1952 and graduating in 1955. SMU moved rather quickly to desegregate other schools: the law school, correspondence courses, and the Graduate School in 1955. On 20 April 1962, it was voted to admit a qualified African-American to the undergraduate school, someone, it was added, not needing dormitory housing. A year later, however, the student moved into the dormitory. In that same year, 1963, the Board of Governors "recognized" black athletes, and Jerry Levias became a celebrated pass receiver for SMU's football team.

Looked at from the perspective of today, all of this seems tame and unforgivably slow in coming. But for those days it was, if not revolutionary, at least progressive. That the progress was not universally welcomed is illustrated by the fact that Levias, the first African-American athlete in the Southwest Conference, received threats.[21]

Full desegregation was still not acceptable to some, even with regard to Perkins. The earliest controversy in Dean Quillian's term of office occurred shortly after he became Dean. A new Director of Housing, Eunice Baab, asked the Dean how she should assign students to roommates in the dormitory. The Dean's response was that they should be assigned as applications for housing came in (unless there were special requests for roommates).

This led to a repetition of the events of 1953, of which Dean Quillian says he had never heard. At that time only two pairings of an African-American and an Anglo-American as roommates occurred, but in 1960 there were four such sets of roommates. Quillian reported this to President Tate who, remembering the events of seven years earlier, became concerned and asked Quillian if he would reconsider this arrangement and quickly change it. Quillian replied that he did not see how that could be done without causing a very negative reaction, and added that he felt he would have to resign if such a move were ordered. Tate replied, "Well, let's not get heroic about it. Let's see what we can do with the Trustee Committee." Tate then took the matter to the Trustee Committee for Perkins School of Theology, where he made a masterful, low-key presentation. During that meeting, Eugene McElvaney, chair of the Board of Trustees, asked, "What's the crisis?" Tate replied that the administration had promised the Board they would consult them before taking additional steps toward full integration. To which Mrs. Perkins replied, saving the situation once again: "Now isn't that grand? We've taken another step, and this is something we can be grateful for. Perkins is known around the world as a progressive school," she added. "Besides, what would I tell my Women's Society in Wichita Falls if we went back on this advance?" This finished the discussion. Dean Quillian adds, "Never did Lois Perkins ever register any loss of confidence in the school" during the various crises which occurred in the 1970s.[22]

The number of African-Americans in the University grew slowly, nor was Perkins overwhelmed by applicants. But the number had grown to the point where in 1969 a list of "Black Demands" was presented to the University administration. The University's response was to pledge an increased effort to recruit African-Americans, the setting up of a review board to review promotions to supervisory positions, a promise that the University would seek out African-American applicants for admission, and to establish immediately a Black Studies program under an African-American coordinator.[23] Perkins responded by stating that the recruitment of African-American students was under way and that preliminary discussions had already begun on a Black Studies program at Perkins.[24]

The first appointment to the faculty was Nathaniel Lacy, who began his work in the fall of 1970.[25] Four years later Zan Holmes became the first African-American appointee to the Intern Staff and also Coordinator of Black Concerns and Associate Professor of Black Theology.[26] The Dean made clear in his 1973–74 report his intention to seek more minority and women faculty members.[27] Meanwhile, students, such as Mel Bailey, began their own push for more minority appointments.[28]

The number of African-American faculty and Intern Staff has not grown significantly in spite of efforts to increase them. The pool of prospects is not large since there was little incentive for them to do graduate work until recently. Standards for faculty remain largely Anglo-oriented, and relatively little effort has been made to determine if there are other standards which would qualify persons with a different cultural background.

In addition to Lacy (who did not remain for long) and Holmes, Charles S. Thomas (faculty) and Richard Stewart (Intern Staff) were recruited during the 1970s. When Dean Quillian retired, two faculty members and one Intern Staff member were African-Americans.[29]

Meanwhile, the number of African-American students has steadily increased but the majority have seldom been United Methodists. In 1973–74, there were eight black students, of whom three were United Methodists, one was Christian Methodist, two were Baptists, one was from the Disciples of Christ, and one was Pentecostal.[30] By 1975, the total had more than doubled, to seventeen, but only five were United Methodists, four were African Methodists, six were Baptists, one was United Church of Christ, and one was from the Disciples of Christ. In 1980 the total was twenty-eight of which thirteen were United Methodist, four were Christian Methodist, two were African Methodist, six were Baptists, two were Disciples of Christ, and one was Lutheran. In 1983 the total was thirty-four, with seventeen United Methodists, one Christian Methodist, four from the African Methodist Episcopal Church, one A.M.E. Zion (a total of twenty-three with a Wesleyan background), four Baptists, one Presbyterian, one Church of God in Christ, one Disciples of Christ, one United Church of Christ, and one Pentecostal.[31]

The official Black Heritage program has not gone nearly so well as the official Mexican-American program. What seems to have happened is that African-American students have increasingly assumed responsibility for their identity in a predominantly Anglo environment. The process is described in a 1978 brochure as "the development of supplementary programs, such as convocations and consultations planned in cooperation with the Black Seminarians."[32] The Black Seminarians organization has grown stronger as the number of students has increased. With the wide variety of denominations represented, what has held the group together is not a common religious heritage but rather a cultural heritage and a search for identity.

The first Black Seminarians retreat was held in 1975.[33] The following year, 1976, the first "Annual Conference on Black Theology" was held,[34] a movement which changed course somewhat when it became Black Emphasis or Black Heritage Week.

The Worship Committee in particular and the Senate in general have continued to struggle with the question of both African-American and Mexican-American emphases in community worship. Should elements of black worship be incorporated into worship on a regular basis and should worship be bilingual, or should special times be set apart for these groups? Both have been tried, neither very successfully, nor has the issue been solved. African-American students have tended to set up their own worship, thus causing further division between them and Anglo students. There is still much soul-searching and experimentation necessary before these problems are solved.

There is, of course, considerable interrelationship between individuals. There are Anglos who espouse the African-American cause, and there are common tasks which the two groups undertake. What the future holds is difficult to predict. Additional minority faculty is at least one important aspect of the solution, and the school continues to try to bring this to pass.

Other Minorities

Some would say that the most neglected minority in American life is the Native American. This may also be true with regard to Perkins School of Theology, though the situation has gradually improved. Few members of the Oklahoma Indian Mission Conference, centered in Oklahoma but with two churches in

Dallas, enroll in the degree program. As in the case of the Rio Grande Conference, the most helpful service is through the Course of Study School. For several years in the 1970s, special courses were held exclusively for members of the Oklahoma Indian Mission Conference, in Oklahoma City. More recently they have been part of the school located on the Perkins campus, with twenty to twenty-five in most sessions. Native American forms of Christian worship form a regular part of the worship in Perkins Chapel during the summer.

An increased minority consists of Asian-American students. Japan and Korea have almost always had students throughout the history of SMU's School of Theology. The new elements, just beginning to be touched, are the Asian-American refugees from Vietnam, Cambodia, and Laos. Dallas has become an important center for such refugees. The East Dallas Cooperative Parish in particular has attempted to deal with these Southeast Asians, even though most of them remain Buddhist. One, a former Buddhist monk, has become a United Methodist minister. What the future of this group is at Perkins remains to be seen.

An international student "community" (often quite small) has existed since the beginning of the school. It is now large enough to have some sense of identity—twenty in 1980 including those in the Ph.D. and M.S.M. programs.[35] Often these students have been lonely and have felt a sense of isolation. Only because of the efforts of individual faculty, especially Richey Hogg, have they at times felt any sense of having an anchor.[36] Language has also been a barrier, and the curriculum is so oriented toward the West that it is at times not as relevant as it might be.

With the emergence of the church in non-Western nations as the dominant force in global Christianity, the number of students seeking admission far exceeds the amount of scholarship money available. In recent years, from among the forty to sixty international applicants, only eight to ten can be admitted with limited funds available to Perkins. Another problem which requires additional attention concerns how Perkins can be of more help to students from another culture. How these and other problems are addressed will help to determine whether Perkins becomes a truly global school of theology in the years ahead.

Minority Concerns in General

Most of the considerations of the special needs of minority and women students were not especially well organized until the mid-1970s. Even the first consultation on racism, although official, was somewhat ad hoc in nature. Thirty-one students and faculty participated in the conference held on 18 May 1972. Racism was defined as "that attitude and/or behavior which fosters and reinforces white male dominance and control and the policy and operations of institutional life at the expense of ethnic and minority group development."[37] The group dealt both with "ideals" (e.g., the creation of a Black Heritage Institute) and with specific suggestions (more participation of minorities in the leadership of worship.)[38] Strangely enough, women's concerns received little attention, although at that time women were often thought of as a minority.

An attachment to the Senate Minutes of 14 February 1975 indicates that a task force of the Committee on Curriculum was working on plans to determine how Perkins could meet the needs of blacks, Mexican-Americans, and women.[39] A few months later an overall task force on minority concerns was elected by the Senate.[40] It reported on 23 April 1976, and made such recommendations as the following: that the Senate at its fall retreat or at some other appropriate time should discuss such matters as all syllabi carrying a special note about possible adaptation of syllabi; that appropriate steps be taken to desegregate the faculty; that increased recruitment of minorities be planned by the Committee on Recruitment and Admissions; that an ongoing plan be developed "to sensitize the total Perkins community regarding the needs and contributions of minority and women students"; and that the Worship Committee really try to make worship "a truly common experience."[41] The report was discussed at length on 12 November 1976, with the primary emphasis being on minority faculty.[42]

During the following two years much additional consideration was given to the problem of minority and women members of the faculty and intern staff.[43] "Guidelines for Enlarging Minority and Women Membership in the Perkins Faculty and Intern Staff" appear in the Senate Minutes for 1 March 1977.[44] Most of the Senate Conference in 1977 was given to such a discussion. Issues relating to the use of sexist language were given due consideration, and the problem of diversity in worship was discussed at some length. Student Senator Tommy Slater held strongly that special weeks for different groups were not adequate.[45] The Community Life Committee proposed an interethnic experience in which a student would participate in the life of a church of a different ethnic background three to four hours per week,[46] and it was later carried out.

So the discussion continued sometimes with one particular group in mind, sometimes with the entire problem linked together.

Women at Perkins

The latest of the "minority" movements to get under way at Perkins concerns the role of women in both church and seminary. The outcome of this movement has been somewhat happier than in other areas.

SMU's School of Theology admitted women from its beginning. Mrs. C. R. Kidd, classified as an undergraduate but under the dual degree plan with the

School of Theology, was in the entering class of 1915.[47] Three candidates for certificates, given to people who pursued the theological course but did not have undergraduate degrees, were Rachel M. Jarratt,[48] Bessie O. Oliver, and Rebecca Gordgin. The first degree students, who did not remain for graduation, were admitted in 1923: Bernice Lee, Mrs. Wood H. Patrick, and Lilia Beth Roberts,[49] with Nina Ogden Calhoun and Sue Bell Mann in 1924.[50]

The first Master of Church Administration degree, a degree that was never popular, went to Anna Lois Todd in 1926, and the same year Opal Bailey was awarded the M.A. degree for work done in the School of Theology.[51] The first female B.D. graduate was Mrs. Steward O'Dell who, along with her husband, graduated in 1928.[52] Ministers' wives had been admitted to courses in 1920 with six enrolled this first year.[53]

The first special degree, the Master of Church Administration, attracted about an equal number of women and men until its discontinuance. Much later the Master of Religious Education degree came into being, in 1950, to prepare men and women for professional lay ministry, and this gradually increased the presence of women on campus.

The number of women in the ordination degree program, then called the Bachelor of Divinity, remained quite small, with only ten as late as 1970.[54] The situation in the Methodist Church changed radically when in 1956 the General Conference voted to ordain women. Women had been licensed to preach in the Methodist Episcopal Church in 1920,[55] and women lay pastors especially from Kansas and Nebraska were often in the Course of Study school. The Methodist Protestant Church had accepted some women into ordination as early as 1880, but the practice did not survive into the twentieth century.[56] The United Brethren in Christ, but not the Evangelical Church, had ordained women since 1889. When all of these churches came together in 1968 the ordination of women was retained.[57]

As we have seen, Perkins was slow in acquiring women students in its basic ordination degree. The climate of the South Central Jurisdiction did not encourage it, and the School made no concerted effort to recruit women for its basic ordination degree. In October 1975, when 28% of all students in United Methodist seminaries were reported to be women, Perkins enrollment included only 47 women (less than 9%),[58] and by 1978 the number was still only 77.[59] The number gradually increased so that in 1985 in a student body of 387 the number of women was 135.[60] Many of these were in other programs than the M.Th. program, and the female percentage in the M.Th. degree program was approximately 30%.[61]

Women students did not become militant until the late 1970s. There had been incidents, of course. For example, on one occasion, when new students at orientation had been advised to wear jackets for the group picture, all the women appeared in men's jackets! (This was largely an effort by M.R.E. students.) In the late 1970s there was still only one woman on the faculty, and the second female member of the Intern Staff was not appointed until 1980.

It is sometimes forgotten that there are many student wives who live on campus and others who live on their husbands' charges. (Male spouses did not become a significant group until the 1980s.) Whitty Cuninggim had had a special concern for spouses during her husband's term as Dean, and had led the way in providing courses and other events to try to help them understand what their husbands were learning in class. A unit of the Women's Society of Christian Service had pre-dated her efforts, and later the Perkins Women's Association came into being.

For several years beginning in 1972 Northaven United Methodist Church, having developed a course on consciousness-raising for women called "Explore," presented it at Perkins. Susan Dean (Streng), Fran McElvaney, and Gayle Smith were the leaders in the enterprise. The course helped to prepare the way for the first Symposium for Women (later "Women's Week") which was led by Letty Russell on 13–18 October 1975.[62] The event has occurred annually from 1975 to the present.[63]

Since the mid-1970s, women had assumed a larger and larger share of responsibility for leadership in the Perkins community. These leaders have come in all ages, some just out of college but others second-career women (with both homemaking and work outside the home being included as first careers).

But the basic question is whether the United Methodist Church and other denominations that ordain women are ready to place women in the church. In the past a majority of M.Div. graduates became associate pastors or assumed other special appointments. This has changed to some extent with women district superintendents and bishops. The first Perkins woman graduate to be elected bishop was Sharon Brown Christopher in 1988. Surveys indicate that lay folk are probably more ready to receive a woman as pastor than the sending agencies (annual conferences) of the United Methodist Church are ready to send them. The truth of the matter is that with a decrease in the number of white males going into ordained ministry, many United Methodist pulpits will be filled by women in the future or else remain vacant. And then another important question arises: Why are the numbers of white males entering the ordained ministry steadily declining?

Conclusion

The changes that have occurred during the past fifteen years at Perkins indicate that it is a different school from what it was in the early 1970s. Changes that began during Dean Quillian's term of office have accelerated during that of his successor, Dean Kirby. Two radical transformations have occurred in the history of SMU's School of Theology: that in the 1950s under Dean Cuninggim and that which began under Dean Quillian and has continued under Dean Kirby. The time is ripe for some serious thinking about what Perkins ought to be and might become by the twenty-first century. Such thinking is already under way and should bear fruit in the years ahead.

13

Controversy, Conflict, and Reconciliation

A school of theology located within a university is probably more likely to be subject to conflict and controversy than one which is independent. As a school of a university, it is an academic institution. But its special relationship with one or more denominations creates a sense of ownership, which often brings a desire to control. So it is not unusual when a clash of school and church evolves.

If a school of theology is, as H. Richard Niebuhr defined it, the "intellectual center of the church's life,"[1] its faculty and students will inevitably raise questions—and sometimes provide answers—that the rest of the church will not like. In a time of rapid change—and whatever else one can say about the twentieth century, it is a time of unprecedented change—the conflict between church, world, and seminary is often intense. Further, as Niebuhr also says, our time is one of "baffling pluralism of Protestant religious life,"[2] a trend which has accelerated unbelievably since Niebuhr's book was published in 1956. Only when a theological school is the product of a unilaterally oriented denomination or sect can this conflict perhaps be minimized.[3]

SMU's School of Theology from its beginning aimed at being a free academic unit of the larger University—and at the same time a servant of its parent denomination. Its intellectual leaders such as Frank Seay, John R. Rice, John H. Hicks, Robert Goodloe, Paul Root, and Fred Gealy—and a host of others including the more recent Albert Outler, Schubert Ogden, and John Deschner—have also been church-oriented people, and that fact has ameliorated external controversy, but not prevented it. Indeed, this linking of church and academy has not been easy, and suspicions have often run high as faculty have sought to express the Gospel in new thought forms and thus relate it to a changed and changing culture.

Unfortunately the conflicts have not always involved the really important questions of life nor the issues of the day. Some of those we will consider in this chapter may seem trivial, or at most not decisive issues. But they were not inconsequential for the participants. The incredible amount of time that Dean Quillian spent in dealing with the conflicts, both internal and external, seems such a waste of energy which could have been used more productively for

students and constituents had they been willing to tolerate diversity, recognize
that seminary students, faculty, and administrators are as imperfect as the
remainder of the church, and negotiate rather than confront.

In any case the decade of the 1970s was a time of conflict such as SMU's
School of Theology had not known since the 1920s when the celebrated Rice,
Workman, and Branscomb events[4] rocked the campus and sent shock waves
throughout the M. E. Church, South. We shall consider first the interior
struggles over the rights of students, the seminary, and the University, and other
inside matters. Second, we will consider the controversies involved with
church and church people; and third the structured efforts, led by Dean Quillian,
to provide a closer working relationship between seminary and church.

Both SMU and Perkins had remained relatively quiet during the student
unrest of the later 1960s and early 1970s. Non-violent confrontations appeared,
but President Tate and Dean Quillian kept open communications with students.
The 1970s were the years of renewed conflict for Perkins.

Student Conflict

In the previous chapter, we looked at the growing power of minorities and
women, and both successes and failures in dealing with the problem. These all
accelerated in the 1970s, and the situations engendered conflict and controversy. Progress that causes deep change is not easy to facilitate, but if the
change is principled right, the struggle has to be considered worth the effort.

Academic freedom was relatively secure, and had been since the days of
President Lee. President Tate upheld the tradition, and there were no more
forced resignations of the Rice, Workman, and Branscomb variety.[5] Even after
the flagrant violations of good taste and University principles by John Beaty,
he was only reprimanded and therefore remained teaching until his retirement.

Conflicts between students and the faculty and administration emerged,
however, and even between different student groups, not quite so easy to
defend. They were often due to a lack of the use of the consultative process,
which both President Tate and Dean Quillian cherished. Both the larger
University and Perkins had their problems, and they were often due to this lack
of consultation because students—and sometimes faculty—wanted to do it
their way without interference.

Although it is usually called academic freedom, there seems to me to be
another kind of freedom which has nothing to do with what happens in the
classroom. For want of a better term I call this civil freedom, which is the right
of a university community to hear controversial speakers outside the classroom.

Early on in Tate's presidency, without consultation, a group of students invited John Gates, former editor of the *Daily Worker*, to speak on campus. President Tate heard of it through the student newspaper. As Marshall Terry describes Tate's decision, "he decided to stand behind the students' invitation to Gates, because he believed that the students should have the right to invite speakers they wished to hear on campus and that 'the truth is affirmed and the fallacious exposed in a free enterprise of ideas.'"[6]

This event, it must be remembered, occurred when Dallas was in the throes of strong right-wing pressure, a stranglehold which was broken only after the Kennedy assassination. Tate interpreted this decision and many others to the Dallas community with consummate skill, and his constant stand for all kinds of campus freedom, as we saw earlier, earned for him the AAUP Alexander Meiklejohn Award in 1965 for "significant support of academic freedom."[7]

Perkins also had its problems with student invitations not carefully considered or without full knowledge of policy, which was often not clearly defined. One such event, in fall 1970, involved the action of the student Social Action Committee to give $125 of its funds to the National Committee to Combat Racism (for feeding children) in connection with an invitation to its head, Curtis Gaines, to speak on campus.[8]

In this case the students were ruled, after careful discussion, to be in the wrong. The issue was whether Perkins funds, which the Social Action Committee received from the Student Council (which in turn had received them from the Perkins budget), could be used for an outside group. Two students, Ed Stevenson and Tom Jones, drew up and distributed widely eleven issues involved in the controversy,[9] and the matter was discussed by the Perkins Senate at length. Out of this discussion came a carefully formulated statement called "Declaration of Principles of the Perkins Community."[10] The declaration affirmed the right of free discussion and encouraged members of the community, students and faculty, to participate in social and political movements *as individuals*. It also denied the School the right to align itself with any such movements. The principles clearly state that no money is to be contributed from the Perkins operating budget to outside social and political movements. This document of academic and personal freedom is a rather remarkable one and has continued to be carried in the *Perkins Catalog*.

Quite a different set of circumstances were involved in an incident in spring 1971. A member of one of the Texas conferences—an able and promising young man who had been considered one of the bright prospects for the future—made the startling decision that he could continue to live in the same house with his wife but also include his mistress in the family. When word got out, his conference quite naturally raised objections to the arrangement, and he was brought to trial by the conference and asked to turn in his ministerial credentials.

On March 13, Dean Quillian heard an announcement on the radio that this alumnus had been invited to speak at Perkins, and on the following day a front-page article appeared in the *Dallas Morning News* to the effect that he had been asked to speak to an ethics class at 10:00 A.M. the following day.[11] As the Dean began to unravel the story, it turned out that a first-year student had invited the alumnus to speak without the knowledge of the professor involved in the class. In the meantime the news media, both print and radio/television, were having a field day concerning the event.

The outcome was that the former student did speak, at an informal discussion in the evening, with some 150 in attendance. The questions raised, as Dean Quillian says, demonstrated that the man's position was "untenable on Scriptural, theological and practical grounds and that the Church had treated him fairly in his trial."[12] The Dean's response to the event was to issue a strong statement for freedom of speech "under controlled situations."

Perkins and the University

On most scores the relationship between SMU's School of Theology and the University has been friendly, supportive, and mutually beneficial. In the early days no one really thought of a separate school, except in the case of financial support. Much of the money that came to the University was not applicable to theology. The move to a separate building in 1924 brought about some separation. Yet as a student in the late 1930s I felt quite at home in the total University. With the opening of the new quadrangle, at the southern extreme of the campus, further separation occurred. Also, the increasing secularization of the University helped to create a barrier between a school whose chief purpose was the training of clergy and the rest of the University, which increasingly aligned itself with the academic community rather than the church.

As we saw in an earlier chapter, the School of Theology had trouble in securing adequate financial backing, and for many years it lived on the edge of poverty. It was not until the Perkins family's money came to the School that other substantial gifts were directed to the School of Theology. Now Perkins is one of the best-endowed schools in the University. With less than five percent of the student body, its income from endowment accounts for nineteen percent of the endowment income of the University.[13]

This endowment has made possible a high quality of education in terms of faculty, academic programs, and the intern program. The expansion has been so great that an active development program in the 1980s has been necessary to keep up with escalating costs.

One of Dean Quillian's concerns was what would happen should SMU dissociate itself from the United Methodist Church and become an independent university. He knew that this had happened in the history of American Methodism on several occasions. At the University of Denver, Iliff School of Theology actually had to close temporarily until matters could be sorted out.[14] He knew also of the problems when the University of Southern California became independent and kept its School of Religion, forcing the establishment of a new seminary, Claremont School of Theology.

Some clarity came out of Quillian's discussions with the University administration, but the issue remains. There is no tendency now for SMU to pull away from the United Methodist Church. The present President, Kenneth Pye, himself a Catholic lay person, has made considerable effort to reconnect SMU with its Methodist roots. Continuing discussion is necessary, however, since one cannot predict the future relationship of SMU with its parent church.

Conflicts with the Constituency

At various times during its history, SMU's School of Theology and its constituency—defined as individual Methodists, both lay and clergy, and groups both official and unofficial—have come into conflict. At times the School of Theology has been singled out for special criticism. At others, for example, in the "Methodism's Pink Fringe" group of the later 1940s, the search for Communist sympathizers, which really meant anyone with "liberal" leanings, included the School of Theology but were not confined to it.

The intellectual search in which a seminary engages will inevitably lead to theological conflicts with persons who do not accept the validity of such an enterprise. The tendency of many clergy, including seminary professors, to align themselves with the poor and dispossessed is one which middle-class Methodists often criticize. It can be argued, I think, that seminary professors—and even pastors—are not always as sensitive to this issue as they might be.

One of the continuing critics of Perkins School of Theology during the 1950s and 1960s, on both of these counts, was Mr. Lynn Landrum, a columnist for the *Dallas Morning News*. He often wrote quite good columns, and in fact when I was a student in the late 1930s we considered him in a broad sense "liberal" on political and social issues. He was a leading member of First Methodist Church, Dallas, and taught the Men's Bible Class for years.

In March 1961 he wrote a column directed toward what he considered to be ideas contrary to Methodist doctrine in the student publication *The Log*.

On 30 March 1961, the Dean wrote a letter to selected clergy and laity enclosing Landrum's column and the article from *The Log*. The reconciling tone of Quillian's approach to such matters is typical of the way he handled controversy. The final paragraph suggested that we not identify individuals like Mr. Landrum as "the enemy." If we cut ourselves off from them, he added, they have no choice except to make us *their enemy*. His hope was that Perkins "can follow a policy of reasonableness and patience in strength" and move to a head-on fight "only if clearly necessary."[15]

He was quite capable of confrontation, of course, and in 1969 reprimanded a student for a nearly, if not actually, obscene poem which he had included in the student newspaper of April 29.[16] He distinguished between freedom and anarchy and on at least one occasion "advised rather ardently the editor of *The Log* to remove a page from the publication." A few copies had already been distributed, one copy of which fell into the hands of William P. Clements, Jr. (later governor of Texas and a long-time supporter of SMU). Quillian, in his usual attempt to be conciliatory, wrote a letter of explanation and apology.[17]

Pornography in the Classroom?

No event in the history of Perkins has created more publicity and controversy than the showing of explicit sex films in the course "Church and World" in October 1971. The course, as we have seen, was part of the curriculum introduced in 1970, and was taught for only two years. It was designed "to enable the seminarian to conceive of the world as the essential stage for God's mission and to prepare him to formulate principles and techniques appropriate for developing an effective ministry."[18]

The films shown were not pornographic in intent, but rather were educational. It is true, however, that they showed explicit sex acts, both heterosexual and homosexual. Two were produced by the Glide Foundation of San Francisco, the third by Dallas's Channel 13 (public television) on the Dallas homosexual community. As Helen Parmley, long-time religious editor of the *Dallas Morning News,* observed, whether the films were considered obscene or educational was in the "eye of the beholder."[19] The intent of Harville Hendrix, director of the course, was to present a slice of life which he deemed not common to the students' experience, or as the *Texas Methodist* put it, the films were part of a series "exposing students to life and its problems" and "help[ing] the students not be shocked when confronted with (e.g.) unusual sex behavior in the parish."[20]

In the major showing, the films were provided with a proper introduction and explanation. Before a second showing for absentees, however, no such introduction was provided. Present at this showing was a top executive of the *Dallas Times Herald* who had been informed by a student who objected to the films. The showing was not open to the public, but he took advantage of the student's invitation and wrote a story in his newspaper on 29 October 1971. The story was picked up by the Associated Press as well as Dallas's Channel 8 television, and soon the world heard that Perkins School of Theology in Dallas, Texas, was showing "pornographic" films to its students![21] For the next weeks Dean Quillian spent most of his time dealing with the problem.

Should the films have been shown? This is still a question on which there is disagreement. They should certainly not have been shown without proper introduction as they were for the second time. So far as I am aware, such films have not been shown since. Perhaps the major problem is that those who opposed the showing protested with confrontation tactics rather than with genuine concern expressed concerning the appropriateness of the films.

Dancing in the Aisle

Before the furor created by the films had subsided, a second event created a similar stir. Although the event was at a University chapel service, the seminary bore the brunt of the criticism because it took place in the Perkins Chapel.

Claude Evans, the University chaplain, believed that Advent should be a time of celebration, looking forward to the coming of the Christ Child. The 1971 service in question was the third of a series of services in which there was a celebration, ending with the throwing of serpentine paper streamers and the choir and congregation shouting, "Advent is here! Christ is coming! The Lord is risen indeed!"[22]

Evans gave his permission for the SMU Public Relations Department to invite the media to the service, and one of the shots caught by the cameras, video and still, was the Chaplain dancing down the aisle with a woman student, a member of the choir, clad in what were then called "hot pants"—tight-fitting short shorts.

The photograph literally was seen around the world, and often with no explanation of what was happening—nothing but a clergyman dancing in the aisle with a scantily clad young woman. Soon Dean Quillian's work of interpretation began all over again.

In a 12 January 1972 letter, he wrote to the *Nashville Banner*:

After having spent a good many weeks this fall answering letters concerning the films on sex that were used in the Church and World course at Perkins and then another big batch of them in connection with the Advent service, I have about come to the feeling that educational institutions would best be served by news media if they simply ignored us altogether.[23]

Theological Controversy

Theological controversy has existed since the beginning of SMU's School of Theology. It led to the resignation of Rice and Workman. It has been between the larger church and the seminary, as well as between some of its students and the faculty. Perhaps Dean Hawk gave the strongest answer to students who came to demand the resignation of a particular faculty member. "The faculty is not on trial, young men; *you* are," was his terse response to their demands.

Controversy again surfaced in the organized movements of evangelicals, known as the "Forum for Scriptural Christianity" or "Good News," in the 1970s.[24] In August 1976, Edmund W. Robb, a United Methodist evangelist from the Northwest Texas Conference, addressed the Good News Convocation at Lake Junaluska and included this sentence: "If we have a sick Church it is largely because we have sick seminaries."[25] In 1977 Quillian did not extend an invitation to the Good News organization to send representatives to Perkins,[26] but a year later he announced to the Senate that Paul Mickey of Duke University Divinity School would speak at Perkins at the request of Good News.[27] In 1980, Robb and Quillian carried on a lengthy correspondence concerning Robb's attempt to raise scholarship funds for evangelical students to pursue the Ph.D. degree at Perkins.[28]

The evangelical-liberal debate continues inside the United Methodist Churches as it does in most of the main-line Protestant churches (and even in the Roman Catholic Church). I am convinced that the Methodist movement can have no reconciliation with fundamentalism—which is a modern form of Calvinism. Yet not all evangelicals are fundamentalists. They have already had some influence on the official structures of United Methodism. There is, I believe, a need for genuine dialogue between the two groups. Unfortunately the discussion often becomes more political than theological, from both sides.

Admission of Known Homosexual Persons

A final major conflict occupied the school's attention during the final years of Dean Quillian's twenty-one years as Dean. It all began when the Committee on Admissions admitted a member of the Metropolitan Community Church in Dallas, a church especially for "gays." Normally, I suppose, the Committee would have consulted the Dean since this was the first of such admissions and might be construed as an "extraordinary" admission. It failed to do so, however, and in March 1980 he discovered what had happened. Two additional applications from the church's membership were pending.[29]

At the 9 May 1980 meeting of the Senate, Quillian used a method he seldom employed and announced arbitrarily that the interim policy of Perkins would conform with the policy of the United Methodist Church. Since General Conference had voted not to ordain known homosexual persons, there would be no admission of such persons to the degree that prepared people for ordination.[30]

The faculty and the student body were divided, and therefore a two-hour discussion on May 15 settled nothing.[31] Three statements by the Dean, on May 9, May 13, and May 19, made clear that he had had considerable opposition to his position, but chose to maintain his decision that Perkins would use no United Methodist funds for the education of known homosexual persons.[32] One of the key questions raised by faculty concerned whether standards for ordination should be different from those for church membership where no ban existed. An evening faculty discussion occurred during May, after which the matter was postponed until the Senate Conference in the fall.

The Senate discussion on 10 October 1980 was more of a philosophical-theological consideration and no decision was reached. Therefore, at a called meeting on November 10, the faculty finally discussed policy. Still no decision was reached except to request "that the Committee on Recruitment and Admissions study the policy of admission of homosexual persons, that the Committee consult in their discussion with all relevant persons, and that it report back to the Senate as soon as reasonable."[33]

The Committee deliberated for almost six months, and finally on 20 March 1981 recommended that "the Senate reaffirm its official statement of policy on admissions as revised in 1977, as the policy of the school and that it direct the Committee on Recruitment and Admissions to act in accordance with this policy as of this date."[34] Basically, this meant that there would be no explicit policy of non-admission of homosexual persons but that inappropriate ways of dealing with one's homosexuality might disqualify a person because of the problems it would generate in intern placement and in future ministry. The statement placed the responsibility for admission squarely on the Admissions Committee where it had been since the Cuninggim deanship.

Quillian accepted the decision—I always suspected not very happily—only three months before his turning the deanship over to James Kirby.

Behind the issue is a fundamental disagreement concerning the responsibility of a United Methodist seminary to make judgments concerning the fitness of a person for ordained ministry. The United Methodist Church's *Book of Discipline* is clear concerning such responsibility, but is it a just requirement? Is a school of theology a school that admits people according to their academic credentials, with the larger church responsible for determining fitness for ministry? Or must the educational institution itself make this kind of decision? The question remains, and no solution is likely to please everyone.

Organized Support: The Alumni Council

One of Dean Quillian's aims as Dean was to secure greater support of Perkins by the church, support that was more than financial. His first emphasis was his own personal efforts to enhance the relationship of the School and the church. Getting to know church people, becoming acquainted with local churches, and developing other personal relationships were important especially in the early days of his deanship when church and school had become estranged.

He realized that more organized support was needed. To this end the first alumni/ae consultation was called for 2 December 1969, and out of this came a permanent Alumni Council with two representatives from each annual conference within the South Central Jurisdiction and one from each of the other jurisdictions. Its purposes were to interpret what the seminary was doing, to help the seminary stay aware of what was happening in the church, to aid in the recruitment of students, to encourage the development of financial resources, and to enhance the relationship between church and school to the mutual benefit of both.[35]

The Council began to function in 1971 with Ray Branton as president and Charles Lutrick succeeding him for 1972–73. Two members of the Council became members of the Senate, and one became a member of the Ministers' Week Committee. Meetings took place in February and October.[36] Among other projects the Council worked on a "Forty-Year Model" to seek to determine what Perkins should do to prepare students for ordained ministry in the twenty-first century.[37]

Out of the Council, together with a proposal from Judge Woodrow Seals of Houston, grew Laity Week in February 1974. Timed to begin as soon as Ministers' Week ended, it includes lectures, worship services, courses, and seminars for lay people. The first attendance was 78 in 1974, and the number more than doubled in 1975 with 175 full-time or part-time participants.

Lay Advisory Council

One year later, in 1972, a second new organization emerged. Dean Quillian readily credited its beginning to Leo Baker, a layman from Lovers Lane United Methodist Church in Dallas. Working with the Dean, Baker coordinated the securing of a group of lay people who began meeting regularly at least once a year to promote better communication between church and seminary, to provide a means whereby a group of laity could come to know Perkins, and to provide a means to bring church concerns to the seminary and seminary concerns to the larger church.[38]

The Lay Advisory Council has proved to be an invaluable means of bringing the seminary and the church into a better relationship with one another. In 1973–74 the Dean reported that the Council "came into its own."[39] Most of the credit for its success goes to Leo Baker and other lay persons who joined him in the enterprise.

Perkins Representatives

A second lay organization, not as closely organized as the Lay Advisory Council, had its first meeting on 25–26 October 1974. Representatives from congregations came together to aid in the financial undergirding of the School of Theology. More than two hundred lay persons accepted appointment. According to a contemporary assessment, both the Lay Advisory Council and the Perkins representatives "are proving invaluable to the seminary in its relationships with local churches."[40]

The Dean's Contribution

James Ward, in the issue of the *Perkins Journal* honoring the Dean at his retirement, commented at length on Dean Quillian's contributions to the work of relating the School to the United Methodist Church. "He has supported the academic freedom and integrity of Perkins unfailingly, and he has also fostered close, effective relations with the United Methodist Church." This came partly through three factors, observed Ward: the Perkins Alumni Council, the Perkins Lay Advisory Council, and the office of Bishop in Residence. But it is also partly the Dean's own nurturing of school relations "by telephone, by mail, and face to face." "For years," Ward writes, "I have been amazed at the time and energy Joe Quillian has poured into this part of his work, and at the skill and good humor with which he has done it."[41]

Conclusion

This has been a chapter on controversy and reconciliation. The controversies have been interesting, varied, and at times quite unpleasant. The reconciling efforts have been extensive and productive. Nothing will ever make it possible for a school of theology, especially if it is part of a university, to please all its constituency. The efforts to interpret, explain, and mollify are never-ending. Dean Quillian made remarkable progress during his twenty-one years as Dean, but he paid a high price for his efforts. No wonder he breathed a sigh of relief when he left Dallas in 1981 for the life of a gentleman rancher and part-time preacher, amid the natural beauty of Washington State!

14

In Service and Action

Most of the first decade of Dean Quillian's term of office was a time of consolidation of past years' gains and preparation for future change. Beginning with the 1968–69 self-study, all of this took quite a different turn. The first major shift in the life of Perkins School of Theology was the institution of shared governance in May 1969. The 1970s were a decade of turbulence, creativity, and building for the future. By the end of the decade, Perkins was quite a different school from what it had been in 1960. Yet its core concern—for the effective preparation of ordained ministers, with a knowledge of the classical Western theological tradition and the ability to minister in the various cultures from which its students derived—remained constant. Some would say that the latter part of this formula was not as effectively done as it might have been.

We have already considered many of the developments of the 1970s, especially in the growth of minority and female influence and the controversies which made the decade one of great ferment. There is much still to be told, and so this chapter will chronicle in brief fashion a wide variety of areas of the School, many not so widely known as other aspects of its life. It is called "In Service and Action" because many of these facets of the life of the school were especially concerned with service to and action in the larger church and community.

Course of Study School

At various places I have mentioned the Course of Study School. Its genesis goes back to the early days of the School when either by correspondence or in special classes, persons pursued a course of study set by the Division of Ministry of the Board of Education in order to qualify them for ordination without a seminary degree.

Then in 1947, under the leadership of A. W. Martin, Professor of Church Administration and Director of Field Education, a more formal school began. It was held in the summer and consisted of four weeks during which a student could complete one year of the five years of the prescribed course.[1] Few enterprises have prospered to the degree this one has. Supported for many years by Highland Park Methodist Church, the students who attend are lay pastors of small churches, either part- or full-time. It is not now possible for them to be ordained except under special circumstances, but they provide the backbone of the supply of pastors for the larger number of rural and urban churches of fewer than one hundred members.

By 1981 there were forty-two faculty members in two terms of four weeks each—some from the Perkins faculty, some from the faculties of colleges or other seminaries, and some from local churches.[2] The largest number of students attended in 1958 with 261 students in two four-week terms. In 1970 the pattern was changed to two two-week terms, with the two together comprising a full year's work.[3] The director of the School has always been the Director of Field Education—A. W. Martin, Marvin Judy, Floyd Curl, Alsie Carleton, Claus Rohlfs, and presently Bert Affleck. The real work of operating the school has been carried on, first, by Mrs. Pat Moxley and later by Mrs. Rosa Marina Barton. The students do not receive university credit, but many are among the strongest supporters of Perkins and consider themselves as alumni/ae.

We saw in an earlier chapter how the Spanish language school developed under the leadership of Roy Barton. There have also been special classes for those whose reading ability was too low for them to comprehend the textbooks required in regular classes.

Seminar for Educational Assistants

It is tempting at this point, at least for me, to write a history of the developing of a similar specialized ministry of lay Educational Assistants in the Methodist Church, but this is not appropriate. Suffice it to say that since 1900, persons not seeking ordination have become staff members of larger churches in Christian education, church music, business management, evangelism, and other fields. Prior to this century there had been choir directors, church visitors, social workers, and others. The Deaconess movement provided personnel for some of these positions, but many came into it because they were recognized as competent laity in local churches. From about 1920 on, this movement greatly increased, especially in Christian education and church music.

As these workers multiplied, church leadership recognized the need for at least minimum training opportunities directed toward the group. The earliest field to receive attention was that of Christian education. R. Harold Hipps, then with the Board of Education and later the Board of Higher Education and Ministry, was the pioneer at the national level of the movement.[4]

Perkins led the way in the actual provision of a seminar. In 1965 the three persons in Christian Education at Perkins—Richard Murray, C. Wayne Banks, and Howard Grimes—met with Hipps to plan a summer seminar for educational assistants in Methodist churches. The four-summer program they worked out—one summer each in Bible, theology, learning and teaching, and administration—became the pattern for other schools to follow.

The seminar in 1966—the first—had some thirty participants. The number grew until there were as many as ninety in several summers. Two of the sources of success have been the use of Perkins professors for lectures in Bible and theology and Murray's ability to take a large group and by using small groups within the larger one to bring off a significant learning experience.[5] The 1979 self-study concluded that the seminar "provides an indispensable service to the United Methodist Church."[6]

Church Musicians' Seminar

Somewhat later a summer seminar for church musicians was begun as a joint enterprise between worship and music people on a national scale and the Master of Sacred Music program at SMU. The two purposes have been to provide background in worship, Bible, and theology for the many church musicians who have no theological education and to provide help in the choice of music and in the increase of knowledge of repertoire, to enhance conducting skills, and to provide a fellowship experience in a theological setting.

This seminar has also proved to be popular and helpful to those who attend. The most visible contribution the participants make to Perkins is in chapel worship. At no time during the year does the music of Perkins Chapel reach the heights that it does during the two weeks of the Church Musicians' Seminar.

Diaconal Ministry Preparation

A third type of special training has been the courses in preparation for the diaconal ministry. Again, some background is required. Until the 1960s lay workers in business management, education, music, evangelism, public relations, and other fields had no status in the Methodist Church. Although "status" is not, or should not be, an end in itself, it does provide a base of operation in what has increasingly become a politicized structure (the United Methodist Church). The first position created, in 1964, was the lay worker, defined as "a person other than clergy whose decision [is] to make a career of work . . . in the employed status of the Church or Church-related agencies. . . ."[7] The 1976 General Conference approved the term "Diaconal Minister," which many hoped would lead to a permanent ordained diaconate in the United Methodist Church.[8] Two ways were provided by the Board of Diaconal Ministry of the Board of Higher Education and Ministry for educational preparation for consecration as a diaconal minister: a degree from a theological school or a series of studies designed to give general theological education (but not skill training) for the work.

Perkins began offering these courses and has continued to do so with some measure of success. The courses offered at Perkins and at other seminaries have provided regular additions to the ranks of consecrated diaconal ministers who are increasingly recognized as an important addition to the United Methodist set-apart ministry. Such persons constitute a corps of full-time (and in some instances part-time) ministers other than the ordained clergy. As yet the United Methodist Church has not been willing to grant them ordination, but many annual conferences provide almost as many benefits to them as they do to the ordained clergy.

Their work varies—"Participating with the elder in the leadership of worship, working in serving professions in the Church, and serving the needs of the poor, the sick, or oppressed. . . ."[9] Serving professions include education, music, business, and the like.

Special Lectureships

Perkins students have the opportunity of attending a wide variety of "occasional" lectures provided by visitors to the campus, with many open to the public. These are in addition to Ministers' Week which serves both as a means of continuing education (now required for both clergy and diaconal ministers) and an "old home" week. The Tate-Willson lectureship under the Graduate Program of Religious Studies was established in 1967 by Dr. and Mrs. J. M. Willson of Floydada, Texas. The Paul Elliott and Mildred Fryar Martin Lectureship in Practical Theology was established by Bishop and Mrs. Martin in 1974 and features a lecturer in various ministry fields. The first was presented by Seward Hiltner, who has been followed by equally prestigious practical theologians.[10]

Continuing Education

Almost from its beginning, SMU's School of Theology has recognized its responsibility for the continuing education of both clergy and laity. We have looked in previous chapters at some of the means it has used. It has never been completely devoid of such activities: for example, Ministers' Week has persisted for many years. In the 1940s and 1950s such efforts were fairly minimal. Then in 1966 Richard T. Murray became part of the Perkins Faculty coming from First Methodist Church, Houston. After a year of further graduate study, he came to Perkins and began setting up a program of Continuing Education involving clergy and laity both on campus and on site.

One of the chief features of his program was the "Guided Reading Program" in which both clergy and laity met regularly to study a particular book using a study guide provided by Continuing Education. Usually the study was completed by an all-day seminar conducted by a Perkins professor or someone in a comparable position elsewhere.[11]

Other events included seminars on campus and other places, Laity Week, seminars during Ministers' Week, and similar events.[12] This means of "reaching out" has proved an indispensable way by which both ordained and diaconal ministers keep up-to-date and fulfill the present requirements for engaging in continuing education. Dick Murray continued with the program until the late 1970s, when for a short time John Holbert took over; more recently Stanley Menking has been brought from Drew University to direct the program.

Research and Planning

One of Marvin Judy's interests was the town and country church, a movement in which he achieved both recognition and competency. His other interest was the analysis of local churches, cities, counties, and annual conferences with an eye to planning for the future.

In order to facilitate this work, the School established the Center for Research and Planning in 1965 with Judy as the Director. He had already made and published fourteen such studies;[13] now that he was freed from Field Education responsibilities and taught only half-time, he was able to continue this work on a larger scale until his retirement in 1977. Later renamed the Center for Research in Parish Leadership and Community Development, the Center also conducted numerous consultations, workshops, and seminars.[14]

Bridwell Library

We have considered the phenomenal growth and progress of Bridwell Library at various places in the chronicle. Max Trent, SMU Director of Libraries, said to the Board of Governors in 1966, "Bridwell is becoming truly outstanding, not only nationally but internationally, due to its addition of rare and very important acquisitions."[15]

This expansion of resources meant that the space in the original building—not really very extensive—had become a serious problem. Dean Quillian began talking with Mr. Bridwell in the mid-1960s concerning an addition to the library. The Dean had learned that Mr. Bridwell did not make contributions lightly, even to causes in which he believed as he did Bridwell Library. He had come to appreciate and treasure rare books, and the library which bore his name had become a real source of satisfaction to him.

Eventually, however, Mr. Bridwell became committed to the idea of enlarging the building, and a high-level meeting was held in Dallas between Mrs. Perkins (who had returned to Texas especially for the meeting), Mr. Bridwell,

Decherd Turner, and Dean Quillian to talk seriously about the addition. After Dean Quillian had presented a tentative plan, Mr. Bridwell replied: "You're planning too small." Whereupon Mr. Bridwell led the others outside and stepped off the limits of what he considered adequate. And this became almost exactly the outside dimensions of the new addition.[16]

Quillian recalls that Mr. Bridwell then asked, "Where are you going to get the money for this?" Mrs. Perkins replied, "Mr. Bridwell, we were hoping that you would give it." Mr. Bridwell then glanced around at the others and said, "Why don't you ask Margaret for it? She has a rich daddy and I don't!"

The Bridwells, father Joseph S. Bridwell and daughter Margaret Bridwell Bowdle, eventually provided from their Foundation the entire amount, something close to $2,000,000. In preparation, Quillian and Turner visited new libraries in Europe, all of which advised more "working space," by which they meant space for such services as cataloging. The building was built, more than doubling the size of the original building. It was dedicated in 1974, and at the ceremonies the announcement was made of the Decherd Turner Endowed Book Fund, also a gift from the Bridwell Foundation.[17] This fund eventually amounted to a million dollars. Joseph Bridwell died on 9 May 1966, long before the completion of the greatly expanded library facility; his daughter Margaret died soon afterward, on 9 November 1976.

Book acquisitions did require a strain on the remainder of the library operation. The ATS report of 26–29 October 1980, just after Jerry Campbell had become Librarian, is less kind to the library than it is to most aspects of Perkins School of Theology. It acknowledges freely the many fine collections in the library but points to places where the operation needed to be improved. Turner had operated with an incredibly small staff because he preferred to use budget and special gifts for the purchase of books. The committee not only pointed to this staffing inadequacy; it also assessed the periodical collection as inadequate. They pointed out the lack of Spanish language materials, indicated the need for a conservator, and recommended better cataloging for Methodist materials. The committee concluded by writing:

> The Bridwell Library is a fine library. Its special collections are outstanding. The working collection is good but needs to be strengthened. In order for the Perkins community to take full advantage of its rich library, services need to be greatly improved.[18]

The task of correcting these weaknesses was begun by Jerry Campbell, who left in 1985 to become head librarian at Duke University. It was continued by Roger Loyd as interim librarian (1985–87). The enterprise is now enhanced by the complete renovation and restoration of the Library, and by the expertise of Robert Maloy, director of the Bridwell since 1987.[19]

This is not to discredit the magnificent thirty years of Decherd Turner's work. His interests and talents lay elsewhere than in administration and organization. He was a superb collector and provided a base for Bridwell Library which gives it a depth that few theological libraries have. By 1981, it held 175,000 volumes.[20]

Ministerial Education Fund

In his report for 1980–81, Dean Quillian acknowledged that he had not been able to give as much time to the financial undergirding of Perkins as he had planned to do.[21] The important part which he played in getting the Ministerial Education Fund under way perhaps made up for his failure to bring in as much new endowment as he had hoped.

Regular gifts came from principal donors—the Bridwells (later the Bridwell Foundation) and Mrs. Perkins after her husband's death in 1960. Other gifts, for the Ph.D. program, for the internship, and for other aspects of the program did materialize. All the while educational costs were escalating. New programs at Perkins, such as the internship, continuing education, the Ph.D. program, the M.S.M. degree, and others further increased the operating budget.[22] By 1974 the budget was more than $2,400,000[23] and the trend continued until in 1987 the amount was $4,435,822.[24]

A major breakthrough in funding occurred in the establishment of the Ministerial Education Fund, at first on a jurisdictional basis and then in 1972 as a responsibility of the General Conference. Annual, Jurisdictional, and the General Conference had increasingly supported the schools of theology of the Methodist Church, but the support was neither fully reliable nor adequate to meet the rising costs of theological education.

In 1960 the Southeastern Jurisdiction, under the leadership of a lay person, D. W. Brooks, adopted a plan calling for one percent of the budget of each local church for the support of ministerial education. One-fourth was retained by the conference, with three-fourths divided between Candler and Duke.[25]

Dean Quillian, Dr. Ewart Watts (Chair of the Commission on Higher Education), Dr. Marvin Boyd (a Northwest Texas Conference pastor), and several lay persons began working on a South Central Jurisdictional Conference plan in the early 1960s. It was presented to the 1964 Jurisdictional Conference and received favorable response from that body. The plan applied only to Perkins and St. Paul School of Theology in Kansas City.[26]

Across the next four years, the group worked out a General Conference plan. Quillian was President of the Association of Methodist Theological Schools, and it fell his lot to present the plan to the General Conference of 1968. Although it did not have the approval of the Commission on World Service and Finance—the financial agency of national Methodism—the new Ministerial

Education Fund was passed by the General Conference by a substantial vote and was implemented in 1970.[27] The plan was included in the 1972 *Book of Discipline*. It involved twenty-five percent of the money raised being returned to the annual conferences for their use in ministerial education, and the remainder being administered by the Division of Ordained Ministry of the Board of Higher Education and Ministry.[28]

Bishop Kenneth Pope, of the Dallas-Fort Worth Area, had put his influence behind the earlier jurisdictional plan, and he now entered with equal enthusiasm into the implementing of the General Conference plan. Perkins received $140,777.64 for 1970 and $249,689.54 for 1971.[29] By 1977–78 the General Conference plan provided $740,000 for Perkins.[30] The M.E.F. has proved to be a lifeline to all United Methodist seminaries including Perkins. It has been said that some United Methodist seminaries might well have gone out of existence without the aid of this fund.

Reaching Out

Quillian's chairing of the Association of Methodist Theological Schools was only one of five major extramural responsibilities he carried during the 1970s. He served two years as the President of the Association of Theological Schools, the accrediting and supervising agency for theological education of the major churches of the United States and Canada. He was a member of the Executive Committee of the Fund for Theological Education. Beginning in 1960 he had been a part of the Wesley Works Project—a plan to publish a definitive edition of John Wesley's writings and still far from compete. He was chair of the Project for a number of years during the 1970s, and, as seems often to have been his lot, had to exert a great deal of influence to keep the Project moving. The Council of Southwestern Theological Schools, a coordinating agency for the schools of theology of the Southwest, elected him president on three occasions.[31] This was in addition to his visits to annual conferences, consultations with church officials, working with University administrators, and similar responsibilities. Although he made a serious attempt to turn over to the Associate Dean the internal workings of the School, it was difficult for him to do so. He was still "Dean of the Faculty," to use Associate Dean Ward's words,[32] a role which often involved his being the pastor in time of crisis and personal problems.[33]

Rank and Tenure/Leave Policy

One of the most personal matters which faculty members face is their promotion in rank—from Instructor to Professor—and their receiving tenure, after which it is difficult to dismiss them except under extreme conditions. In the early days of the School, most faculty were employed as full professors. If they were not, their promotion was at the discretion of the Dean.

This practice prevailed even through Dean Cuninggim's time, and therefore it was 1960 before an ad hoc Rank and Tenure Committee was appointed to advise the Dean on matters of promotion and tenure.[34]

The policies of the Committee evolved during the next decade, and on 8 May 1970, a firm policy much like what had been stated as early as 1961 was approved by the Senate.[35] The three factors given most weight were teaching, scholarly productivity (writing), and service to Perkins, with service to SMU, the church, the academy in general, and the civil and cultural community the other criteria to be considered.[36] The larger University did not regularize its criteria until a decade later.

In both instances a question must be raised as to whether the legitimate concern for scholarly production (writing) has not led to a "publish or perish" policy. It would appear that occasionally an excellent teacher is not promoted or given tenure on the basis of his or her lack of published material. To be sure, it would seem that any teacher alert to his or her subject matter would find both time and inclination to do some writing. Yet some of the best teachers I have known have done little or no writing. Is the primary business of a university to develop students or to encourage professors to do the kind of writing which will bring it recognition?

Perkins has, to be sure, increasingly provided incentives for both junior and senior faculty to do scholarly work through its leave policy. New faculty are provided with time for writing in the early parts of their career, and a generous leave policy continues throughout one's teaching at Perkins. Yet as one who did engage in writing during his teaching career, I can be sympathetic with those who for one reason or another do not find it possible to do so—especially if I hear the students repeatedly extol their virtues as inspired teachers who care for students.

Ecumenical and Interdenominational Concerns

From its beginning SMU's School of Theology has been thoroughly grounded in the Methodist tradition and has recognized its first priority to be the preparation of a Methodist clergy for its ministry. Yet it has never been narrowly sectarian; its curriculum, as we saw earlier, was modeled after the German pattern of the "classic" theological disciplines with greater emphasis than in German universities on "training for the ministry."

Most of the student body of the School of Theology was at first Methodist. As new degrees were added—especially the Ph.D., the M.S.M., and the D.Min.—an increasing number of non-Methodist students received degrees.

There have also been ways of helping students look beyond their own denomination, the earliest of these for students being the Interseminary Movement. Consisting of students from seminaries throughout the country, it provided students with an ecumenical experience they received nowhere else.[37] In 1946, W. Richey Hogg, then a recent Duke Divinity School graduate serving as the Traveling Secretary of the Interseminary Movement, addressed a regional conference at SMU organized and chaired by Neill McFarland, at that time a senior student at Perkins.

A variety of special emphasis weeks have emerged, many of which help provide ecumenical experiences for students: for example, Missionary Emphasis, Third World Theology, International Students' Week, Women's Week, Black Emphasis Week, and Mexican-American Emphasis Week. The providing of a global perspective on the church is still far from adequate, but at least some progress has been made in that direction.

Two official interdenominational efforts originated in the 1950s and 1960s. The Council of Southwestern Theological Schools was formed in 1958 as a vehicle for the Southwestern seminaries to work together and to sponsor summer seminars for participants of the schools.[38] After retiring from Perkins, Herndon Wagers became part-time director of C.O.S.T.S. and served in that capacity for several years.

The Institute of Religion, its founding director being Dawson Bryan of the Texas Conference, was established to correlate the Clinical Pastoral Education certification program of the Houston Medical Center. At first related to the S.T.M. degree, it later became the principal means of doing the D.Min. at Perkins.

Growing out of the leadership of Albert Outler of Perkins and David Balas of the Cistercian Seminary at the University of Dallas, the Seminar on the Development of Catholic Christianity began in 1967. Its concern at its four yearly meetings is that period of church history between the last of the New Testament writings and the more systematic works of the third and fourth centuries. Partly because of this seminar, a good working relationship developed between the two seminaries.[39]

Another ecumenical organization grew out of the interest of William R. Farmer, a New Testament professor at Perkins, and Father Bernard Orchard, a Benedictine monk in England. They were later joined by David Dungan from the University of Tennessee. After some ten years of discussion with special concern for the order in which the Gospels were written, the International Institute for the Renewal of Gospel Studies was chartered in 1980. Three of the seven fellows selected by the Institute have been related to Perkins: alumni Phillip Shuler and David Peabody, and faculty member William Farmer. One recent publication of the Institute, a bibliography of all materials dealing with the Synoptic problem since 1915, was done by Page Thomas.[40]

In addition, Perkins faculty members have participated in existing ecumenical movements. These have included the Dallas Community of Churches, the Texas Council of Churches, the National Council of Churches, and the World Council of Churches. Albert Outler's leadership especially in the WCC began in 1952 when he was a delegate to the Third World Conference on Faith and Order at Lund, Sweden. He became actively involved in the Faith and Order Commission, and from 1953 to 1963 was chair of the American Section of the Theological Commission on Tradition and Traditions, an attempt to relate the different denominational traditions to the one tradition of the Christian faith. He was instrumental in the New Delhi statement (1961) on "The Unity We Seek" and continued his intensive activity for two more years.[41]

By the early 1960s he was also active in the theological preparations for the Consultation on Church Union, an attempt of churches to understand what kind of unity could be achieved. His participation in Vatican Council II took him beyond Protestant ecumenism and was important for the Council, since he not only understood the Catholic tradition better than many bishops but also helped them with their Latin, in which he was a specialist.[42] A story—I'm sure apocryphal—is that at the opening meeting of one of the sessions of Vatican II, the Pope scanned the assemblage carefully and finally, with gusto, asked, "Where's Albert?"

John Deschner became a member of the Faith and Order Commission of the World Council of Churches in 1968 and its Moderator in 1982. This activity has kept Deschner busy in two ways: It has taken him to meetings of the Faith and Order Commission throughout the world, and it has required an unbelievable amount of writing to interpret the body's decisions. He has been one of the principal architects of statements from the Commission, and under his leadership decisions have been reached on a number of tough problems confronting the ecumenical church. We are far from unity, but remarkable progress has been made.

The National Council of Churches has had less Perkins faculty participation than other councils. The work of Bishop William C. Martin occurred while he was still bishop of the Dallas-Fort Worth Area. His courage in standing up for what was then—and still is—a controversial organization cannot be emphasized too much.

Nothing has been said, although it is important, of the ecumenical experiences of individual faculty in scholarly and professional organizations. My own experience in attending such meetings was that I not only learned of new and exciting developments in my field but also came to know persons of all communions, including during the last few years especially Roman Catholic scholars.

The Perkins faculty itself has become increasingly ecumenical in nature. Although some Methodists are not pleased with this movement, the faculty believes that this diversity helps prepare students for the pluralistic religious world they face in the parish today.

Student Life

Students were never quite so busy as they were during the first years of the shared governance plan. With twelve (later fifteen) students as members of the Senate and twenty-one additional ones involved in committees, almost one-tenth of the student body had an official position. In addition the Student Association involved about an equal number (some of whom duplicated those participating in the Senate or Senate committees).

Worship Committee. Perhaps the most hard-working committee, related both to Senate and Student Council, has been the Worship Committee (which also has faculty members). It is so far as I can determine one of the oldest functioning student groups on campus, the oldest being the Student Council. The Worship Committee was a fully established and recognized committee when I was a student from 1937 to 1940, and goes back at least to the early 1930s when the faculty, who had been in charge of worship, either tired of the job or gave up trying to get the work done, and turned it over to the students. The committee's task includes all official services of worship except those under the auspices of minority groups, and requires a great deal of student time in spite of the unusually good organization of the Committee into various work groups.[43]

Seminary Singers. Also an enduring student organization has been the Seminary Singers, now fifty years old. In its present form, the Singers were organized by Fred Gealy in 1939 and made their first trip, a weekend in West Texas (in a school bus!), the following spring.[44] They presented a program of Christmas music in 1948 as the last chapel service of the semester.[45]

In 1970 the Singers made a goodwill trip to Mexico in addition to their yearly tour. The Dean at the 10 April 1970 Senate meeting commended them "not only for their performance but also for the fine manner in which they served as emissaries from the United Methodist Church and the nation."[46] In 1971 women became members of the Singers, singing the tenor parts.[47] A few years later the Singers became a mixed chorus.

Christmas Worship Service. In the fall of 1959 Richey Hogg, who then chaired the Community Affairs Committee, stated to that body that he felt keenly the lack at Perkins of a Christmas worship service for the whole community, alluding to the traditional Christmas services he remembered from Yale Divinity School, and suggested that the committee authorize a similar and ongoing Christmas observance at Perkins.

Following the Yale pattern, he proposed a Christmas dinner, which spouses could also attend, in the evening in the Perkins Hall Cafeteria, and then going into the Chapel for the community celebration of Christmas. The latter would include Scripture and prayers, choral music and congregational singing, and the presentation of a Christmas sermon from the treasury of the church's history.

The committee responded positively, agreed that this should be an annual event, and asked committee member Lloyd Pfautsch to be responsible for the music and requested Grady Hardin to arrange for the sermon and prayers. The community's response was enthusiastic, and Dean Cuninggim began to speak of "Perkins' annual traditional Christmas worship service."

From the outset Pfautsch set the pattern by including together the Seminary Singers and the University Choir. After two years, the committee dropped the dinner as too unwieldy. From 1960, the *Catalog*'s calendar has listed the date for the Christmas worship, and from 1961 the observance has required two services, at 4:00 P.M. and 8:00 P.M. Each year the designated preacher has chosen one of the seven short sermons or reflections from Prof. Roland Bainton's *The Martin Luther Christmas Book*,[48] but across the years it seems that no one has sought to go much beyond this collection.

Over three decades, Lloyd Pfautsch (1959–64), Carlton R. (Sam) Young (1964–75), and Roger N. Deschner (1975–90) have directed the Seminary Singers and have taken major responsibility for the music. Yet, except for one year, Pfautsch from the beginning has provided shared leadership annually, has directed the University Choir, and has been a creative enabler throughout. Moreover, Robert T. Anderson, performing at the organ each year from 1960, has made his own notable contribution to the glory and beauty of this unique worship experience.

The Christmas worship service has now entered its fourth decade, and has become an integral, traditional part of Perkins School of Theology and of SMU.[49]

Student Spouses. Another group that has been active in a variety of ways has been the student spouses (student wives for most of its history). Begun as early as the 1940s, it was especially encouraged by Whitty Cuninggim during the 1950s. Study groups (to help them keep up with what their husbands were learning), interest groups, service projects, a Women's Society of Christian Service circle, and other programs have been a part of the activities sponsored.[50]

Perkins Student Foundation. Although begun slightly later than the period with which we are concerned in this chapter, the Perkins Student Foundation is too important not to be mentioned at this time. The only organization with a restricted membership, some of its members represent other organizations and some are elected at large. It performs a variety of services to the School, including the recruitment of students, assisting in Perkins development programs such as the annual Phonathon, speaking to campus visitors, and similar activities. Perkins puts its best foot forward in the Student Foundation and selects some of its top students to represent the school at various functions and to become partners with staff in enhancing the work of the School.[51]

Special Interest Groups. As we saw in a previous chapter, during the late 1960s and the early 1970s special interest groups emerged. Among these were the Black Seminarians, the Chicano Seminarians, the Perkins Women's Association, the Evangelical (Wesleyan) Fellowship, and others.[52] It was inevitable that this should happen, and they have served a useful purpose of giving a sense of belonging to persons with special interests. It appears to me, however, that some of the groups give preference to "their" group over the interests of the larger School. Theological education at Perkins is just not what it once was, with the large variety of interests among older students, town students who pursue the M.T.S. degree, and the fact that most students, and many spouses, work at secular as well as church jobs. Nor am I sure that the problem has been faced creatively by the school. We talk a great deal about community but have found ourselves relying mostly on the special interest groups to bring it about.

Student Awards and Prizes. A word should be said about student awards and prizes. As of 1981 the following were awarded annually: the B'nai B'rith Award in Social Ethics; the Dr. and Mrs. J. P. Bray Award in Hebrew; the W. B. DeJernett Award in Homiletics; the Albert C. Outler Award in Theology; the Senior (Dr. and Mrs. Glenn Flinn) Award; the Charles T. and Jessie James Bible Award; the Paul W. Quillian Award in Homiletics; the Charles Claude Selecman Award in New Testament Greek; the Karis Stahl Fadely Scholarship Award; the Elsa Cook Award; and the Master of Sacred Music Award.[53] In addition to these are the John M. Moore Fellowship for students doing graduate work, and a host of other scholarships provided by individuals, local churches, Sunday school classes, and annual conferences.

Conclusion

How does one adequately tell the story of an institution? It may be impossible. I am aware that lapses in content exist in what I have said. Indeed, some parts of this account may have bored the reader, but they seemed necessary to understand the life and ethos of Perkins School of Theology. The Quillian years have been especially difficult to write about because so much of interest took place. Yet really to know the School, one needs the material incorporated in this chapter.

We will close this long account of the 1960s and 1970s with a statement Dean Quillian made in his 1980–81 report. He wrote:

The best years of Perkins School of Theology are yet ahead. The foundation on which to build is sound. With the relative inner health of the school and with the present favorable relationships with the University, Church and region, this seminary should make more progress in the next ten years than has been made in the past thirty years. I happily conclude my part in the succession of deans with that confident expectation.[54]

Epilogue I

The Kirby Years: 1981–

In the ten academic years between the coming of James E. Kirby, Jr., as Dean and this writing, 1981 to 1991, change has been a constant. No recapitulation of such recent events can pretend to stand at sufficient historical distance to see the decade clearly. But too much of importance has occurred to allow this volume to end with the year 1981, where Howard Grimes laid down his narrator's pen.

James E. Kirby

On 1 July 1981, James E. Kirby, Jr., came to Perkins School of Theology as Dean. Son of Dr. and Mrs. J. Edmund Kirby, his father a Northwest Texas Conference Methodist pastor, Kirby was educated at McMurry College (B.A., 1954), Perkins School of Theology of Southern Methodist University (B.D., 1957; S.T.M., 1959), and Drew University (Ph.D., 1963). His dissertation topic was "The Ecclesiastical and Social Thought of Matthew Simpson."

Dean Kirby's professional career includes service as a Methodist pastor (Roby, Texas, 1958–60; Milford, Pennsylvania, 1960–61). He taught in the Religion department at Sweet Briar College (1963–67) and at Oklahoma State University (1967–76); there, he was Head of the Department of Religion (1967–70) and then Director of the School of Humanistic Studies (1970–76). From 1976 to 1981, Kirby was Dean and Professor of Church History at Drew Theological Seminary, Drew University, Madison, New Jersey.

Among other distinctions, Kirby holds the honor of being the first graduate of Perkins School of Theology to return as its Dean. Kirby is married to Patty Boothe Kirby, herself a Perkins graduate (M.R.E., 1956); they have two children.[1]

Changes in Faculty and Administration[2]

1981–82. During the year, new additions to the faculty and staff were James E. Kirby, Jr., Dean and Professor of Church History; Joan Ronck, Director of Perkins Development; and Laura H. Randall, Catalog Librarian. In June 1981, Richard Stewart resigned from the Intern Staff. In June 1982, James F. White joined the Notre Dame faculty. Charles Allen moved to the SMU Development Office; Barbara Ruth, Director of Community Life, took an appointment in the

Southwest Texas Conference, as did Dale Hensarling in Mississippi. C. Wayne Banks retired.

1982–83. Joining the faculty and staff were Guy D. Garrett, Director of Academic Procedures and Professor of Missions and Ecumenics; Susanne Johnson, in Christian Education; Lynn Mims, in the Intern faculty; and Linn M. Richardson (now Caraway), as Director of Admissions. David Lowes Watson added duties as Director of Community Life to his teaching. Claus Rohlfs retired after fall 1982; James Gwaltney left his part-time Intern Staff position at year's end to pursue a private consulting practice.

1983–84. New members of the faculty and staff were Bert Affleck, as Director of the Intern Program, Director of the Course of Study School, and teaching Practical Theology; Marjorie Procter-Smith, in Worship; Patsy Affleck, Secretary to the Librarian; and Alice Mongold, Periodicals Librarian. John Deschner was named Lehman Professor of Christian Doctrine. Four faculty members were named as University Distinguished Professors: John Deschner, Theology; Victor P. Furnish, New Testament; Schubert M. Ogden, Theology; and Robert Anderson, Organ and Sacred Music. John Holbert became Director of Continuing Education and of the Doctor of Ministry Program. In November, Lois Craddock Perkins died in Wichita Falls[3] (see this chapter's end). In June 1984, Douglas E. Jackson retired; Joan Ronck left for family reasons; David Lowes Watson went to the staff of the United Methodist Church's Board of Discipleship.

1984–85. David Maldonado joined the faculty in Church and Society; John Holbert was reassigned to teach Preaching; Virgil Howard joined the Intern Faculty. In January 1985, Stanley Menking came as Director of Continuing Education, Director of the Doctor of Ministry Program, and Professor of Practical Theology. New staff members were Beverly Sawyer, as Associate Dean of Community Life; James Lewis, as Director of Development; and Linda K. Umoh, Catalog Librarian. On 22 February 1985, the Texas Conference of the United Methodist Church formally presented the Albert C. Outler Chair in Wesley Studies to SMU, complete with a $1 million endowment.[4] Richard Heitzenrater was named the first Albert Cook Outler Professor of Wesley Studies, effective 1 September 1985. The family of Lois Craddock Perkins announced their gift of $1.25 million to endow a chair in homiletics in her memory.[5] Also, the Bridwell library director's position was endowed with a gift of $1 million to fund the J. S. Bridwell Foundation Endowed Librarian. In spring 1985, Saul Trinidad Camargo, of the Latin American Biblical Seminary in Costa Rica, was a visitor and offered lectures and workshops.

In June 1985, three faculty members left to join other faculties: Harold Attridge (Notre Dame), Phyllis Bird (Garrett-Evangelical Theological Seminary), and Charles B. Thomas (University of Pennsylvania). Jerry D. Campbell became Director of Libraries of Duke University; Roger Loyd was named acting Director of Bridwell Library. On 31 May 1985, John Hooper retired as Head of the library's Circulation Department, in which position he is believed to have been the first African-American member of the SMU staff in a role other than custodian or groundskeeper. Bishop William C. Martin, long-time friend of Perkins and its second Bishop in Residence, died in Little Rock, Arkansas, on 30 August 1984. Rabbi Levi A. Olan, distinguished visiting member of the faculty until 1980, died in Dallas on 17 October 1984.

1985–86. James Wharton was installed as the Lois Craddock Perkins Professor of Homiletics. William K. McElvaney, previously President of the St. Paul School of Theology, joined the faculty as the LeVan Professor of Preaching and Worship. William J. Abraham came as McCreless Associate Professor of Evangelism. Ellen Lethcoe (later Frost) joined the library as Acquisitions Clerk (Acquisitions Manager from 1987), as did Craig Haynes (Circulation). Leaving were Jane Marshall, to private teaching, and Craig L. Emerick, to a private consulting practice.

1986–87. New faculty and staff members were Mary Lou Santillán Baert in the Intern faculty; Jouette Bassler, in New Testament; Theodore D. Walker, Jr., in Ethics and Society; and Mary (Mimi) Davis, in Reference, Bridwell Library. W. Richey Hogg retired at the end of the academic year. James Lewis accepted a development position with Millsaps College; Martha Gilmore accepted a North Texas Conference appointment; Alice Mongold left the library staff.

Early in the academic year, the National Collegiate Athletic Association placed SMU on probation for violations associated with the football program, then in February suspended the football program from competition for two years and assessed other penalties;[6] further description of these events is beyond the scope of this chapter. President L. Donald Shields resigned due to ill health; William B. Stallcup was named President *ad interim.* In late May, A. Kenneth Pye of Duke University was named as SMU's ninth President.[7]

SMU celebrated the 75th anniversary of its founding during the year, notably with a Founders Day Convocation on 19 January 1987.

1987–88. New Perkins faculty and staff members were Danna Nolan Fewell, in Old Testament; Kenneth W. Hart, Director of the Master of Sacred Music Program and Professor of Sacred Music; Robert Maloy, first holder of the newly endowed chair as the J. S. Bridwell Foundation Endowed Librarian (Director of the Bridwell Library) and Professor of Church History; and M. M. Thomas (of India), Visiting Professor of World Christianity. Lillie Jenkins-Carter joined the library staff as Manager of Loans (previously called Circulation), following Craig Haynes's resignation to accept a library position elsewhere. In summer 1987, Lynn Mims accepted appointment to a church in the Oklahoma Conference. In the spring, H. Neill McFarland retired, and W. McFerrin Stowe retired as Bishop in Residence. Beverly Sawyer resigned for health reasons; Susanne Johnson was appointed to be Associate Dean of Community Life. Patsy Affleck took new responsibilities as Coordinator of Perkins Chapel.

1988–89. New faculty and staff were Marilyn Spurrell Atkins and Thomas W. Spann, in the Intern faculty; John Wesley Hardt, as Bishop in Residence; Bishop James S. Thomas, as Distinguished Visiting Professor of Practical Theology; Yap Kim Hao (of Malaysia and Singapore), as Visiting Professor of World Christianity. David J. Lawrence became Secretary to the Librarian; in January, Laura Randall transferred within the library to become Reference Librarian. In June 1988, Ruth T. Barnhouse retired; Mary (Mimi) Davis left the library staff. Bishop W. McFerrin Stowe, who had served both as Bishop in Residence and as a member of the teaching faculty, died in November 1988.

1989–90. The faculty additions for the year were C. Clifton Black, in New Testament; Ruben L. F. Habito, in History of Religions; and in January, Edward W. Poitras, in World Christianity. New library staff were Russell Morton, as second Reference Librarian; Jon Speck, Exhibits Curator; and Roberta Cox, Coordinator for Public Events. D. Lyle Dabney taught during the year as an adjunct member of the faculty, in Systematic Theology. In June 1989, J. William Matthews left to join the North Texas Conference Council staff. Schubert Ogden ended his service as Director of the Graduate Program in Religious Studies; William S. Babcock succeeded him in the office.

During the academic year, death removed several long-time Perkins leaders from the scene. Bishop W. Kenneth Pope, who had been another of the Bishops in Residence, died in June of 1989. Albert C. Outler died in September;[8] Lewis Howard Grimes died in December 1989. Former Associate Dean of Community Life Beverly Sawyer died in an Arkansas automobile accident in January 1990.

1990–91. Millicent C. Feske joined the faculty in Systematic Theology. James M. Ward returned to full-time teaching; Dean Kirby appointed Charles M. Wood as Associate Dean for Academic Affairs and Marilyn Alexander as Director of Alumni Relations. New members of the Bridwell Library staff were Isaac Gewirtz, in Special Collections, and Jan Sobota, in Conservation. The end of the academic year was marked by the retirements of John Deschner and William R. Farmer. Herndon Wagers, first Director of the Graduate Program in Religious Studies, died in October 1990.

At the March 1 faculty meeting, Dean Kirby announced that two searches for faculty had been successfully concluded. In Christian Education, Susanne Johnson (after a term as Associate Dean for Community Life) rejoined the full-time faculty. In Systematic Theology, Ellen T. Charry agreed to join the faculty in September 1992. And at the final faculty meeting, May 3, Dean Kirby announced the completion of the faculty search in Pastoral Care with the appointment of Patricia H. Davis. Thus, for the first time in several years, there remained no active search committees for faculty vacancies.

Curricula and Degrees

On 20 February 1981, the Perkins Senate renamed the M.Th. as the Master of Divinity (M.Div.) degree, in conjunction with the new curriculum.[9] On 16 April 1982, the Senate adopted the new curriculum, including a new Master of Theological Studies degree.[10] Joseph L. Allen chaired the Committee to Study the Curriculum.

Requirements to graduate included 72 semester hours of course work and an internship, for which 12 semester hours of credit were awarded. In addition, each student was required to be involved in an interethnic experience, in which one would spend up to 40 hours per semester in an ethnic setting other than one's own. A notable addition to course requirements was the one-hour course in Formation, for first-year students. Required courses were:[11]

Bible		12 s.h.
History of Christianity		6 s.h.
History and Phenomenology of Religion		3 s.h.
Theological Studies		12 s.h.
Systematic Theology	6 s.h.	
Moral Theology	3 s.h.	
Advanced course	3 s.h.	
The Church and Its Ministry		15 s.h.
Introduction to Ministry	5 s.h.	
Formation	1 s.h.	
Preaching in Christian Worship	3 s.h.	
Courses in two other functions	6 s.h.	
of ministry		
Advanced seminar in theology and ministry		3 s.h.

The United Methodist Church required all candidates for ordination to complete six additional hours in United Methodist history, doctrine, and polity.

The new Master of Theological Studies degree was designed "to offer sustained theological study at the master's level for persons who wish to pursue such study for personal or professional reasons, but who do not seek, or are uncertain about seeking, ordination."[12] It required the completion of 48 semester hours of approved course work, including a minimum of six semester hours per division. M.T.S. students often transferred into other degree programs, especially the M.Div. (and vice versa), since the courses taken were the same.

Minor revisions in curricular requirements continued to be made. But on 26 January 1990, the faculty approved a major revision of the curriculum, recommended by the Curriculum Review Committee chaired by Charles M. Wood. It added a new required course (Introduction to Theological Studies), reduced the total number of required hours to 39, expanded the number of elective hours to 30 (33 in the first version adopted) and provided for "concentrations" within each student's studies, and modified the requirements for the Internship so that a two-year internship might be taken concurrently with one's course work.

The required courses of the 1990 version of the curriculum were:[13]

Introduction to Theological Studies		3 s.h.
Division I: The Biblical Witness		9 s.h.
Interpretation of the Bible	6 s.h.	
Biblical exegesis course	3 s.h.	
Division II: The Heritage of the Christian Witness in Its Religious and Cultural Context		9 s.h.
History of Christianity	3 s.h.	
Intermediate course in history	3 s.h.	
Religion in a Global Perspective	3 s.h.	
Division III: The Interpretation of the Christian Witness		9 s.h.
Interpretation of the Christian Message	6 s.h.	
Moral Theology	3 s.h.	
Division IV: The Witness of the Church and Its Ministry		9 s.h.
Introduction to Preaching	3 s.h.	
Introductory courses in two other areas of ministry	6 s.h.	

Each student was required to propose and complete a 12-semester-hour "concentration," a group of courses related to each other to permit the student to pursue some particular area of interest. Usually, concentrations would involve more than one division's courses. In its curricular proposal, the Committee suggested the following as illustrative of concentrations: Christian Spirituality, Church and Society, Pastoral Leadership, Christian Preaching and the Biblical Witness, The Christian Faith and Other Faiths, and Hebrew Old Testament.

In addition to the new curriculum, the faculty adopted strategies for making it possible for persons with difficult schedules to attend and graduate from the M.Div. curriculum. For example, in 1989–90, the required courses were scheduled so that first-year part-time students could attend on Tuesday and Thursday only, and so that second-year students could attend on Wednesday and Friday only. A further refinement, scheduled to begin in 1991–92, is the offering of significant numbers of courses in the evenings.

Student Enrollment

Student enrollment (measured in the fall semester) grew toward mid-decade, then declined, both in persons and in full-time equivalents (FTE):[14]

Year	M.Div.	Persons	FTE
1980	330	439	330
1981	315	436	312
1982	297	431	300
1983	314	483	312
1984	286	519	335
1985	279	497	331
1986	298	475	347
1987	270	448	320
1988	271	425	303
1989	250	401	281
1990	239	365	261

Enrollment in the fall of 1989 in all programs was as follows: M.Div., 250; M.R.E., 17; M.S.M., 24; M.T.S., 29; D.Min., 54; Ph.D., 19; M.A., 2; non-degree, 6; auditor, 2.[15]

The 1990 ATS self-study analysis revealed that, in the 1989–90 student body of 326 in masters-level degree programs, 298 were Methodist (91%), with 276 being United Methodist (85% of all students). There were 188 men (57%) and 138 women (43%). There were 38 African-Americans (12%), 11 Hispanics (3%), 7 Asian-Americans (1%), 1 Native American, and 18 international students (6%). The entering class of 1989 averaged 33.6 years of age; for the first time in the School's history, there were more students in their thirties (42%) than in their twenties (31%).[16]

The 1990 ATS self-study also provided data concerning students in the Graduate Program in Religious Studies. The report lists 6 graduates with the M.A. in Religious Studies and 37 graduates with the Ph.D. in Religious Studies (through 1988); of the Ph.D. graduates, 24 then held positions as professors in universities, seminaries, or other academic institutions.[17]

Bridwell Library[18]

One of the salient aspects of the 1990 ATS self-study is the thorough discussion of the Bridwell Library's development during the previous decade. The report, prepared by the faculty's Committee on the Library in consultation with library director Dr. Robert Maloy, sets forth the renewed vision for the library's role, out of which emerged plans for and accomplishing of the library's total renovation. The faculty adopted a Statement of Mission for the library, setting forth the renewed vision in succinct form, on 6 November 1989.

From the arrival in August 1987 of Robert Maloy as the Bridwell Library's third director, a high priority became the renovation of the total library building. The J. S. Bridwell Foundation gave a multi-million dollar gift for the renovation, supplemented by an additional major gift from Charles N. Prothro of Wichita Falls to provide a major exhibition gallery, named the Elizabeth Perkins Prothro Galleries in honor of his wife and celebrating their fiftieth wedding anniversary.

The architectural firm of Hellmuth, Obata & Kassabaum designed the renovation in consultation with the librarian. Construction forced closing of the library facility from June 1988 until June 1989, with some renovations continuing into November 1989. Library services were provided in the basement rooms of nearby S. B. Perkins Hall, known as "Bridwell-in-exile."

Features of the renovated facility, which was formally rededicated in ceremonies on 19 October 1989, include comfortable seating in quiet reading rooms, individual studies for persons with long-term research projects, electrically operated movable bookstacks (to conserve space), a rare book reading room, and the refitting of restrooms and other modifications to provide more adequate access for persons who use wheelchairs or who have other disabilities. Also in 1989, the university libraries (including Bridwell) began offering the library catalog in computer-based form, naming the service "PONI" (Public ONline Information).

Moreover, the library staff has grown and provides new services: a reference librarian is available to assist readers; a conservator works to preserve bindings and paper; a special collections librarian devotes full time to guiding the library's distinctive and important special collections. Also, staff members prepare and promote exhibitions in the new Prothro Galleries, which were formally dedicated on 14 January 1990; fittingly, the first exhibition was "The Bible: 100 Landmarks from the Elizabeth Perkins Prothro Collection."

A Death in the Family

Lois Craddock Perkins died on 20 November 1983 in Wichita Falls, Texas. With her death, none of the principal benefactors who made possible the present campus of Perkins School of Theology remained. In tribute to her years of dedication to the work of Perkins School of Theology, a busload of faculty and students attended her memorial service in Wichita Falls on 22 November, with former Dean Joseph D. Quillian offering the sermon eulogy. On 19 January 1984, the Perkins community joined in a memorial service in the Perkins Chapel, with Dean James E. Kirby offering the sermon, entitled "Making the Vision a Reality."[19]

Bridwell Library staff members prepared a small exhibition of letters and other memorabilia marking the contributions of the Perkins family to the School of Theology. In one letter, dated 4 March 1960, Mrs. Perkins greets newly appointed Dean Quillian:

> For myself and my husband, who is not able to write, I want to welcome you to the Deanship (if there is such a word) of Perkins Seminary. . . .
>
> Perkins School and SMU are the two greatest interests of our lives. We have been proud of the progress made since we gave the physical plant. But we are also aware, that buildings do not make a great Seminary. It has to turn out great Spiritual ministers.
>
> I want to assure you that in spite of our interest in Perkins, we will never interfere in the least. Just our prayers and best wishes will be with you.[20]

Perhaps the most fitting memorial to Lois Perkins comes from another of her letters to Dean Quillian, dated 9 February 1967, in which she sends thanks for a book of tributes given her, including one by former Dean Eugene B. Hawk. Mrs. Perkins wrote:

> One said to Dr. Hawk, "Dean Hawk, how did you know where to go to find all of this money?" Dean Hawk's answer was, "I didn't go out looking for money. I went out looking for a man and a woman with generous impulses in whose hearts I could plant a vision and whom I could inspire to respond to make the vision a reality."
>
> If I am worthy I would like to have that on my tombstone.[21]

Roger Loyd

Epilogue II

Toward 2000

It would have been impossible for most to have imagined, or for even the best-informed persons to have predicted, the nature or the magnitude of the changes which have occurred in theological education during the four decades Howard Grimes taught at Perkins. Except for the fact that seminaries today continue to prepare persons for work in the various forms of ministry, and carry on the mission of theological research and reflection on the life and witness of the Church, little else is the same.

The once-traditional student—an Anglo male, fresh out of college—is now the exception. In mainline Protestant student bodies they number somewhere on the average between one-fourth to one-third of the total enrollment. General interest in the ministry itself has diminished. Among today's college freshmen, somewhere between one and two percent indicate a willingness to consider any form of ministry as a life's work. The bulk of today's typical student body consists of females, ethnic persons, and international students. Our typical seminarian is a second- or third-career person in their mid-thirties.

The cost of theological education has soared. In the early years of Howard Grimes's career there was no tuition at Perkins. The church, through the seminary, expected to provide for the education of prospective clergy. Today a serious question for our students is how much debt they can prudently assume to meet the cost of a theological education, and how much of its cost they can be expected to bear. These ever-increasing costs coupled with the nature of our new student population have shifted every seminary to a regional focus. Even the best-known schools in the country now tend to draw students from the immediately surrounding area. Any serious claim to be a national seminary is difficult to support. Persons choosing a seminary look first at institutions which are in proximity to their homes. Despite the existence of thirteen denominational seminaries located from coast to coast, one-half of United Methodist seminarians are enrolled in schools which are not United Methodist. The option to select the very best school without regard to location and move to it in order to enjoy an extended time in a new environment is simply unavailable to many of today's students. Moreover, after they arrive most of them are required to spend blocks of time in church-related or secular employment in order to pay their bills.

These practical considerations have changed the nature of the seminary experience, and have made a dramatic impact on the way in which the educational task itself is conceived. In no form of professional education is it more essential for the student to interact with faculty and peers; to have extended time for reflective thought and meditation; to worship in the chapel; and to participate in the variety of activities which are common in our communities.

Today's class schedule is designed to accommodate a part-time, commuting student. Many of them can spend no more than two days a week on campus. There is more concern among them to learn the "practical" skills which will enhance their ministry, and to get out as soon as possible. And, as a result, faculties are less satisfied with the learning environment than they were in the past. If they could change it to be more like it was forty years ago, they probably would.

In the ordinary course of M.Div. studies there is a new emphasis in Protestant seminaries on formation. It has always been a part of the Roman Catholic tradition, but has only been adopted by us in recent years. Moreover, there is today a great deal more attention given to education which should take place after the student graduates from the seminary—education during the probationary years and continuing education. Among United Methodists, a regular and approved program of continuing education is required by annual conferences for all active clergy. The seminary, in concert with the judicatories, is expected to assume a pivotal role in providing these opportunities. We are more alert to the issues of what should be taught when, where, and by whom than ever in the past. New degree programs, especially the Doctor of Ministry, have been created in response to the demand for more structured continuing education among active clergypersons. Howard Grimes was the first Director of the Doctor of Ministry program at Perkins.

Most annual conferences in the United Methodist Church now offer extended programs which are required of seminary graduates in the process leading to ordination. Many practical skills required for effectiveness in ministry can be better taught by experienced practitioners to persons who are engaged in their ministry. Other subjects are better considered in the traditional classroom setting. The future will surely demand of both school and denomination a larger commitment to work together in the educational task. At the moment, however, we lack the full and interactive dialogue which will make it effective. The decade of the nineties requires that to change.

Given the fundamental shifts which have already taken place in theological education, what can we expect in the years ahead? What opportunities and challenges await us as we seek to work in closer cooperation with the groups we are committed to serve?

Surely one of these will be to do our part to insure that enough persons enter both the general and the ordained ministry to meet the needs of the church. We are experiencing a decline in the number of seminarians, and in the United Methodist Church somewhere between forty-five and fifty percent of active clergy will retire before the year 2000. The number of persons being ordained is at a net of zero growth. Younger persons with the gifts needed for effective work in ministry are opting for other professions. The status accorded to clergy by society as a whole has diminished. It is not true in every profession. While both theology and medicine have seen declines in the number of applications for places in their educational institutions, law schools continue to experience a significant increase.

New ways to attract persons to ministry must be found soon. Church and seminary can cooperate in this effort. It is no longer adequate for theological schools to assume that the responsibility for enlistment belongs to the church alone. Over the past four decades, the traditional streams which led persons into ministry have dried up. Church youth and student organizations which once encouraged younger persons to consider ministry either no longer exist or do not include the emphasis in their programming. College Wesley Foundations, for example, lost much of their appeal to students during the decade of the sixties. "Baby boomers," who make up the bulk of today's seminary population, have different loyalties.

The polity of churches must also be examined to see what influence it has on the supply of clergy. In the United Methodist Church, the long-honored "itinerant" system, which guarantees appointments to clergy requiring them to serve wherever assigned, is in need of revision. Employed spouses, both male and female; a desire to serve in urban rather than rural areas; declining membership; inability of local congregations to support the high cost of a full-time pastor; and older clergy have all created new pressures on its traditional way of operating. Groups with congregational polity have faced a shortage of both clergy and openings. Among them it is virtually impossible for a new seminary graduate to be called to a single congregation these days.

New forms of ministry will have to be developed, too. Lay persons employed in secular jobs who serve congregations on the weekends, various forms of cooperative and team ministries, longer terms of service, and new ways of recognizing and rewarding it are possibilities. The days when a small congregation could expect to have an Anglo male in his mid-thirties are by and large history. The fact that ten percent of the members in the United Methodist

Church are in forty-five percent of its churches indicates that some new provision will have to be made for small congregations.

In today's church, there is no shortage of exciting examples of vital and growing ministries led by persons who once would have been unacceptable to traditional congregations. Ordained women continue to grow in numbers in the United Methodist Church. But we have a long way to go before the barriers are finally down. Seminaries and those they serve must seek to find new ways both to enhance the openness to new forms of ministry and to increase the readiness of persons to serve in them.

The last chapters of Howard Grimes's book are yet to be written. His story is of days past and honored; what is on the horizon is both exciting and daunting. It is well never to forget that the future of the church is not in our hands alone.

James E. Kirby, Jr.
Dean, Perkins School of Theology

Notes

Chapter 1

1. *Texas Christian Advocate,* 30 September 1915.
2. I have used various sources for this information: the 1915 *Catalog* for the School of Theology, President Hyer's handwritten account of the founding of SMU, articles in the *Texas Christian Advocate,* and other sources.
3. At first called a "Department of Theology," it soon became known as a separate school. Perhaps more than the School of Music, this designation provided at least some reason to use the term "university."
4. Quoted in Vernon 1967, 234.
5. Hyer 1915.
6. Moore and Nelson 1906, 7–9.
7. Moore and Nelson 1906, 189.
8. Moore and Nelson 1906, 225.
9. Hyer 1915, 2–3. A later account says that his promise was for $10,000 and forty acres of land *(Campus,* 23 March 1932).
10. Hyer 1915, 3.
11. Hyer 1915, 4.
12. See a photograph of Bishop Ward in Nail 1961, 4.
13. Vernon 1967, 174–76; Brown 1957, 27–29; Campbell 1906, 71–78.
14. *Texas Christian Advocate,* 22 August 1907.
15. Vernon 1967, 230.
16. *Texas Christian Advocate,* 19 September 1907.
17. *Texas Christian Advocate,* 5 August 1908, 5 November 1908.
18. *Texas Christian Advocate,* 22 August 1922.
19. *Dallas Morning News*, obituary of Frank Seay, 15 February 1920.
20. Thomas 1974.
21. Thomas 1974, 8.
22. Thomas 1974, 5–8.
23. Henderson 1966, 27:895. Curiously, this article, written by the then-business manager of the university, says nothing about Vanderbilt's Methodist roots. Rather, he states that Cornelius Vanderbilt founded Vanderbilt as Central College, giving $500,000 in 1873 and another similar sum in 1875. Various gifts from the Vanderbilt family followed.
24. Thomas 1974, 34; see *Texas Christian Advocate,* 26 March 1914. In a letter on 31 August 1922 to Bishop E. D. Mouzon, Bishop Collins Denny says that at the time

Vanderbilt was founded, the laws of Tennessee did not permit any church to own and control educational institutions. (Letter in Mouzon Papers.) In response, Mouzon agrees with Denny that the loss of Vanderbilt "gave the church a deep wound from which it has not yet recovered."

25. See *Texas Christian Advocate,* 2 September 1911.

26. *Texas Christian Advocate* is the principal source for this conclusion.

27. *Texas Christian Advocate,* 21 November 1907.

28. *Texas Christian Advocate,* 27 February 1908.

29. *Texas Christian Advocate,* 28 June 1908.

30. Brown 1957, 126–127.

31. Hyer 1915, 5; Moore 1948, 211.

32. *Texas Christian Advocate,* 24 March 1910, 7 April 1910, and 21 April 1910. These articles are included in full in Blair 1926. See also Hyer 1915, 6.

33. *Texas Christian Advocate,* 22 September 1910.

34. Henning 1934, 1:8.

35. See Thomas 1974, 171, for a list of commission members. Later a member of the German Methodist Conference was added. See Executive Committee Minutes for 15 May 1912.

36. *Texas Christian Advocate,* 26 January 1911.

37. Hyer 1915, 7. Thomas 1974 has provided a detailed and apparently accurate account of these events, fuller than my own sketch of them here.

38. Thomas 1974, 31.

39. Thomas 1974, 31–32.

40. *Texas Christian Advocate,* 19 September 1912. The Armstrongs had previously offered land for a Presbyterian university which never materialized.

41. Thomas 1974, 30. See *Texas Christian Advocate,* 16 June 1910, which states that the real estate was valued at $75,000. It also says that $325,000 had been pledged by the citizens of Dallas.

42. Hyer 1915, 8.

43. The Board of Trustees and Executive Committee Minutes are located in the office of the Secretary of the University.

44. Hyer 1915, 7.

45. The Executive Committee Minutes state that it was some years later when the General Board of Education was convinced that $800,000 for endowment had been raised. They had paid part of the $200,000 earlier, and later made another pledge even larger which they also paid after SMU officials convinced them that they had fulfilled their matching obligation.

46. Hyer 1915, 10.

47. *Texas Christian Advocate,* 2 November 1911.

48. *Texas Christian Advocate,* 5 November 1914.

49. *Texas Christian Advocate,* 16 January 1913, and other issues.

50. Thomas 1974, 195, n. 50.

51. Executive Committee Minutes, 1 June 1913.

52. Trustee Minutes, 30 June 1913. See Hyer 1915. See also *Bulletin,* School of The-

ology, 1942–43, 6.

53. Building Committee Minutes, 10 July 1913.

54. *Texas Christian Advocate,* 15 January 1914.

55. *Texas Christian Advocate,* 18 June 1914.

56. *Texas Christian Advocate,* 3 December 1914. "Old Master McKenzie" was very likely the Rev. J. W. P. McKenzie, who came to Texas in the late 1830s as missionary to Indians and became what Walter Vernon calls a "great pioneer" and a North Texas "stalwart" until his death in 1891. (Vernon 1967, 46, 96–97.)

57. *Texas Christian Advocate,* 2 April 1914.

58. *Texas Christian Advocate,* 3 December 1914.

59. *Texas Christian Advocate,* 17 September 1914.

60. Executive Committee Minutes, 14 May 1912.

61. Executive Committee Minutes, 14 May 1912.

62. Executive Committee Minutes, 4 April 1914.

63. Bishop n.d., 10.

64. Executive Committee Minutes, 8 December 1911 and 6 May 1912.

65. *Mustang,* May–June 1972, in an article on SMU's presidents.

66. Gambrell 1951.

67. *Texas Christian Advocate,* 26 March 1914.

68. White 1966, 3–4.

69. *Texas Christian Advocate,* 11 September 1913, 29 June 1913.

70. Hyer 1915, 15.

71. *Texas Christian Advocate,* 24 October 1912, 28 November 1912. The original date was October 16 but it was postponed because of rain. See also Minutes, North Texas Annual Conference, 1912, 68–69.

72. Executive Committee Minutes.

73. Brown 1957.

74. *Campus,* 3 April 1929.

75. *Dictionary of American Biography,* s.v. "Hyer, Robert." Manuscript of Gambrell's original article in the Kern Papers.

76. Brown 1957, 43.

77. Brown 1957, 43.

78. Brown 1957, 74.

79. Brown 1957, 40–41.

80. *Dictionary of American Biography,* s.v. "Hyer, Robert."

81. *Dictionary of American Biography,* s.v. "Hyer, Robert."

82. *Campus,* 10 October 1929; Board of Trustee Minutes, 20 February 1920.

83. *Texas Christian Advocate,* 11 February 1915.

84. *Texas Christian Advocate,* 15 January 1914.

85. Hyer 1915, 16.

86. "The Influence of the Universities," an address by Hyer after he became President Emeritus, in the archives of Bridwell Library.

87. Board of Trustee Minutes, 6 November 1964.

Chapter 2

1. Thomas 1974, 61.
2. Thomas 1974, 46.
3. *Texas Christian Advocate,* 27 May 1915, 11 September 1915, 23 September 1915.
4. *Texas Christian Advocate,* 27 May 1915.
5. Executive Committee Minutes, 30 June 1917.
6. *Texas Christian Advocate,* 2 September 1915; see Vernon 1967, 239–240.
7. Executive Committee Minutes, 13 July 1915. According to Henning (1934, 1:92), there was no card catalog until April 1916. It had been developed with the help of the Dallas Public Library's librarian, Laura Alexander.
8. Board of Trustee Minutes, 8 June 1916; see *Texas Christian Advocate,* 20 November 1914, 2 July 1915, 5 August 1915.
9. Faculty Minutes, 10 February 1916.
10. *SMU Times,* 18 September 1915.
11. Faculty Minutes, 17 November 1915.
12. Faculty Minutes, 12 January 1916.
13. Faculty Minutes, 8 April 1916.
14. Faculty Minutes, 10 February 1916.
15. Nowhere have I found an explanation of the faculty chair's responsibilities, other than to preside in Mouzon's absence.
16. So far as I know this became standard practice in the School of Theology chapel several years after the opening of Perkins Chapel in 1951.
17. W. Martin 1965, 4–5.
18. W. Martin 1965, 6.
19. W. Martin 1965, 5–6.
20. Thomas 1974, 171.
21. Thomas 1974, 84, 119. Kilgore was actually acting dean longer than anyone else had been dean up to his time.
22. Hackney 1969, 148.
23. *Service* 1, no. 1 (May 1920): 9–10.
24. W. Martin 1965, 4.
25. *Texas Christian Advocate,* 6 July 1916.
26. Trustee Minutes, 9 June 1916.
27. *Bulletin,* 1916–17.
28. Faculty Minutes, School of Theology Archives, Bridwell Library.
29. Faculty Minutes, 19 January 1917.
30. Faculty Minutes, October 1916.
31. For their election see Executive Committee Minutes, 17 February 1917.
32. Faculty Minutes, 10 April 1917.
33. All of these faculty appointments are from various sources in Faculty Minutes and Trustee Minutes listing faculty appointments.
34. Gambrell 1951, 18.
35. *SMU Times*, 28 September 1915.

36. *SMU Times*, 3 October 1915.
37. Trustee Minutes, 8 June 1916.
38. Faculty Minutes, 24 February 1916.
39. *Texas Christian Advocate,* 2 September 1916.
40. Faculty Minutes, 15 February 1916.
41. *Campus*, 12 May 1919.
42. Faculty Minutes, 8 December 1915.
43. Trustee Minutes, 9 June 1916.
44. Trustee Minutes, 9 June 1916.
45. The early image of SMU, according to the *Texas Christian Advocate,* was of a "poor boy's school." Most early applicants, the *Advocate* observed, were determined to get an education whether they had the money or not (9 September 1915).
46. Trustee Minutes, 9 June 1916.
47. Faculty Minutes, 24 February 1916; Trustee Minutes 7 June 1917. At one period as much as one–third of the work could be done by correspondence (Faculty Minutes, 7 June 1919).
48. See Faculty Minutes, 10 December 1918; Vernon 1961, 118. Apparently this Sunday School assembly was modeled after the one at Lake Junaluska, and was continued in the later-established Mount Sequoyah, at Fayetteville, Arkansas.
49. Faculty Minutes, 24 February1916.
50. Faculty Minutes, 7 December 1917.
51. Faculty Minutes, 15 February 1918; Executive Committee Minutes, 4 April 1918.
52. Executive Committee Minutes, 1 June 1919.
53. Executive Committee Minutes, 16 December 1920.
54. Executive Committee Minutes, 6 January 1921.
55. Executive Committee Minutes, 17 February 1921.
56. Roestline 1966, 24:357. It is ironic that this same scenario was played out in the 1980s when Scarritt, for fiscal reasons, was forced to make a move that ultimately closed the institution. Perkins was again one of the unsuccessful "bidders" in seeking to bring the school and its assets to the SMU campus.
57. Trustee Minutes, 10 June 1919.
58. For records of these funds see the Trustee Minutes for 7 June 1917 and 7 and 10 June 1918. See the *Texas Christian Advocate,* 2 May 1916 and 2 May 1917. One gets the impression that the M. E. Church, South, made no concerted effort to support its School of Theology financially. The people in the churches either would not or could not provide adequate funds.
59. *University Bulletin*, June 1916 (catalog for 1915–16; announcements for 1916–17).
60. See Johnson 1966, 24–26.
61. *SMU Times*, 28 September 1915.
62. *SMU Times*, 28 September 1915.
63. *SMU Times*, 9 October 1915.
64. *Texas Christian Advocate,* 27 April 1916.
65. *Texas Christian Advocate,* 27 April 1916.
66. *Texas Christian Advocate,* 24 February 1916.

67. A. Frank Smith, letter in Kern Papers.
68. A. Frank Smith, letter in Kern Papers.
69. Trustee Minutes, 27 June 1916.
70. A. Frank Smith, letter in Kern Papers.
71. Johnson 1966, 21.
72. Johnson 1966, 29. This number was later drastically reduced, but there is no explanation as to why this was the case.
73. See photographs of pastors in Johnson 1966, opposite 64.
74. Trustee Minutes, 7 June 1917.
75. Trustee Minutes, 7 June 1917.
76. Trustee Minutes, 8 June 1918.
77. Trustee Minutes, 8 June 1918.
78. *Campus*, 5 February 1918.
79. *Campus*, 5 February 1918.
80. *Campus*, 29 January 1919.
81. *Campus*, 2 April 1919.
82. *Campus*, 10 March 1920.
83. Trustee Minutes (Called Meeting), 20 February 1920.
84. Letter dated 17 February 1920, in Kern Papers.
85. Trustee Minutes, 20 February 1920.
86. Trustee Minutes, 20 February 1920.
87. Brown 1957.
88. Brown 1957, 163–167.
89. Brown 1957, 162–163.
90. Brown 1957, 165.
91. A facsimile of the program is contained in Brown 1957, 69–72.
92. Trustee Minutes, 20 February 1920.
93. *Dallas Morning News*, Sunday, 15 February 1920.
94. From Faculty Minutes.
95. *Mustang*, February 1920.
96. Faculty Minutes, 8 April 1919 and 22 April 1919.
97. See Seay 1925a, especially Ch. 11 and 12. Also see Seay 1925b, especially Ch. 1–3.
98. Interview by Norman Spellmann with O. W. Moerner, at Georgetown,Texas, 19 October 1973; in the archives of Bridwell Library.
99. *Dallas Morning News*, 14 February 1920.
100. *Mustang*, February 1920.
101. *Campus*, 20 March 1920.
102. Executive Committee Minutes, 5 December 1952.
103. *Texas Christian Advocate,* 12 November 1914.
104. *Bulletin*, 1916–17.
105. Trustee Minutes, 7 June 1917.

Chapter 3

1. Thomas in her history of the early years of Southern Methodist University has a full and, so far as I can determine, an accurate record of this process. There is one discrepancy between my statistics and hers. She gives the indebtedness of the University when Hyer resigned as $339,122 while the Board of Trustee Minutes of 20 February 1920 give $207,691.34. Her source is a 1922 Board meeting, and is therefore a later figure. See Thomas 1974, 71–83.

2. Trustee Minutes, 22 May 1922.

3. Executive Committee Minutes, 1 June 1920.

4. Thomas 1974, 80.

5. *Campus*, 16 January 1924.

6. *Campus*, 16 January 1924. See also Thomas 1974, 81. Thomas says that the Pires gift was made in 1922. These larger gifts were nothing like the money being raised at that time by eastern schools but were large in relation to the many small gifts of the past.

7. Thomas 1974, 80.

8. Executive Committee Minutes, 21 March 1924.

9. Thomas 1974, 82.

10. Trustee Minutes, 13 June 1921.

11. Trustee Minutes (Called Meeting), 11 October 1922.

12. *Campus*, 31 March 1923; see Trustee Minutes, 21 March 1923.

13. *Campus*, 10 March 1920.

14. Kern 1921, 3. *Service* was published for several years by the School of Theology as a means of acquainting the Methodist Episcopal Church, South, with its School of Theology in Dallas. Copies are in the School of Theology Archives, Bridwell Library.

15. Trustee Minutes, 12 June 1920. It may be noted that it is difficult to construct an accurate record of the dates of faculty appointments. Thomas's SMU list (1974, 174–189) was based on SMU catalogs, but the list is not always reliable. For example, she includes Gross Alexander, who died before the 1915 session began, and Fitzgerald Parker, who changed his mind and remained in Nashville before the opening session. The Board of Trustees records are reliable as far as they go, but some known faculty, especially those who were visiting professors, are not easily found in the Trustee Minutes (if they are there at all).

16. Executive Committee Minutes, 12 June 1919; *Campus*, 1 October 1919.

17. *Campus*, 1 October 1919.

18. *Campus*, 8 December 1920.

19. Thomas 1974, 97–98.

20. *Campus*, 22 September 1920.

21. *Campus*, 22 September 1920. See also Faculty Minutes, 20 May 1921.

22. Trustee Minutes, 13 June 1921.

23. Executive Committee Minutes, 19 September 1921; *Service* 1, no. 4 (December 1921).

24. Trustee Minutes, 13 June 1921.

25. Trustee Minutes, 13 June 1921.

26. Faculty Minutes, 19 September 1922.

27. Executive Committee Minutes, 19 September 1921.

28. Faculty Minutes, 4 November 1921.

29. Executive Committee Minutes, 19 September 1921.

30. Thomas 1974, 55.

31. Trustee Minutes, 13 June 1921. They were apparently at the School of Theology from 1920 to 1921.

32. *Bulletin*, 1923. The listing of Seneker, Goodloe, and Hicks in this order means that Goodloe's one year in 1920–21 as Visiting Professor was not counted as the beginning of his teaching.

33. *Service* 2, no. 1 (December 1922).

34. *Campus*, 28 September 1923.

35. *Campus*, 24 September 1924.

36. *Campus*, 24 September 1924.

37. Faculty Minutes, 27 May 1924.

38. Thomas 1974, 177.

39. Typed list, in Kern Papers.

40. Executive Committee Minutes, 11 February 1924.

41. *SMU Ex-Students' Magazine,* October 1924, 6.

42. Faculty Minutes, 4 November 1921. One source in the School of Theology Archives says that she began work at the School of Theology immediately after her graduation.

43. Letter from the Dean's Secretary, Kern Papers.

44. Information from Kern Papers.

45. From a typed list, 10 October 1924, Kern Papers.

46. Henning 1934, 1:192.

47. *Bulletin*, May 1926.

48. *Campus*, 15 March 1933.

49. *Bulletin*, May 1926.

50. Bradfield 1925.

51. Document in Kern Papers.

52. *Campus*, 31 March 1923.

53. *Campus*, 3 October 1923.

54. *Service*, January 1924.

55. The School of Theology publication *Service*, for January 1924, gives three as the total number of buildings needed. Kern said to the Board of Trustees on 22 May 1924 that the School also needed a dormitory, a chapel, and a library building (Minutes, 22 May 1924.)

56. Letter from Dean Kern, 5 April 1924, in Kern Papers.

57. To indicate how inextricably Lillian Jennings was involved in the operation of the School, her letter to Dr. Bradfield, studying at the University of Chicago in the summer of 1924, describes in some detail the status of the work on Kirby Hall and

the tunnel through which utility lines would be run. Dr. Bradfield was interested in the building to a greater extent than most, since it was through him that the gift was made. In Kern Papers, dated 25 August 1924.

58. In Kern Papers.
59. Letter to Dr. W. D. Bradfield, 26 March 1923, in Kern Papers.
60. *Bulletin*, 1924–25.
61. Faculty Minutes, 14 January 1925.
62. Trustee Minutes, 24 March 1926.
63. *Bulletin*, May 1926.
64. Faculty Minutes, 5 March 1926.
65. *Bulletin*, 1925.
66. *Service*, May 1920.
67. *Bulletin of the Extension School*, December 1924; *SMU Ex-Students' Magazine*, January 1925.
68. Trustee Minutes, 1 June 1925.
69. *SMU Ex-Students' Magazine*, January 1925.
70. Typed document in Kern Papers, dated 26 May 1925.
71. Material from Kern Papers.
72. Document in Kern Papers.
73. *Campus*, 23 February 1921.
74. *Campus*, 23 February 1921.
75. *Campus*, 7 January 1926.
76. According to a statement from Kate Warnick while she was still actively at work at Bridwell Library.
77. Trustee Minutes, 12 June 1923.
78. Executive Committee Minutes, 2 September 1920.
79. Trustee Minutes, 4 June 1935. I remember this red brick building from my childhood, when I visited an aunt who lived across the street on Rosedale.
80. Trustee Minutes, 2 July 1922.
81. *Service,* February 1923.
82. *Campus*, 11 February 1926.
83. *Campus*, 13 February 1926.
84. *Campus*, 11 February 1926.
85. *SMU Ex-Students' Magazine*, June 1926.
86. See, for example, a letter from Kern to Bishop McMurry in the Kern Papers, dated 31 March 1926.
87. Executive Committee Minutes, 6 March 1922, 27 April 1922.
88. *Campus*, 19 January 1922.
89. Trustee Minutes, 2 May 1922.
90. Trustee Minutes, 12 June 1923. See also the *Campus*, 26 May 1923, concerning the possibility of relocating Scarritt to the SMU campus.
91. Faculty Minutes, 28 September 1922.
92. *Campus*, 9 December 1925.

93. *Campus*, 20 October 1920.

94. *Campus*, 7 November 1925.

95. I am assuming that the condition which existed when I was a student in the late 1930s had been the case all along. My extracurricular life was almost altogether on the university campus and at Highland Park Methodist Church.

96. P. Martin 1973, 5.

97. *Campus*, 31 October 1925.

98. P. Martin 1973, 4–5.

99. P. Martin 1973, 6.

100. Trustee Minutes, 13 June 1921.

101. See Vernon 1967, 321–322.

102. *SMU Alumni Directory*, 1986, 9.

103. Although this comes from my own memory, which I tend not to trust, it is so indelibly stamped there that I am reasonably sure of its authenticity.

104. *SMU Alumni Directory*, 1986, 4.

105. I am relying on the *Semi-Weekly Campus* for this breakdown. See issue for 27 October 1922.

106. *SMU Alumni Directory*, 1986, 4.

107. There was for many years a campaign for "Little SMU in Brazil," later combined in the Campus Chest. The *Campus* always gave it good publicity, and often the campaign reached its goal. See, for example, *Campus*, 16 April 1924.

108. *Campus*, 19 January 1924.

109. *SMU Alumni Directory*, 1986, 8–9.

110. In 1922, there were nine student pastors in the North Texas Conference. These students were expected to meet with Prof. Ormond one hour per week. (*Campus*, 27 October 1922).

111. *Campus*, 13 November 1926.

112. This was the opinion of Mrs. John (Kate) Warnick, who worked closely with Dean Kern for several years.

113. Pope 1976, 46.

Chapter 4

1. See Thomas 1974, 86–87.

2. Thomas 1974, 85–91.

3. Thomas 1974, 86.

4. Thomas 1974, 87–88.

5. Thomas 1974, 91.

6. See Quebedeaux 1974, 5ff.

7. Quebedeaux 1974, 9. These five fundamentals are not always identical, but the first line (the verbal inspiration of the Bible, or a literalistic view of biblical revelation) is crucial for all fundamentalism. See, for example, Packer 1974, chs. III–V.

8. Harnack 1957. The first German edition was published in 1900, and by 1927 had gone through fourteen printings. See "Introduction" by Rudolf Bultmann, vii.

9. Vernon 1967, 279.

10. Whether this term was used as far back as the 1920s, I do not know.

11. Pope 1976, 44.

12. Thomas 1974, 82–83.

13. Published by the Macmillan Co., 1920.

14. *Campus*, 8 December 1920.

15. "A Plain Statement of Fact." No publication information; located in the Kern Papers, 3–4.

16. "A Plain Statement of Fact," 4.

17. "A Plain Statement of Fact," 14–15.

18. "Lower criticism" dealt with the text itself. Many other varieties of biblical study have developed since the Rice affair.

19. Rice 1920, xxxi.

20. Rice 1920, 320.

21. Rice 1920, 1–6.

22. Rice 1920, 8–24. Speaking of the biblical text in the mid-eighth century B.C., Rice says: "There is no Old Testament book yet in its present form" (24).

23. Rice 1920, 27–109.

24. Rice 1920, 113–188.

25. Rice 1920, 191–253.

26. Rice 1920, 257–289.

27. Rice 1920, 293–320.

28. "A Plain Statement of Fact," 10.

29. Rice 1920, 134.

30. Rice 1920, 134–135.

31. "A Plain Statement of Fact," 11.

32. Rice 1920, 34.

33. Rice 1920, 30.

34. "A Plain Statement of Fact," 11ff.

35. "A Plain Statement of Fact," 11ff. See also Executive Committee Minutes, 4 October 1921.

36. "A Plain Statement of Fact," 4.

37. "A Plain Statement of Fact," 4.

38. "A Plain Statement of Fact," 5.

39. Faculty Minutes, October 1921.

40. Executive Committee Minutes, 4 October 1921.

41. Faculty Minutes, October 1921.

42. Executive Committee Minutes, 11 October 1921.

43. Executive Committee Minutes, 25 November 1921.

44. Executive Committee Minutes, 12 December 1921.

45. Thomas (1974, 98–102) has documented the Workman case in great detail.

46. *Campus*, 2 May 1923.

47. *Campus*, 5 May 1923.

48. *Campus*, 5 May 1923.

49. Thomas 1974, 100. Her source is the *Dallas Times Herald*, 7 May 1925. See also *Campus*, 6 May 1925.

50. *Campus*, 6 May 1925.

51. *Campus*, 6 May 1925.

52. *Campus*, 9 May 1925.

53. *Campus*, 13 May 1925.

54. Thomas 1974, 101.

55. Thomas 1974, 101.

56. Thomas's sources are partly from personal correspondence.

57. *Campus*, 12 May 1923.

58. Thomas 1974, 101.

59. Thomas 1974, 102.

60. Thomas 1974, 202, n. 140.

61. This incident is recorded in detail in Thomas 1974, 85–91. Shuttles, like Cockrell, chair of the Board of Trustees during the event, believed that the University should be controlled by businessmen on the board, especially its Executive Committee.

62. Neither letter of the first interchange between Branscomb and Kern has been found. They are known only from Branscomb's letter of 19 January 1924, in the Kern Papers.

63. See Branscomb's letter of 19 January 1924, in Kern Papers.

64. Branscomb's letter of 19 January 1924.

65. Kern's letter to Branscomb, 22 January 1924, in Kern Papers.

66. Branscomb's letter to Kern, from Dallas to Oklahoma City, where Kern was fulfilling an assignment, dated 22 May 1925, Kern Papers.

67. Letter from Kern to Branscomb, 25 May 1925, Kern Papers.

68. It is possible that this is the committee to which Judge Cockrell had been appointed.

69. Article of Religion V includes these words: "The Holy Scripture *containeth* all things necessary to salvation, so that whatsoever is not read therein, nor may be proved thereby, is not to be required of any man that it should be believed as an article of faith, or be thought requisite or necessary to salvation. In the name of the Holy Scripture we do understand those canonical books of the Old and New Testament of whose authority was never any doubt in the Church." (Emphasis added.) There follows a list of the Old Testament books, which does not include those of the Apocrypha, and a statement that the New Testament includes those "commonly received." Since the Bible itself does not claim inerrancy, it is difficult, if not impossible, to prove the inerrancy or literal interpretation of Scripture from Scripture itself. See *Book of Discipline*, 1988, 61–62.

70. Handwritten letter from Branscomb to Kern, dated 18 January 1926, Kern Papers.

71. Quoted in Thomas 1974, 102.

72. Thomas 1974, 101.

73. *Campus*, 29 November 1922.

74. *Campus*, 6 October 1922.

75. *Campus*, 28 November 1923.

76. *Campus*, 4 November 1925.

77. Letter in Kern Papers.

78. Typed document in Kern Papers.

79. Typed document in Kern Papers, 2.

Chapter 5

1. *Campus*, 9 April 1930.

2. Trustee Minutes, 4 June 1934.

3. See *Campus*, 22 June 1932.

4. Letter from James A. Kilgore (Dean Kilgore's son) to D. E. Kilgore, Corpus Christi, Texas, 30 August 1968, in SMU Archives.

5. Typed document, written by Herbert Gambrell, in SMU Archives.

6. Letter from James A. Kilgore to Eva B. and O. Eugene Slater, 13 March 1987.

7. Gambrell typescript, SMU Archives.

8. Thomas 1974, 146.

9. Thomas 1974, 147.

10. Thomas 1974, 147.

11. Thomas 1974, 146.

12. *Mustang*, June 1938. See *Campus*, 3 April 1929.

13. *Campus*, 3 April 1929.

14. *Campus*, May 1938.

15. *Campus*, May 1938.

16. Thomas 1974, 157. Since this material is not central in the history of the School of Theology, I have relied considerably on Thomas's history of SMU in this section.

17. Thomas 1974, 159.

18. Thomas 1974, 146–147.

19. Thomas 1974, 148–154.

20. Thomas 1974, 148–151.

21. Trustee Minutes, 4 June 1934.

22. *Bulletin*, May 1927.

23. *Bulletin*, May 1928; *Campus*, 5 October 1927.

24. *Bulletin*, July 1929.

25. Letter in Kilgore Papers.

26. *Bulletin*, April 1933.

27. *Bulletin*, April 1931.

28. See *Bulletin*, 1931–32. There were 81 B.D. students, three of whom were women; 12 M.A. students, three of whom were women; three in the certificate program; and 11 in the Correspondence Division. There were some twenty fewer students reported for the following year, seeming to indicate a high drop-out rate.

29. Faculty Minutes, 6 April 1927.

30. *Campus*, 19 October 1932.

31. Trustee Minutes, 3 June 1929.

32. *Summer Campus*, Fall 1931.

33. *Campus*, 8 January 1930.

34. *Campus*, 4 January 1930.

35. *Bulletin*, 181–183.

36. Faculty Minutes, 2 October 1929.

37. From an undated document following the Faculty Minutes of 22 August 1930.

38. *Bulletin*, 147.

39. *Campus*, 11 January 1930, 5 June 1931.

40. Trustee Minutes, 7 June 1927. No explanation is provided for the remainder of ordained clergy.

41. *SMU Ex-Students' Magazine,* January 1927.

42. Faculty Minutes, January 28 1927; *Campus*, 15 April 1931.

43. The original name in the nineteenth century was Interseminary Missionary Alliance, with a meeting held in New Brunswick, New Jersey, in 1880. The organization was revived a few years later, and eventually became the Interseminary Movement. See Hogg 1952, 83–86. Also see Hogg 1945 and Love 1930.

44. *Campus*, 1 October 1927.

45. *Campus*, 9 March 1929.

46. *Campus*, 19 April 1929.

47. *Campus*, 6 November 1929. In the late 1930s, I attended meetings at which I am fairly certain the implications of "Interseminary" were carried out.

48. *Campus*, 6 November 1929.

49. See note 28.

50. *Campus*, 7 May 1927; *SMU Ex-Students' Magazine,* May 1927.

51. *Campus*, 21 March 1928.

52. From the files of Mrs. John Warnick, Warnick Papers; *Campus*, 21 April 1928 and 9 May 1928.

53. Banquet programs from Warnick Papers.

54. *Campus*, 7 December 1928.

55. *Campus*, 19 December 1928.

56. *Campus*, 30 April 1930; see Slater 1988, 29–30.

57. *Campus*, 27 April 1932.

58. Slater 1988, 34.

59. Slater 1988, 34.

60. *Campus*, 28 May 1932.

61. *Campus*, 6 April 1930.

62. *Campus*, 9 January 1929.

63. Faculty Minutes, 26 September 1931.

64. Faculty Minutes, 21 October 1931.

65. Faculty Minutes, 6 April 1932.

66. Faculty Minutes, 13 September 1933.

67. Letter from Mrs. John H. Warnick to Miss Nell Anders, 3 March 1930, in Warnick Papers.

68. *Bulletin*, April 1931.

69. Although Robert E. Goodrich, Jr. (later a bishop) has often received the credit for

this transformation of the band, he told me not long before his death that it was Cy Barcus who began the process. Barcus came to SMU after being solo cornettist with the Culver Military Institute Band. His association with the SMU band lasted for some years. In 1988 he was living in retirement in Dallas, Texas.

70. *Campus*, 3 December 1930.

71. *Campus*, 28 September 1932. It is my impression that his arrangement was similar to the one which the band currently uses.

72. *Summer Campus*, Fall 1933.

73. *Summer Campus*, Fall 1933.

74. *Campus*, October 1934.

75. Their association at SMU led to Meeker's providing numerous State Fair Musical stars for Goodrich's Chautauqua series at First Methodist Church of Dallas during the 1950s.

76. *Campus*, 7 November 1934.

77. *Summer Campus*, October 1934.

78. *Campus*, 18 February 1933, 9 December 1933.

79. *Campus*, 24 March 1934.

80. I had always thought it was the New York Palace, but I have found no record of this.

81. *Campus*, 2 September 1935. If this story is true—and I am reasonably sure it is—the decision was a fortunate one for the Methodist Church. During Goodrich's twenty-six years as Pastor of First Methodist Church, Dallas, he did the kind of innovative programming which was widely copied and led to significant national changes. The ideas were not always original with Goodrich, but he gave them a flair which was distinctly his own. He later served for eight years as Bishop of the Missouri Area, then as Bishop in Residence at St. Luke's United Methodist Church in Houston, and finally back at First Church, Dallas, where he died on 30 October 1985, soon after returning to the church he had influenced so deeply.

82. Kilgore Papers, 3 September 1930.

83. Trustee Minutes, 1 June 1931; quoted by Thomas 1974, 137.

84. Thomas 1974, 137.

85. Moore Papers.

86. Moore Papers. Tuition was minimal; perhaps, as in the late 1930s, it was not required at all, only fees.

87. Trustee Minutes, 22 March 1927.

88. *Campus*, 26 March 1927.

89. Trustee Minutes, 22 March 1927.

90. Moore Papers; *Bulletin*, April 1931. I have found no indication as to why Mrs. Lehman willed her estate to the School of Theology. A purely speculative guess is that W. D. Bradfield was instrumental, as he had been for the money for Kirby Hall. The chair disappeared when Bradfield retired, and did not resurface until the 1980s when Professor John Deschner was elected to it. Presumably, the money had been used as general endowment between the two dates.

91. Moore Papers.

92. Minutes of a meeting of the committee, 21 November 1930, in Kilgore Papers.

93. "Foundations of the Future," 1 January 1931, in Kilgore Papers.

94. *Campus*, 6 January 1937.
95. *Campus*, 27 February 1932. I have recently heard that this identification has been called into question.
96. Faculty Minutes, 2 March 1928.
97. *Campus*, 18 January 1933.
98. *Campus*, 18 January 1933.
99. *Campus*, 2 March 1929.
100. *Campus*, 20 February 1932.
101. For example, E. Stanley Jones appeared on campus on 31 March 1933, and later at a mass meeting at First Baptist Church: *Campus*, 29 March 1933.
102. *Campus*, 18 February 1933.
103. *Campus*, 19 March 1932.
104. *Campus*, 3 April 1929.
105. *Campus*, 30 October 1929.
106. *Campus*, 5 May 1926.
107. *Campus*, 28 September 1929.
108. *Campus*, 22 February 1928.

Chapter 6

1. Faculty Minutes, 25 January 1936.
2. When St. Paul School of Theology was established in Kansas City in 1959, it was understood that Perkins School of Theology would relate primarily to the southern part of the jurisdiction.
3. Faculty Minutes, 28 June 1933.
4. *Mustang*, 1 October 1938.
5. When I came back to teach in 1949, one faculty member told me quite frankly that the school was not as good as it was when I was a student (1937–40).
6. Trustee Minutes, 9 May 1951.
7. *Bulletin*, 1939–40.
8. Trustee Minutes, 9 May 1951.
9. Executive Committee Minutes, 7 February 1939.
10. A letter to A. W. Martin dated 22 October 1945, in Hawk Papers.
11. *Campus*, 9 November 1938, 8 February 1939; Trustee Minutes, 7 November 1938.
12. *Campus*, 21 November 1923; Weiss and Proctor 1971, 82.
13. Statement prepared by Herbert Gambrell, Trustee Minutes, 6 November 1958.
14. Gambrell statement; Weiss and Proctor 1971, Chap. V.
15. Gambrell statement.
16. *Campus*, 7 October 1942.
17. Trustee Minutes, 9 May 1951.
18. *Mustang*, December 1938.
19. Quoted in Weiss and Proctor 1971, 225.
20. Trustee Minutes, 25 January 1945.
21. Trustee Minutes, 26 June 1943.

22. Weiss and Proctor 1971, 163–164. Lee, of course, was not directly responsible for securing the money for many of these buildings.

23. Trustee Minutes, 6 February 1940.

24. Trustee Minutes, 4 January 1940.

25. *Campus*, 23 September 1949. George Baker also taught Homiletics at Perkins School of Theology.

26. Trustee Minutes, 26 January 1943.

27. *Campus*, 10 January 1942.

28. Faculty Minutes, 15 January 1942.

29. Trustee Minutes, 6 February 1945. Also, personal communication from H. Neill McFarland.

30. Trustee Minutes, 24 June 1946.

31. Executive Committee Minutes, 2 April 1946; Trustee Minutes, 4 February 1947; *Campus,* 1 August 1946.

32. Trustee Minutes, 2 June 1947.

33. *Bulletin,* April 1935, April 1936.

34. Trustee Minutes, 4 June 1934.

35. He later dropped most of his teaching in order to be Vice-President of the University.

36. *Bulletin*, April 1934, 1935, 1936; Trustee Minutes, 4 June 1934; Trustee Minutes, 29 January 1935; Executive Committee Minutes, 22 February 1935. All of those remained until retirement except Paul Root, who resigned in 1947 to become Dean of Duke Divinity School but died before moving to North Carolina.

37. This material is compiled from a variety of sources—*Bulletins*, Trustee Minutes, Executive Committee Minutes, and other resources of the period. Some of it comes from my personal knowledge since I was a student from 1937 to 1940.

38. I went from SMU for a year's study (S.T.M.; 1940–41) at Union in New York. Although I had some good professors there—e.g., Reinhold Niebuhr—others who were well-known scholars were not as stimulating as I had found most professors at SMU to be.

39. See, for example, the report to the Board of Trustees, January 1936 (found in Faculty Minutes, 22 January 1936), in which it is frankly stated that the President and the Dean "in cooperation with the faculty may assign members of the faculty to serve in Bible Conferences, Training Schools, etc. . . ." I do not think this prerogative was often if ever exercised, but this at least shows the seriousness with which such work was taken.

40. Trustee Minutes, 25 June 1938.

41. Report of the Theology Committee to the Board of Trustees, 26 June 1944.

42. *Campus*, 7 September 1955; letter to Dr. Martin, dated 30 January 1945, Hawk Papers.

43. Trustee Minutes, 25 June 1945; letter from Dean Hawk, Hawk Papers.

44. Trustee Minutes, 24 June 1946.

45. Trustee Minutes, 24 June 1946.

46. Letter from Umphrey Lee, dated 8 December 1945, Hawk Papers.

47. Some of the material in this section comes from my memory, which I normally do

not trust but which for these general statements I believe is trustworthy.

48. *Bulletin*, 1948–49.

49. Faculty Minutes, 10 November 1948.

50. Faculty Minutes, 6 October 1948.

51. For example, after I had accepted a place on the faculty, I had a letter from Sweet saying he understood I was to begin teaching in 1949 and asking what I was to teach.

52. Letter from Dean Hawk, 23 January 1941, Hawk Papers; Faculty Minutes, 11 December 1943.

53. *Bulletins*, 1943–44, 1944–45, 1945–46, 1946–47, 1948–49; Faculty Minutes, 31 October 1947, 3 December 1947, 8 January 1948, 6 April 1949.

54. *Campus*, 12 March 1949; Trustee Minutes, 10 May 1949.

55. My name is also included in this list, and I know that I did not come as a visitor at this time; Faculty Minutes, 31 October 1947.

56. Trustee Minutes, 10 May 1949.

57. *Bulletin*, 1951–52.

58. *Bulletin*, 1951–52; Trustee Minutes, 10 November 1950.

59. Faculty Minutes, 6 April 1949.

60. *Bulletin*, April 1935.

61. Faculty Minutes, May 1937. This was the curriculum I pursued as a student.

62. *Bulletin*, 1942–43.

63. Faculty Minutes, 28 February 1947.

64. Trustee Minutes, 10 May 1952.

65. *Bulletin*, 1950–51.

66. *Campus*, 1 July 1949.

67. Faculty Minutes, 16 August 1951; information in the files of Mrs. John Warnick, Warnick Papers.

68. Trustee Minutes, 1 June 1936; *Bulletin*, 1937–38.

69. Document establishing the lectureship, Hawk Papers.

70. *Campus*, 11 January 1946; Executive Committee Minutes, 25 January 1946.

71. Executive Committee Minutes, 17 February 1938; material in Hawk Papers.

72. Vernon 1967, 336.

73. Thomas 1974, 111.

74. Faculty Minutes, 22 January 1936.

75. Faculty Minutes, 19 October 1940.

76. Turner Papers.

77. Turner Papers.

78. Faculty Minutes, 28 September 1949.

79. *Campus*, 24 April 1940.

80. *Campus*, 22 April 1950.

81. This comes from my own experience of having been on the Worship Committee one quarter and its chair the next, in 1939–40.

82. More than 200 were expected for the 22 April 1938 banquet, at the Melrose Court Hotel; *Campus*, 20 April 1938.

83. *Campus*, 17 April 1940.
84. I was his M.A. advisor, and few students have impressed me as much as Mr. Liu. In 1948, according to a *Campus* interview, Mr. Liu traveled 3,000 miles in America visiting churches and youth groups. *Campus*, 25 September 1948; see also *Campus*, 11 January 1950.
85. *Campus*, 17 April 1940. My recollection is that we were not very good that first year, but it was the beginning of a long tradition that has meant more to many students than any other student activity.
86. *Campus*, 11 December 1946.
87. Faculty Minutes, 24 September 1935.
88. Faculty Minutes, 12 October 1938.
89. Faculty Minutes, 29 September 1942.
90. Faculty Minutes, 8 January 1948.
91. Faculty Minutes, 15 July 1948.
92. Correspondence in Kilgore Papers, 8 July 1926. This negotiation had to do with the C. M. E. Church (Colored, later Christian, Methodist Episcopal Church).
93. *Campus*, 14 May 1928; 1 November 1930; 21 February 1948.
94. *Campus*, 17 January 1940.
95. *Campus*, 9 January 1952.
96. During my first year of teaching at Perkins (1949–50) I offered two courses to a black student who lacked them in the completion of his degree at Oberlin School of Theology, then sent his grades to that school. I have heard that other professors did the same thing.
97. Faculty Minutes, 6 December 1950
98. Faculty Minutes, 3 January 1951.
99. An editorial in the same issue commended Perkins for taking the step. *Campus*, 6 January 1951.
100. See Vernon 1967, 243–245. See also Moore 1948, 211–215.
101. Moore 1948, 211.
102. Moore 1948, 211.
103. Moore 1948, 103.
104. The judgment of Walter N. Vernon, 1967, 245.
105. See Grimes 1951, 121–122.
106. More will be said about this in the following chapter.
107. Spellmann 1979, 332. Spellmann's source is a letter from Umphrey Lee to Smith.
108. This issue will be discussed in a later chapter. See Spellmann 1979, 328–330.
109. Spellmann 1979, 336.
110. Spellmann 1979, 333.

Chapter 7

1. Moore 1948, 212–213.
2. Executive Committee Minutes, 30 September 1938.
3. Hawk Papers.

4. Hawk Papers.

5. Hawk Papers.

6. Trustee Minutes, 11 April 1944.

7. Vernon 1967, 241–243.

8. Trustee Minutes, 20 March 1928.

9. Trustee Minutes, 20 March 1928.

10. Executive Committee Minutes, 2 November 1920.

11. P. Martin 1973, 25–29.

12. Moore 1948, 213.

13. Trustee Minutes, 4 November 1960 (at the time of Mr. Perkins's death).

14. Trustee Minutes, 20 March 1928.

15. For this account I have used both primary sources and Spellmann's account (1979, 320–328). Unfortunately no one seems to have kept a running account of the negotiations with Mr. and Mrs. Perkins (except in Bishop Smith's diary to which Spellmann had access). Spellmann's, reconstructed from various sources, is the best account that I have found. It is written from the Smith perspective, of course, and probably does not give Paul Martin (later a bishop) sufficient credit. For an account from Bishop Martin's perspective, see Vernon 1973, 114–123.

16. Spellmann 1979, 320–321.

17. Spellmann 1979, 321. This is verified by an entry in Bishop Smith's diary for 11 April 1944.

18. Spellmann 1979, 321; based on an interview with Bishop Smith.

19. P. Martin 1973, 28–29.

20. Trustee Minutes, 6 February 1945.

21. Spellmann 1979, 325; from Bishop Smith's diary.

22. Legal document, dated 6 February 1945, Hawk Papers.

23. Pencil drawing available in Moore Papers.

24. Holograph in Moore Papers.

25. Quoted in Spellmann 1979, 326, from a letter dated 23 September 1947, Moore to Smith.

26. Quoted in Spellmann 1979, 327.

27. Spellmann 1979, 327.

28. Spellmann 1979, 327.

29. Spellmann 1979, 328; quoted from the *Dallas Morning News*, 9 February 1951.

30. Executive Committee Minutes, 28 January 1949.

31. Loggie 1967, 68–69.

32. According to information from the SMU Business Office.

33. For several weeks after we began having worship in Perkins Chapel in the spring of 1951, two workers always had to stop their work on these rails during worship.

34. Trustee Minutes, 24 June 1946.

35. Trustee Minutes, 4 November 1954. The actual numbers given are 1952—390; 1953—383; and 1954—378.

36. Grimes 1986, final page.

Chapter 8

1. I have relied considerably in this chapter on my own memory of what was happening during my first years at Perkins School of Theology as teacher. Especially do my prejudices show through when I evaluate what was taking place. I do not trust my memory, nor for that matter that of most people, and so I have where possible checked not only dates and other facts but sources which help me understand what was happening. In some instances I have noted that I cannot verify a particular story. The facts in the section on Cuninggim come from *Who's Who in the Methodist Church* and *Encyclopedia of World Methodism*.

2. *Campus*, 17 March 1954.

3. Minutes, Special Meeting of the Board of Trustees, 30 March 1954.

4. Minutes, Board of Trustees, 6 May 1954.

5. Minutes, Board of Trustees, 6 May 1954.

6. *Campus*, 21 September 1954.

7. Minutes, Board of Trustees, 25 June 1954.

8. *Campus*, 7 May 1954.

9. Terry 1978, xxii.

10. Beaty's principal book on this subject was *The Iron Curtain over America* (Dallas: Wilkinson Publishing Co., 1951). See Terry 1978, xxl. This episode began during the presidency of Umphrey Lee, and the trauma of having to deal with it, so some people feel, brought about his resignation.

11. Terry 1978, xxiii–xxv.

12. J. Grimes 1978 provides many clues and insights into Tate's presidency through his speeches and otherwise. Though not a biography, it provides an important source for one.

13. *Catalog*, 1951–52. Paul Root died in 1947 and had not been replaced.

14. *Catalog*, 1951–52. Sweet, of course, also acted as "Chairman of the Faculty," which was not a clearly defined position as we saw in a previous chapter.

15. *Catalog*, 1951–52. Baker's primary job, of course, was as chaplain to the University, but he valued greatly his association with the School of Theology.

16. *Catalog*, 1951–52. There is need for a biography of Outler. His papers, deposited in the Bridwell Library archives, will make this possible.

17. He edited and wrote a brilliant introduction to *John Wesley* (Oxford University Press, 1964), a one-volume edition of Wesley's writings in the "Library of Protestant Thought" series. His four-volume edition of Wesley's sermons, published by Abingdon Press from 1984 to 1987, is likely to remain the definitive edition of the sermons for generations to come. His painstaking checking of every quotation (most of which Wesley did not cite), with the assistance of Wanda Smith, was an exacting and time-consuming labor of love which he saw as part of the effort to secure respect for Wesley as an able and creative theologian in eighteenth-century England.

18. *Catalog*, 1951–52.

19. *Catalog*, 1951–52.

20. Faculty Minutes, 19 March 1952.

21. *Catalog*, 1952–53; also Faculty Minutes, 24 September 1952.

22. *Catalog,* 1952–53. I have not included those who taught in the non-credit (so far as Perkins was concerned) Approved Supply School. This would be desirable—and their names are listed in the catalogs—for the School was an integral part of the life at Perkins. A decision not to include them was based simply on the many additional names this would have required, added to a chapter that at times already appears to be only a chronicle of the names of faculty of Perkins School of Theology.

23. Faculty Minutes, 23 April 1953.

24. *Catalog,* 1953–54; also various faculty minutes for 1952–53.

25. Faculty Minutes, 26 September 1953.

26. *Catalog,* 1954–55. See also various faculty minutes for 1953–54, where names of those invited to interview and their disposition are included for 1954–55.

27. *Catalog,* 1955–56. See also various Faculty Minutes, 1954–55.

28. *Catalog,* 1956–57. See also various Faculty Minutes, 1955–56.

29. *Catalog,* 1957–58. See also various Faculty Minutes, 1956–57.

30. *Catalog,* 1957–58.

31. *Catalog,* 1958–59. See also various Faculty Minutes for 1957–58.

32. *Catalog,* 1959–60. See also various Faculty Minutes for 1958–59 and Board of Trustee and Executive Committee Minutes.

33. Faculty Minutes, 4 March 1960.

34. Faculty Minutes, 22 January 1960.

35. *Catalog,* 1960–61. See also Faculty Minutes for 22 January 1960; Trustee Minutes, 5 November 1959.

36. This information comes from various sources. That concerning the M.R.E. degree is partly my own recollection of a process for which I was responsible.

37. Faculty Minutes, 2 April 1954.

38. Attachment to Faculty Minutes of 17 February 1956. See also the Minutes for 28 November 1956.

39. Attachment to Faculty Minutes of 24 April 1959.

40. These dates are assembled from the catalogs of the nine years.

Chapter 9

1. Faculty Minutes, 22 September 1951.

2. Attachment to Faculty Minutes, 3 April 1959.

3. Since I chaired the Admissions Committee prior to there being an Admissions Officer, I sometimes wrote letters of rejection in the absence of the Dean.

4. This maximum enrollment of 400 was never officially adopted, and it was only an unofficial figure which seemed right to me. On one occasion in fact, prior to Cuninggim's deanship, the faculty set 500 as the maximum.

5. *Catalog,* 1951–52.

6. See the report from Dean Cuninggim to the Provost, 1953–54, in Cuninggim Papers.

7. Faculty Minutes, 8 October 1952.

8. Faculty Minutes, 20 May 1952.

9. Faculty Minutes, 22 October 1952, 21 November 1952.

10. Faculty Minutes, 2 January 1953. Apparently no minutes were kept of the 22

December 1952 meeting. At least they are not included in the bound volumes of Faculty Minutes.

11. Davis 1953, 10.
12. Davis 1953, 11–12.
13. "Report to the Provost," Cuninggim Papers; see also Davis 1953.
14. *Catalog,* 1953–54, 43–44.
15. *Catalog,* 1953–54, 44.
16. *Catalog,* 1953–54, 47.
17. "Report to the Provost." See also Davis 1953.
18. For example, in *Christian Century,* 28 April 1954.
19. *Catalog,* 1957–58.
20. Faculty Minutes, 22 May 1959; *Catalog,* 1960–61.
21. See, for example, Faculty Minutes for 30 May 1955, 27 June 1955, 23 May 1956, 2 May 1957, 28 March 1958, 24 October 1958, and 3 April 1959. The experiments included a yearly "Parish Week," at first during Holy Week, later in the fall; attempts to get the faculty to be either supervisors or advisors (at first, all the faculty, later selected faculty); and so on. One thing that becomes clear in reading the Faculty Minutes during the 1950s: the faculty tried to make something out of the integration of field education and the on-campus curriculum. Sometimes it worked, but often it did not.
22. Faculty Minutes, 15 November 1951.
23. Attachment to Faculty Minutes, 25 May 1956.
24. *Catalog,* 1954–55.
25. *Catalog,* 1959–60.
26. I have not found the exact date of their being demolished. The 1955–56 *Catalog* is the first not to list them among housing units at Perkins.
27. My most important source for this section is the address which Cuninggim made to the Ministers' Week Luncheon during Ministers' Week, 4 February 1987, and entitled "Far-Off Things and Battles Long Ago" (Cuninggim 1987). See also Cuninggim 1956, 109–115.
28. Cuninggim 1956, 109.
29. Logan 1957, 16.
30. Cuninggim 1987, 3. For an account of these events from the point of view of one of the students involved, see Williams 1980, 57–66.
31. Cuninggim 1987, 3–4.
32. Cuninggim 1987, 4.
33. Cuninggim 1956, 111.
34. Cuninggim 1987, 5.
35. Cuninggim 1987, 6.
36. Cuninggim 1987, 6.
37. Other accounts of these events are found in Weiss and Proctor 1971, 174–176. There is a record from Bishop A. Frank Smith's perspective in Spellmann 1979, 328–330. Bishop Paul Martin also has remarks about the resolution of the affair (1973, 29–30). Although the sources from the time in which it was happening, such as the Faculty

and Trustee Minutes, mention the matter, they contain surprisingly little which is of help in understanding it. I have drawn upon my own memory of my participation in many of the events to supplement what others have said.

38. From an interview with Bishop Smith, by Charles Braden, reprinted in Spellmann 1979, 329.
39. Weiss and Proctor 1971, 175.
40. Cuninggim 1987, 9.
41. Cuninggim 1987, 9–10.
42. Cuninggim 1987, 10.
43. P. Martin 1973, 30.
44. From an interview quoted in Spellmann 1979, 330.
45. Cuninggim 1987, 11.
46. Cuninggim 1987, 11.
47. Cuninggim 1987, 11.
48. Weiss and Proctor have dealt with this incident in some detail (1971, 176–186).
49. Weiss and Proctor 1971, 178.
50. Weiss and Proctor 1971, 179.
51. Grimes 1954, 3.
52. *Campus*, 13 November 1953. See also the issues for 18 November 1953, 20 November 1953, 10 February 1954, 17 February 1954, 19 February 1954, and 24 February 1954.
53. *Campus*, 19 February 1954.
54. Faculty Minutes, 19 February 1954.
55. Grimes 1954, 3–4.
56. Trustee Minutes, 30 March 1954.
57. Trustee Minutes, 6 May 1954.
58. See Weiss and Proctor 1971, 185.
59. I am drawing on my memory here and do not remember the date.
60. Cuninggim 1952b, 4.
61. Cuninggim 1952b, 5.
62. Cuninggim 1952a, 3.
63. "Mrs. Warnick Honored" 1954, 19.
64. Turner 1951b, 16; Faculty Minutes, 17 October 1951.
65. Turner 1951a, 14.
66. Turner 1952, 16.
67. Faculty Minutes, 20 April 1956.
68. Faculty Minutes, 28 September 1956.
69. See Executive Committee Minutes for 7 November 1952, 6 March 1953, and 8 September 1961. These gifts were later to prove fairly substantial according to records of the business office for 1988.
70. Faculty Minutes, 17 January 1952.
71. The Faculty Minutes for 5 December 1953 record that the budget for 1952–53 was $221,358. Receipts for the previous year had been $166,719.71.

72. *Catalog,* 1951–52, 1954–55.
73. *Catalog,* 1957–58; Trustee Minutes, 6 May 1954.
74. Cuninggim 1953b, 3.
75. *Catalog,* 1954–55.
76. Cuninggim Papers.
77. Executive Committee Minutes, 1 June 1956.
78. As late as 1988 cuts in budget for the entire University were ordered by the President.
79. Faculty Minutes, 17 October 1951; *Campus,* 30 September 1955.
80. Later, in 1955, one of the chapel periods was a convocation in Lois Perkins Auditorium, and still later chapel was held twice a week with other worship services scheduled at various times.
81. Faculty Minutes, 19 March 1952.
82. *Campus,* 14 March 1952.
83. Faculty Minutes, 22 October 1952.
84. Wicker 1954, 19.
85. *Campus,* 17 October 1952.
86. *Campus,* 29 April 1955. There may have been others whom I have neither located nor remembered.
87. Irwin 1953, 19.
88. *Campus,* 6 February 1957.
89. Hawk 1947, 3.
90. *Catalog,* 1958–59.
91. Quillian 1979.
92. Cuninggim 1953a, 9.

Chapter 10

1. Trustee Minutes, 9 November 1962.
2. J. Grimes 1978, 4–5 and passim.
3. Trustee Minutes, 3 November 1961.
4. "Growth Through Two Quadrennia 1960–68" (SMU Report to the South Central Jurisdiction Conference of the United Methodist Church, 24–27 July 1968).
5. Executive Committee Minutes, 12 January 1962.
6. Orientation of New Trustees (in Trustee Minutes), 3 October 1964.
7. Names are available but not used. The communications are in the Quillian Papers.
8. Letter from President Tate, 26 February 1960, giving the details of the procedures, in Faculty Minutes.
9. Faculty Minutes, 16 January 1960.
10. Letter from President Tate, 26 February 1960, in Faculty Minutes.
11. *Who's Who in Methodism,* s.v. "Quillian."
12. Tate 1960; *Who's Who in the Methodist Church* and *Encyclopedia of World Methodism.*
13. Letter from President Tate, 26 February 1960, in Faculty Minutes.
14. Quillian 1979.

15. Quillian 1979.

16. Quillian 1979, 3.

17. Quillian 1979. Mr. Perkins died on 15 September 1960, and Mrs. Perkins then took his place as a member of the Board of Trustees and a direct supporter of Perkins School of Theology and of its Dean.

18. Quillian 1979, 2.

19. Attachment to Faculty Minutes, 11 September 1963.

20. Attachment to Faculty Minutes, 21 September 1962.

21. Attachment to Faculty Minutes, 21 September 1962.

22. "Report of the Dean to the Faculty," Lake Sharon Retreat, 29 September 1961; Quillian Papers.

23. "Report to the Perkins School of Theology Committee of the Board of Trustees of Southern Methodist University," October 1961.

24. Carbon copy of a document with no details given, dated 20 June 1960. Quillian Papers.

25. "Report of the Dean to the Faculty," Lake Sharon Retreat, 29 September 1961.

26. Trustee Minutes, 12 May 1964.

27. *Catalog,* 1960–61.

28. Quillian 1979.

29. *Catalog,* 1961–62; Faculty Minutes, 11 September 1963.

30. *Catalog,* 1961–62.

31. Faculty Minutes, 13 January 1961.

32. *Catalog,* 1962–63.

33. Faculty Minutes, 29 March 1963.

34. *Catalog,* 1963–64; Faculty Minutes, 11 September 1963.

35. I have not been able to establish whether this was the first of the "Bishops in Residence" programs in seminaries. If it was not the first, it was assuredly one of the earliest.

36. *Catalog,* 1965–66.

37. *Catalog,* 1965–66; Trustee Minutes, 12 May 1964.

38. Material from Quillian 1981.

39. Minutes, Board of Governors, 11 September 1964. This was one of Dean Quillian's appointments made without faculty consultation. Although primarily an administrator, Dr. Carleton also did some teaching. The necessity of secrecy in the appointment process, as well as the administrative nature of the appointment, Dean Quillian believed, justified his decision not to consult the faculty.

40. *Catalog,* 1965–66; Trustee Minutes, 7 May 1965.

41. *Catalog,* 1966–67.

42. Trustee Minutes, 4 November 1960.

43. *Catalog,* 1967–68; Trustee Minutes, 5 May 1967.

44. The Elsa Cook Award is chosen by members of the senior class, and the award is made at the Spring Banquet. See *Catalog,* 1979–80, 105.

45. *Catalog,* 1969–70; Faculty Minutes, 2 February 1969, 9 May 1969.

46. Senate Conference Minutes, 27 September 1969.

47. "Report of the Dean to the Faculty," Lake Sharon Retreat, 29 September 1961, 1.
48. Faculty Retreat Minutes, 30 September 1961.
49. Faculty Minutes, 9 November 1962.
50. Faculty Minutes, 7 December 1962.
51. Faculty Minutes, Fall 1964.
52. Faculty Minutes, 12 February 1965.
53. *Catalog,* 1964–65.
54. I can rely on my memory, which is vivid concerning this event. Faculty Minutes for 10 May 1966 confirm the decision.
55. Faculty Minutes, 10 May 1966.
56. Faculty Minutes, 10 May 1966.
57. Attachment to Faculty Minutes, 10 February 1967.
58. Faculty Minutes, 9 October 1966, 9 February 1968.
59. Faculty Minutes, 6 September 1966.
60. *Catalog,* 1959–60 and 1963–64.
61. *Catalog,* 1963–64.
62. *Catalog,* 1963–64.
63. Itals. mine. *Catalog,* 1965–66.
64. *Catalog,* 1965–66.
65. *Catalog,* 1966–67.
66. *Catalog,* 1969–70.
67. *Graduate School of Humanities and Sciences Catalog,* 1965–66, 25.
68. *Catalog,* 1971–72.
69. Attachment to Faculty Minutes, 16 April 1971; also 1979 "Self-Study," Appendix.
70. Attachment to Faculty Minutes, 16 April 1971.
71. 1979 "Self-Study," Appendix.
72. At a special dinner honoring his work at Bridwell, just before going to the University of Texas, Austin, he made this point of view quite clear.
73. My principal source is Quillian 1981. See also Turner 1969.
74. "Proposed Policy Concerning Rare Books in Bridwell Library," 9 May 1980, proposed to and approved by the SMU Board of Trustees; Turner Papers. Also see Hazel 1989, 11.
75. Ortmayer 1963, 3.
76. Turner 1963a, 27.
77. Ortmayer 1963, 3.
78. Turner 1963d, 43–45.
79. Turner 1963b, 47.
80. Turner 1963c, 48.
81. Report of Decherd Turner, Attachment to Faculty Minutes, 16 April 1971. Also see Hazel 1989, 11.
82. "Proposed Policy Concerning Rare Books." 9 May 1980, Turner Papers. The list is included in the Appendix.
83. Turner 1961, 486.

84. J. Grimes 1978, 40.

85. *Dallas Times Herald*, 10 May 1972, SMU Archives.

86. Attachment to Faculty Minutes, 27 November 1963.

87. Attachment to Faculty Minutes, 6 February 1964.

Chapter 11

1. *Americana Annual 1971*, s.v. "United States."

2. J. Grimes 1978, 41.

3. J. Grimes 1978, 41.

4. *Campus*, 1 May 1969.

5. *Campus*, 2 May 1969.

6. *Americana Annual 1971*, s.v. "Education."

7. Since I participated in this project, I can attest even now to my feeling of hopelessness and almost despair.

8. *Dallas Morning News*, 6 May 1970. In SMU Archives.

9. Tate 1978a, 60.

10. *Dallas Times Herald*, 10 May 1972. SMU Archives.

11. *Dallas Morning News*, 11 May 1972. SMU Archives.

12. Tate 1978b, 61.

13. Attachment to Faculty Minutes, 8 December 1967.

14. Faculty Minutes, 15 March 1968.

15. Attachment to Faculty Minutes, 18 April 1969.

16. "A Sketch Profile of Perkins School of Theology." Dean's Report to the Board of Trustees, 1980.

17. Attachment to Faculty Minutes, 18 April 1969.

18. Faculty Minutes, 9 May 1969.

19. Senate Minutes, 16 May 1969. (From this point forward to the mid-1980s, the Minutes are primarily from the Senate. Faculty Minutes tended to cover routine matters of admission to candidacy, approving candidates for graduation, and the like.)

20. The earliest edition is dated 12 September 1969.

21. All quotations are from the original document. Changes were made over the years in details, but the essential design remained intact for over a decade.

22. Some administrators were voting members; others had no vote.

23. Pioneer student senators were Roy May, Jim Noland, Fred Haustein, Mel Morgan, Mike Harper, John Bengel, Benny McGee, Garry Ritzky, Guillermo Chavez, Keith Thompson, Rex Shepperd, Carol Cotton. It is interesting that only one was a female, a fact which soon changed as the number of women in the student body increased. Additional committee members included Roger Loyd, Carl Clarke, Joe Eldridge, Howard Savage, Bob Hayes, Alice Flint, Joe Reams, Mark Matheny, David Harrington, Cindy Calderon (spouse), John Holbert, and Rick Hebert. Leighton Farrell and Wilfred Bailey were alumni representatives.

24. I have tried throughout this account not to allow my memory of events to be the sole source of information. The two factors which follow note 25 are not fully recorded

(if at all), and in this cases my memory is quite vivid, and I think accurate. I do not mean to imply that I present an unprejudiced view of anything unless I do it in the words of someone else. I am certain that some events would receive a different interpretation were someone else writing the record!

25. Allen 1981, 18.

26. Allen 1981, 19–20.

27. Allen 1981, 20–22.

28. Allen 1981, 22.

29. *Catalog,* 1970–71. The curriculum was introduced in 1970.

30. "Course Descriptions," *Catalog,* 1970–71; Attachment to Senate Minutes.

31. "Course Descriptions," *Catalog,* 1970–71. A few years after this attempt to do a course called "Practical Theology," we developed a Doctor of Ministry seminar with the same name, with John Deschner providing the basic structure. This was for me one of the most exciting courses I ever taught. It consisted basically of a theological critique of the church's life and ministry, drawing heavily on the case study approach.

32. "Course Descriptions," *Catalog,* 1970–71.

33. Attachment to Senate Minutes, 9 March 1972.

34. *Catalog,* 1973–74.

35. The Bachelor of Divinity name was changed to Master of Theology in 1969, and a year later provisions were adopted to make it possible for the B.D. diploma to be exchanged for a retroactive M.Th. See Attachment to Senate Minutes, 4 May 1970.

36. *Catalog,* 1970–71, p.45.

37. See *Catalogs,* 1976–66, 1977–78, and 1979–80.

38. Ward 1981, 9.

39. Attachment to Senate Minutes, 18 April 1969.

40. Attachment to Senate Minutes, 18 April 1969.

41. Quillian 1981. Also see a memorandum addressed to the faculty concerning the importance of worship, 18 September 1969. Bridwell Archives.

42. Senate Minutes, 14 September 1973; *Catalog,* 1974–75.

43. Senate Minutes, 25 January 1974; *Catalog,* 1974–75.

44. *Catalog,* 1975–76.

45. Senate Minutes, 21 March 1980.

46. "ATS Institutional Self-Study," 1980, 13.

47. "ATS Institutional Self-Study," 1980, 15.

48. "Report to the Senate," 22 September 1978, Attachment to Senate Minutes.

49. "Report from the Task Force on the Ministry Core," Attachment to Senate Minutes.

50. *Catalog,* 1973–74, 52. See also Senate Minutes, 4 May 1972.

51. "ATS Study," 26–29 October 1980. Quillian Papers.

52. Attachment to Senate Minutes, 16 March 1981.

53. These statistics are taken from the ATS Institutional Self-Study done by Perkins, 1980. In other instances I have used catalog data.

54. ATS Institutional Self-Study done by Perkins, 1980.

55. *Catalog,* 1979–80, 108–09.

56. "Self-Evaluation, 1979," Prepared for the Southern Association of Colleges and Universities; *Catalog, 1979–80.*

57. *Catalog, 1979–80.*

58. *Catalog, 1970–71;* Senate Minutes, 11 September 1970.

59. Senate Minutes, 16 April 1971.

60. *Catalog, 1971–72;* Senate Minutes, 2 May 1971; 9 September 1971; 9 December 1971; and 13 April 1972.

61. Senate Minutes, 15 September 1972.

62. Senate Minutes, 9 May 1972.

63. Senate Minutes, 15 September 1972. So far as I can find, this is the first use of the term "Bishop in Residence." It is probable that it was actually used earlier than 1972 but was not recorded.

64. Senate Minutes, 15 September 1972.

65. Senate Minutes, 15 September 1972.

66. Senate Minutes, 28 January 1972.

67. A field unit consisted of three to eight students in geographical proximity who met together weekly. Field Instructors were local church clergy who worked directly with the student.

68. Senate Minutes, 13 October 1972.

69. Senate Minutes, 4 May 1973.

70. Senate Minutes, 19 November 1972.

71. Senate Minutes, 14 March 1973.

72. Senate Minutes, 14 September 1973.

73. Senate Minutes, 6 May 1974.

74. Terry 1978, xxvi. Additional information from President Tate.

75. *Catalog, 1974–75.*

76. Senate Minutes, 14 February 1975.

77. *Catalog, 1974–75.*

78. Senate Conference Minutes, 26–27 September 1975; Senate Minutes, 19 October 1975.

79. *Catalog, 1975–76;* "Dean's Report to the Senate," Attachment to Senate Minutes, 9 May 1975.

80. Information from the Pastoral Care Office, Highland Park United Methodist Church.

81. Information from M.S.M. office.

82. Dean's Report, 9 May 1975.

83. Senate Minutes, 10 October 1975.

84. *Catalog, 1975–76.*

85. Senate Minutes, 12 December 1975.

86. *Catalog, 1976–77;* Senate Minutes, 7 May 1976, 8 October 1976.

87. *Catalog, 1977–78;* Senate Minutes, 9 May 1977, 26 August 1977.

88. *Catalog, 1978–79;* Senate Minutes, 27 January 1978, 24 February 1978, 14 April 1978.

89. Senate Minutes, 11 May 1979, 13 October 1978.

90. Attachment to Senate Minutes, 20 April 1979. One woman had already been considered but was not invited to join the faculty.
91. Attachment to Senate Minutes, 20 April 1979.
92. Attachment to Senate Minutes, 7 May 1979.
93. *Catalog,* 1979–80.
94. Dean's Annual Report, 1980, Quillian Papers; Senate Minutes, 26 October 1979.
95. Dean's Annual Report, 1980.
96. Dean's Annual Report, 1980.
97. *Catalog,* 1980–81.
98. *Catalog,* 1980–81.
99. Senate Minutes, 26 October 1979; *Catalog,* 1980–81.
100. Senate Minutes, 9 May 1980; *Catalog,* 1980–81.
101. *Catalog,* 1980–81.
102. Senate Minutes, 14 February 1980.
103. *Catalog,* 1981–82; Dean's Report, 1980 (Attachment to Senate Minutes, 8 May 1981); Senate Minutes, 8 May 1981.

Chapter 12

1. Attachment to Senate Minutes, 7 December 1979.
2. See Chapter 11.
3. "Hispanic" is a general term now widely recognized as the most appropriate to refer to all persons of Spanish descent. The largest group of Hispanics in the United States is Mexican-American, but increasingly Cubans have come to the country, and there are Puerto Ricans, Mexicans, Central Americans, and so on. Since the Perkins program is largely directed toward Mexican-Americans, we will often use that term. See Miranda 1987, 188.
4. *Catalogs,* 1916–17, 1917–18, 1918–19; Trustee Minutes, 10 June 1919.
5. These dates come from the Alumni listing.
6. See Nañez 1981, esp. 101ff. See also Lafontaine 1978, 10–11. See also Sylvest 1987, 53–61.
7. Cooke 1973, 36–38.
8. For more information see Nañez 1981, 82–84, and Nañez 1977, esp. 63ff.
9. Barton 1978, 20. See also Nañez 1981, 113–116.
10. *Texas Christian Advocate,* 19 September 1907, 10.
11. Barton 1978, 20; Barton 1980.
12. Senate Conference Minutes, 27 September 1969.
13. Attachment to Senate Conference Minutes, 11–12 October 1974.
14. Conversation with Roy Barton; see also Barton 1978, 21; also "The Mexican-American Course of Study . . ."
15. "Training for Ministry," 21–22.
16. *Five Centuries . . .,*1987 contains the results of the symposium.
17. "Programa de Administradores Laicos," 15–17 April 1988.
18. "The Mexican-American Program."

19. The term "black" was the designation used nationwide for at least two decades, until in 1988, Democratic Presidential candidate the Rev. Jesse Jackson used and recommended the term "African-American." One cannot be certain whether it will prevail, though it has become quite quickly a much-used term.

20. These dates come from the SMU Archives.

21. How well I remember the TCU-SMU game at Daniel Myers Stadium in Fort Worth, with police officers at every entrance. Threats had been received on Jerry Levias, and the game was tense not only because it decided SMU's ranking in the Southwest Conference that football season, but also because there was always the possibility that the threats would be carried out. They were not.

22. So far as I have found, no record of this event has been published. My source of information is Quillian 1981.

23. These were ambitious aims and were not all realized immediately. See document dated May 1969, in Quillian Papers; also *Dallas Times Herald,* 4 May 1969.

24. Senate Minutes, 3 May 1969.

25. Senate Minutes, 10 April 1970.

26. Senate Minutes, 1 April 1974.

27. Report of Dean, 1973–74, attached to Senate Minutes.

28. Senate Minutes, 10 May 1974.

29. Ward 1981, 13.

30. I cannot be certain these statistics are accurate. My source consists of student directories for the year indicated, which do not include additions for the second semester.

31. None of these statistics include native Africans.

32. "The Perkins Report, 1978," pages not numbered.

33. Senate Minutes, 14 March 1975.

34. Senate Minutes, 15 February 1980.

35. This count is taken from the 1980–81 Student Directory, and its accuracy cannot be guaranteed.

36. My life has been greatly enriched by dealing with students from other countries. The first was D. G. Liu, in 1950, who returned to the People's Republic of China in 1950 and did not surface again until the end of the Cultural Revolution. At that time he re-established contact with the school. Some of my last students were Norman Hudson, now a bishop in the Methodist Church of South Africa; Daniel Brewer, a prominent leader of the church in Liberia; and Jong Chul Chang, who teaches at the Methodist Seminary, in Seoul, Korea. The last three were all D.Min. students.

37. Minutes of the Consultation, Howard Grimes, Reporter.

38. Minutes of the Consultation, Howard Grimes, Reporter.

39. Senate Minutes, 14 February 1975.

40. Senate Minutes, 9 May 1975.

41. Senate Minutes, 23 April 1976.

42. Senate Minutes, 12 November 1976.

43. See "Community Life Committee and Minority Concerns," Senate Minutes, 18 February 1977, 11 March 1977.

44. Although the discussion occurred at the Senate meeting on 11 March 1977, the original document was amended and dated 14 March 1977.
45. Senate Conference Minutes, 17 September 1977.
46. Attachment to Senate Minutes, 11 April 1980; Senate Minutes, 10 April 1981.
47. *Catalog,* 1915–16.
48. *Catalog,* 1917–18. How they qualified for a certificate with only one year of work is not known. Ordinarily it was the completion of the theological program that caused the certificate to be awarded.
49. *Catalog,* 1923–24.
50. *Catalog,* 1924–25.
51. *Catalog,* 1925–26.
52. *Catalog,* 1927–28.
53. *Catalog,* 1920–21.
54. Attachment to Senate Minutes, December 7 1979.
55. Will 1982, 2:290.
56. Will 1982, 2:290.
57. Will 1982, 2:295.
58. According to a statistic (in Peck 1975, 39) furnished by Robert Thornburg (then executive of the Division of Ordained Ministry, Board of Higher Education and Ministry, United Methodist Church), reported in a memorandum from Phyllis Bird to the faculty, attached to the Senate Minutes of October 1975.
59. Attachment to the Senate Minutes, 7 December 1979.
60. Perkins Student Handbook, 1986 edition.
61. Information from Linn Caraway (formerly Richardson), Director of Recruitment and Admissions, Perkins School of Theology.
62. Senate Minutes, 9 May 1975.
63. Senate Retreat Minutes, 26–27 September 1975.

Chapter 13

1. Niebuhr 1956, 107.
2. Niebuhr 1956, 6.
3. The conflict between moderates and fundamentalists in the Southern Baptist Convention and the effort, sometimes successful, for the fundamentalists to take over the seminaries of that body, have demonstrated that some churches that we tended to think of as relatively stable are not free of the conflict of which I speak. Perhaps even a greater surprise was the surfacing of disagreement within the Roman Catholic Church after Vatican II and its continuation today. The same kind of conflict is evident in the Episcopal Church over questions relating to ordination of women.
4. Chapter 3.
5. Chapter 3.
6. Terry 1978, xxiii.
7. Terry 1978, xxiv.
8. This presentation is based on a document in the Quillian Papers giving the details of

the event.

9. In "Controversy" file, Quillian Papers.

10. First carried in the *Catalog* in 1972–73. It was dropped for a few years and included again, in 1981–82, without change. See Senate Minutes, 16 April 1971, for draft statement, and Senate Minutes, 7 May 1971, for the final form of the statement as adopted.

11. Dean Quillian, in his careful, analytical manner, has provided a complete chronology of the events, even to the exact time of many of them. In "Controversy" file, Quillian Papers.

12. Quillian narrative of controversy (see note 11), 6.

13. Information furnished by SMU's business office, 1988.

14. Quillian 1981.

15. The letter is in the "Controversy" file, Quillian Papers.

16. "Controversy" file, Quillian Papers.

17. "Controversy" file, Quillian Papers.

18. "Controversy" file, Quillian Papers.

19. *Dallas Morning News*, 2 November 1971.

20. "The Seminary and the Church," *Texas Methodist*, 14 January 1972.

21. The Dean's summary in the "Controversy" file, Quillian Papers. The event was exaggerated beyond recognition. For example, the *Arizona Republic* carried this statement in its 31 October 1971 issue: "A Methodist minister said yesterday that Southern Methodist University is offering a course in 'raw' pornography to its ministerial students." (A UPI release.) See "Controversy" file, Quillian Papers.

22. See Evans 1971 for his own account. The context of the service is the experimental worship atmosphere that prevailed at the time. Some rather bizarre things were done in the spirit of working on more meaningful forms of worship.

23. Letter in "Controversy" file, Quillian Papers.

24. Many of us resent the fact that this group does not consider the rest of us "evangelical" if we do not accept the theological position which they espouse. The truth is that most of that position is orthodox catholic Christianity. Whether they are setting up a "straw man" in the form of the drift of Methodism in the late nineteenth and early twentieth century toward German liberalism is a matter of opinion. That there is some truth in their accusations seems obvious, but that the truth is exaggerated seems also without doubt.

25. Robb 1975.

26. Senate Minutes, 13 October 1978.

27. Senate Minutes, 13 October 1978.

28. In "Controversy" file, Quillian Papers.

29. I have no reason to believe that the three applications were not legitimate. It is possible that they were "test cases" by the Metropolitan Community Church, but this information did not come out in any of the public discussion.

30. Senate Minutes, 9 May 1980.

31. Senate Minutes, 15 May 1980.

32. 9 May 1980 document, 13 May document, 19 May document; "Controversy" file, Quillian Papers.

33. Senate Minutes, 10 November 1980.

34. Senate Minutes, 20 March 1981.

35. See attachment to Senate Minutes, 12 December 1969; also Senate Conference Minutes, 10 October 1980.

36. Senate Minutes, 10 November 1980; *Catalog,* 1972–73, 23.

37. Senate Minutes, 20 March 1981; *Catalog,* 1973–74.

38. Attachment to Senate Minutes, 8–9 October 1971; *Catalog,* 1973–74.

39. Dean's Report, 1973–74, included in Senate Minutes.

40. *Catalog,* 1978–79.

41. Ward 1981, 9.

Chapter 14

1. *Catalog,* 1979–80.

2. *Catalog,* 1981–82. I have not listed the members of this faculty since the sheer number would be too great. It has, in fact, been difficult to find ways of listing the seminary's regular faculty.

3. Information from Rosa Marina Barton of the Intern Office.

4. L. F. Sensabaugh, Director of Religious Education for Highland Park Methodist Church and Director of Religious Activities for SMU for many years, deserves at least a footnote in this account. It was partly his insistence on the legitimacy and his recognition of lay workers on church staffs that paved the way for later developments. Pioneers have a way of being forgotten, and "Dr. S," as he was affectionately known, is certainly one of those pioneers.

5. Richard Cookson, formerly with the United Methodist Board of Discipleship, was also a regular participant in the seminars for many years.

6. Attachment to Senate Minutes, 11 April 1980

7. *Book of Discipline,* 1968, 149–150.

8. As of 1989, there still had not occurred such a move in spite of the growing importance in the Roman Catholic, Episcopal, and other churches.

9. *Book of Discipline,* 1988, 192–193. The section on the Diaconal Ministry now occupies more than fourteen pages.

10. *Catalog,* 1981–82.

11. See any of the catalogs of this period.

12. See *Catalog,* 1981–82, for a more extensive description of these and other activities of Continuing Education.

13. Attachment to Senate Minutes, 23 January 1970.

14. Attachment to Senate Minutes, May 1973.

15. Minutes, Board of Governors, 6 February 1966.

16. Quillian 1981 and Quillian Papers.

17. Dean's Report, 1973–74.

18. ATS Report, 26–29 October 1980, 15.

19. ATS Report, 26–29 October 1980, 11–15.

20. *Catalog,* 1980–81.

21. Dean's Report, 1980–81, an Attachment to the Senate Minutes.

22. This incomplete list is derived from the Senate Minutes and attachments for 8 December 1978, 8 October 1966, 12 September 1974, 11–12 October 1974, and 11 April 1980; also from the Dean's Report for 1978–79.

23. Attachment to Senate Conference Minutes, 11–12 October 1974.

24. Data from the SMU Business Office.

25. Dean Quillian's report to the Perkins Trustees Committee, 1980; Quillian 1981.

26. Quillian 1981.

27. Quillian 1981.

28. *Book of Discipline,* 1972, 277–278.

29. Attachment to Senate Conference Minutes, 8–9 October 1971.

30. Report of the Dean to the Faculty, 1977–78; attachment to Senate Minutes.

31. Dean's Report to the Committee on Faculty, 1973–74, 5; Quillian Papers.

32. Ward 1981, 8–14.

33. See Grimes 1981, 25–26.

34. Faculty Minutes, 4 November 1960.

35. Attachment to Senate Minutes, 8 May 1970.

36. Attachment to Senate Minutes, 8 May 1970, 2.

37. See, e.g., Senate Minutes, 13 May 1964 and 23 January 1970.

38. *Catalog,* 1965–66 and 1975–76.

39. Information from Prof. William R. Farmer.

40. Information from Prof. William R. Farmer.

41. Deschner 1975, xv–xvi.

42. Deschner 1975, xvi–xvii.

43. See Bylaws of "The Worship Committee," 1970, Quillian Papers. There have no doubt been changes since that time but this document describes the work of the Committee.

44. The year 1935 has recently been used as the founding date of the Seminary Singers. Apparently, this was the year that Mrs. Kate Warnick began either a quartet or double quartet, and therefore this organization is a predecessor of the Seminary Singers. Although I do not usually trust my memory, in this case I do. I joined the Seminary Singers under the leadership of Dr. Fred Gealy in 1939, and there was, so far as I can remember, no group which formed the nucleus of the new group. I do remember that Mrs. Warnick mentioned a group she had led at an earlier time. My recollection is that there were fifteen original Singers members. One of them was Dr. Durwood Fleming, later President of Southwestern University and after his retirement from that institution on the Development staff of Perkins School of Theology. Had it not been for him, my bass would have been more discordant than it actually was!

45. *SMU 71,* 8 February 1971.

46. Senate Minutes, 10 April 1970.

47. *SMU 71,* 8 February 1971.

48. Published by Westminster Press, 1948.

49. Data and dates contributed by Roger Deschner, Richey Hogg, and Lloyd Pfautsch. Deschner and Pfautsch each have complete files of the annually printed programs. For membership of the authorizing committee, see the Perkins *Catalog,* 1959–60, 10.
50. See "Besides the Books: A Guide to Life in the Perkins Community," 1969, 34.
51. "Perkins Student Handbook," 1986–87; pages unnumbered.
52. See "The Perkins Report," 1978; also see "Perkins Student Handbook," 1986–87.
53. *Catalog,* 1981–82, 109–110.
54. Attachment to Senate Minutes, May1981.

Epilogue I

1. *Perkins Perspective,* Summer 1981, 1, 5. Also see Kirby Papers.
2. Information in this section, unless otherwise noted, is drawn from the Kirby Papers and from Catalogs for the years 1981–82 through 1990–91.
3. *Dallas Morning News,* 20 November 1983, B16.
4. *Perkins Perspective,* Spring 1984, 1.
5. *Perkins Perspective,* Spring 1984, 1.
6. *Dallas Morning News,* 26 February 1987, A1.
7. *Dallas Morning News,* 30 May 1987, A1. Also see *Daily Campus,* 7 June 1987, 1.
8. See Deschner 1989, the text of a statement by John Deschner at the memorial service for Albert Outler, at Highland Park United Methodist Church in Dallas, 7 September 1989.
9. Senate Minutes, 20 February 1981.
10. Senate Minutes, 16 April 1982.
11. Senate Minutes, 16 April 1982; attachment from Committee to Study the Curriculum, dated 13 April 1982.
12. Senate Minutes, 16 April 1982.
13. *Catalog,* 1990–91, 15–16.
14. Perkins Self-Study, 1990, 2. (In Kirby Papers)
15. Perkins Self-Study, 1990, 2.
16. Perkins Self-Study, 1990, 3–5.
17. Perkins Self-Study, 1990, Appendix 21.
18. Perkins Self-Study, 1990, Appendix 22 with attachments.
19. Kirby Papers.
20. Letter in Quillian Papers.
21. Letter in Quillian Papers.

Bibliography

Allen, Joseph L.

1981 "The Policy Process at Perkins in the Quillian Years." *Perkins Journal* (Spring): 15–23.

Bailey, Wilfred.

1969 "Will Success Spoil Perkins?" *Perkins School of Theology Journal* (Winter): 13–15.

Barton, Roy D.

1978 "Training for Ministry." *e/sa Forum-41* (June): 19-23.

1980 "The Mexican-American Program at Perkins School of Theology." Dallas: Perkins School of Theology. English and Spanish.

Beaty, John O.

1951 *The Iron Curtain over America*. Dallas: Wilkinson Publishing.

Bishop, Horace.

n.d. "Semi-Centennial Sermon." In *Sketches from the Life of Dr. Horace Bishop*, edited by Ralph Masterson. N.p.

Blair, John Edward.

1926 "The Founding of Southern Methodist University." M.A. thesis, Southern Methodist University.

Book of Discipline.

1968 *The Book of Discipline of The United Methodist Church, 1968*. Nashville: United Methodist Publishing House.

1972 *The Book of Discipline of The United Methodist Church, 1972*. Nashville: United Methodist Publishing House.

1984 *The Book of Discipline of the United Methodist Church, 1984*. Nashville: United Methodist Publishing House.

1988   *The Book of Discipline of The United Methodist Church, 1988.*
          Nashville: United Methodist Publishing House, 1988.

Bradfield, W. D.
1925   "Our Benefactors: Mr. and Mrs. Harper Kirby." *Southern Meth-
          odist University Ex-Student's Magazine* (Jan.): 4, 16.

Brown, Ray Hyer.
1957   *Robert Stewart Hyer: The Man I Knew.* Salado: Anson Jones
          Press.

Bulletin.
          Bulletin, School of Theology, SMU. See *Catalog.*

Campbell, James.
1906   "The Southwestern University History." In *Texas Methodist
          Education Convention: Proceedings and Addresses*, edited by
          John M. Moore and John R. Nelson. Dallas: Blaylock Publishing
          Company.

Campus.
          The SMU student newspaper; available on microfilm in Fondren
          Library, SMU. Title history: *SMU Times* (1915), *Campus* (1916–
          22, 1937–38, 1940–41, 1943–45, 1946), *Semi-weekly Campus*
          (1923–37, 1938–40, 1941–43), *SMU Campus* (1945–46, 1946–
          69), *SMU Daily Campus* (1981–84), *Daily Campus* (1969–81,
          1984–).

Catalog.
          Catalog, School of Theology, SMU (1915–45); and *Catalog*,
          Perkins School of Theology, SMU (1946–). Also named *Bulletin.*

Cooke, Alistair.
1973   *America.* New York: Alfred A. Knopf.

Cuninggim, Merrimon.
1952a   "Dean's Page." *Perkins School of Theology Journal* (Winter): 3.
1952b   "The State of the School." *Perkins School of Theology Journal*
          (Spring): 3–6, 9.
1953a   "A Commencement Address." *Perkins School of Theology
          Journal* (Spring): 3–9.
1953b   "Dean's Page." *Perkins School of Theology Journal* (Winter): 3.
1956   "Integration in Professional Education: The Story of Perkins,
          Southern Methodist University." In *Racial Desegregation and*

Integration, edited by Ira De A. Reid. *Annals of the American Academy of Political and Social Science* 304: 109–115.

1960   "Blueprint for Breakthrough." *Christian Century* 77 (20 April): 485–487.

1987   "Far-Off Things and Battles Long Ago." Speech given at Alumni Luncheon, Ministers' Week, 4 Feb. 1987. (Available from the Office of the Dean, Perkins School of Theology.)

Papers   Merrimon Cuninggim Papers, Perkins School of Theology Archives, Bridwell Library.

Davis, Wesley C.

1953   "The New Curriculum." *Perkins School of Theology Journal* (Spring): 10–16.

Deschner, John.

1975   "Albert Cook Outler: A Biographical Memoir." In *Our Common Heritage as Christians: Essays in Honor of Albert C. Outler*, edited by John Deschner, Leroy T. Howe, and Klaus Penzel, ix–xxi. New York: Oxford University Press.

1984   "Where Honor Rests."*Perkins Journal* (Spring): 27–30.

1989   "Remember in Christ Albert Outler." *Perkins Journal* (October 1989): 9–10.

Dobbs, Hoyt M.

Papers   Hoyt M. Dobbs Papers, Perkins School of Theology Archives, Bridwell Library.

"Education."

1971   *Americana Annual*.

Encyclopedia of World Methodism.

1974   Edited by Nolan B. Harmon. Nashville: United Methodist Publishing House.

Evans, J. Claude.

1971   "The Advent Celebration Service at SMU." December 1971. In "Controversy" file, Quillian Papers.

Five Centuries . . .

1987   *Five Centuries of Hispanic American Christianity 1492–1992*. Dallas: Hispanic Instructor Program, Perkins School of Theology.

Gambrell, Herbert.

1951   "The Way I Remember It." *Mustang* (Oct.): 18.

Goodloe, Robert W.

1951   "Welcome to Dean Merrimon Cuninggim and Dr. Albert C.
        Outler." *Perkins School of Theology Journal* (Fall): 3.

Grimes, Johnnie Marie, editor.

1978   *Willis M. Tate: Views and Interviews*. Dallas: SMU Press.

Grimes, Lewis Howard.

1951   *Cloud of Witnesses: A History of First Methodist Church,
        Houston*. Houston: First Methodist Church.

1954   "Is Being Brotherly Subversive?" *Perkins School of Theology
        Journal* (Spring): 3–4.

1981   "The 'Quillian Years': With Appreciation and with a Look to the
        Future." *Perkins Journal* (Spring): 25–31.

1983   "How I Became What I Am as a Christian Religious Educator." In
        Modern Masters of Religious Education, edited by Marilyn Mayr,
        135–159. Birmingham, Ala.: Religious Education Press.

1986   "The Perkins 40th Story, 1946–1986." Dallas: Perkins School of
        Theology, SMU.

Hackney, Sheldon.

1969   *Populism to Progressivism in Alabama*. Princeton, N.J.: Princeton
        University Press.

Harnack, Adolf.

1957   *What Is Christianity?* Translated by Thomas Bailey Saunders;
        introduction by Rudolf Bultmann. New York: Harper & Brothers.

Hawk, Eugene B.

1947   "Why This Journal?" *Perkins School of Theology Journal* (Fall):
        3.

1949   "Expanding Program of the University." *Perkins School of
        Theology Journal* (Spring): 3.

Papers   Eugene B. Hawk Papers, Perkins School of Theology Archives,
         Bridwell Library.

Hazel, Michael, compiler.

1989   "Special Collections in the Libraries at Southern Methodist
        University." Dallas: SMU Publications.

Henderson, Gerald D.

1966   "Vanderbilt University." *Encyclopedia Americana*.

Henning, Albert F., compiler.

1934?   "The Story of Southern Methodist University, 1910–1930." N.p.
         Typed two-volume manuscript; in Fondren Library.

Hogg, William Richey.

1945   *Sixty-five Years in the Seminaries: A History of the Interseminary
         Movement.* N.p.

1952   *Ecumenical Foundations.* New York: Harper & Brothers.

Howe, Leroy T.

1982   "Beginnings in Practical Theology: An Account of a Journey."
         Perkins Journal (Summer): 22–27.

Hyer, Robert S.

1915   "Dallas and the University." Manuscript, written by Dr. Hyer in
         1915 but not made public until after his death; copied by Mrs.
         Hyer. Copies in the SMU Archive and the Archives of the School
         of Theology, Bridwell Library.

Irwin, William A., editor.

1953   "Quadrangle News." *Perkins School of Theology Journal* (Fall):
         19.

Johnson, Doris Miller.

1966   *Golden Prologue to the Future.* Dallas: Highland Park Methodist
         Church.

Kern, Paul B.

1921   "What We Are Driving At: A Little Talk Where We Take You
         into Our Confidence." *Service* 1, no. 4: 3.

Papers   Paul B. Kern Papers, Perkins School of Theology Archives,
         Bridwell Library.

Kilgore, James A.

Papers   James A. Kilgore Papers, Perkins School of Theology Archives,
         Bridwell Library.

Kirby, James E.

1987   "A Vision of the Future: Looking into the 90's." Copy filed with
         Faculty Minutes, 18 Sept. 1987.

Papers   James E. Kirby Papers, Perkins School of Theology Archives,
         Bridwell Library.

Lafontaine, Edith.

1978   "An Image of the Past." *e/sa Forum-41* (June): 10–11.

Lee, Umphrey.

1947   "The Perkins School of Theology and the University." *Perkins School of Theology Journal* (Fall): 4–5.

Logan, Rayford W.

1957   "The United States Supreme Court and the Segregation Issue." *Annals of the American Academy of Political and Social Science* (March): 10–16.

Loggie, Mary Basham.

1967   "Joseph Sterling Bridwell." M.A. thesis, Midwestern University, Wichita Falls, Texas.

Love, Joe Brown.

1930   "The Interseminary Movement in the United States." B.D. thesis, Southern Methodist University.

McCulloh, Gerald O.

1980   *Ministerial Education in the American Methodist Movement.* Nashville: United Methodist Board of Higher Education and Ministry, Division of Ordained Ministry.

Martin, Paul E.

1973   "The Humanness of the Ministry: Some Informal Reflections." Typescript, 1973, in Paul E. Martin Papers.

Papers   Paul E. Martin Papers, Bridwell Library

Martin, William C.

1965   "The Origin of the School of Theology of Southern Methodist University." Manuscript, 10 July 1965, in William C. Martin Papers.

Papers   William C. Martin Papers, Archives, Bridwell Library.

Miranda, Jesse.

1987   "Toward a Hispanic Pastoral." In *Five Centuries of Hispanic American Christianity 1492–1992.* Dallas: Hispanic Instructor Program, Perkins School of Theology.

Moore, John M.

1948   *Life and I: Or Sketches and Comments.* Nashville: Parthenon Press.

Papers   John M. Moore Papers, Archives, Bridwell Library.

Moore, John M., and John R. Nelson, editors.

1906   *Texas Methodist Education Convention: Proceedings and Addresses*. Dallas: Blaylock Publishing Company.

Mouzon, Edwin D.

Papers   Edwin D. Mouzon Papers, Archives, Bridwell Library.

"Mrs. Warnick Honored."

1954   *Perkins School of Theology Journal* (Spring): 19.

Mustang.

Alumni magazine, SMU. Variously named: *Mustang* (1920, 1936–40, 1950–84), *Southern Methodist University Alumni Quarterly* (1922–23), *Southern Methodist University Ex-students' Magazine* (1924–27), *SMU Ex-students' Bulletin* (1947–48), *SMU Alumni Bulletin* (1948–50), *SMU Alumnus* (1950), *SMU Mustang* (1985–87), *SMU Magazine* (1987–).

Nail, Olin W., editor.

1961   *History of Texas Methodism, 1900–1960*. Austin: Capital Printing Co.

Nañez, Alfredo.

1977   "Methodism Among the Spanish-speaking People in Texas and New Mexico." In *One in the Lord: A History of Ethnic Minorities in the South Central Jurisdiction, The United Methodist Church*, edited by Walter N. Vernon, 50–94. Oklahoma City: Commission on Archives and History, South Central Jurisdiction, United Methodist Church.

1981   *Historia de la Conferencia Rio Grande de la Iglesia Metodista Unida*. Dallas: Bridwell Library. Simultaneously published as *History of the Rio Grande Conference of the United Methodist Church*.

Niebuhr, H. Richard.

1956   *The Purpose of the Church and Its Ministry*. New York: Harper.

Ortmayer, Roger.

1963   "About This Issue." *Perkins School of Theology Journal* (Winter-Spring): 3.

Outler, Albert C.

Papers   Albert C. Outler Papers, Archives, Bridwell Library.

Packer, J. I.
1974   *"Fundamentalism" and the Word of God.* Grand Rapids: W. B.
        Eerdmans Publishing Co., 1958.

Peck, J. Richard.
1975   "Seminary Mergers: What Happened to the Plan?" *Interpreter* 19
        (Oct.): 36–39.

"A Plain Statement of Fact."
        No publication information, circa 1921; located in the Perkins
        School of Theology Archives, Bridwell Library.

Pope, W. Kenneth.
1976   *A Pope at Roam: The Confessions of a Bishop.* Dallas: The
        author.
Papers W. Kenneth Pope Papers, Archives, Bridwell Library.

Quebedeaux, Richard.
1974   *The Young Evangelicals.* New York: Harper & Row.

Quillian, Joseph D., Jr.
1961   "The Seminary for Tomorrow." *Perkins School of Theology
        Journal* (Spring): 33–38.
1979   "Concerning the Office of Dean of Perkins School of Theology."
        30 January 1979. In Quillian Papers.
1981   "Joseph D. Quillian, Jr.: A Video History Interview" (Parts I &
        II). 19 May 1981. Available at SMU Media Center.
Papers Joseph D. Quillian Papers, Perkins School of Theology Archives,
        Bridwell Library.

Rice, John A.
1920   *The Old Testament in the Life of Today.* New York: Macmillan.

Robb, Edmund W.
1975   "The Crisis of Theological Education in The United Methodist
        Church." Address to the Good News Convocation, Lake
        Junaluska, N. Car., 22 July 1975. Copy in "Controversy" file,
        Quillian Papers.

Roestline, Henry.
1966   "Scarritt College for Christian Workers." *Encyclopedia Ameri-
        cana.*

Rohlfs, Claus H.

1978   "A History of the Development of the Perkins Intern Program."
        Perkins Journal (Winter): 1–31.

Seay, Frank.

1925a   *An Outline for the Study of Old Testament Prophecy, Wisdom,
        and History.* Nashville: Publishing House of the M. E. Church,
        South.

1925b   *The Story of the Old Testament: A Primer of Old Testament
        Introduction.* 4th ed. Nashville: Cokesbury Press.

Selecman, Charles C.

Papers Charles C. Selecman Papers, Archives, Bridwell Library.

Slater, Oliver Eugene.

1988   *Oliver's Travels: One Bishop's Journey (A Chronological
        Account of the Comings and Goings of Oliver Eugene Slater,
        1906–).* Dallas: The author.

Spellmann, Norman W.

1979   *Growing a Soul: The Story of A. Frank Smith.* Dallas: SMU Press.

Sweet, William Warren.

Papers William Warren Sweet Papers, Archives, Bridwell Library.

Sylvest, Edwin E., Jr.

1987   "Rethinking the 'Discovery' of the Americas: A Provisional
        Historical-Theological Reflection." In *Five Centuries of Hispanic
        American Christianity 1492–1992.* Dallas: Hispanic Instructor
        Program, Perkins School of Theology.

Tate, Willis.

1960   "Letter to Ministers of The Methodist Church in the South Central
        Jurisdiction." 26 Feb. 1960. In Faculty Minutes, 26 Feb. 1960.
        Perkins School of Theology Archives, Bridwell Library.

1978a   "Kent State Memorial Service." Speech, Memorial Service in
        Perkins Chapel, May 6, 1970. In *Willis M. Tate: Views and
        Interviews*, edited by Johnnie Marie Grimes. Dallas: SMU Press.

1978b   "Shared Decision-Making." In *Willis M. Tate: Views and Inter-
        views*, edited by Johnnie Marie Grimes, 61–62. Dallas: SMU
        Press.

Terry, Marshall.

1978   "Introduction: Willis Tate, A Recollection of Character." In *Willis M. Tate: Views and Interviews*, edited by Johnnie Marie Grimes, xvii–xxvi. Dallas: SMU Press.

Texas Christian Advocate.

Weekly newspaper of Methodism in Texas. Microfilm and paper copy available in Bridwell Library. Publishing history: *Texas Christian Advocate and Brenham Advertiser* (1847), *Texas Christian Advocate* (1848), *Texas Wesleyan Banner* (1849–54), *Texas Christian Advocate* (1854–61, 1864–1931, 1949–60), *Southwestern Christian Advocate* (1932–49), *Texas Methodist* (1960–83), *United Methodist Reporter* (1983–present).

Thomas, Mary Martha Hosford.

1974   *Southern Methodist University: Founding and Early Years.* Dallas: SMU Press.

Turner, Decherd, Jr.

1951a   "From the Library." *Perkins School of Theology Journal* (Winter): 14.

1951b   "The Sadie and David Lefkowitz Collection of Judaica." *Perkins School of Theology Journal* (Fall): 16.

1952   "The Steindorff Collection." *Perkins School of Theology Journal* (Fall): 16.

1961   "Bridwell Library." In *History of Texas Methodism, 1900–1960*, edited by Olin W. Nail, 483–486. Austin: Capital Printing.

1963a   "A Bibliographic View of 'The Chronicle.'" *Perkins School of Theology Journal* (Winter-Spring): 24–30.

1963b   "First Aldine Dante." *Perkins School of Theology Journal* (Winter-Spring): 47.

1963c   "The Last Bishops' Bible." *Perkins School of Theology Journal* (Winter-Spring): 48.

1963d   "The Levi A. Olan Collection." *Perkins School of Theology Journal* (Winter-Spring): 42–46.

1969   "Incunabula and Bridwell Library." *Perkins School of Theology Journal* (Spring): 33–49.

1980   "Decherd Turner: A Video History Interview." 28 May 1980. Available at SMU Media Center.

Papers   Decherd Turner Papers, Archives, Bridwell Library.

Vernon, Walter N.

1961   "Christian Teaching in Local Churches." In *History of Texas Methodism, 1900–1960*, edited by Olin W. Nail, 112–141. Austin: Capital Printing.

1967   *Methodism Moves Across North Texas*. Dallas: Historical Society, North Texas Conference, Methodist Church.

1973   *Forever Building: The Life and Ministry of Paul E. Martin*. Dallas: Southern Methodist University Press.

Papers   Walter N. Vernon Papers, Archives, Bridwell Library.

Vernon, Walter N., Robert W. Sledge, Robert C. Monk, and Norman W. Spellmann.

1984   *The Methodist Excitement in Texas: A History*. Dallas: Texas United Methodist Historical Society.

Ward, James M.

1981   "Dean Quillian as Dean of the Perkins Faculty." *Perkins Journal* (Spring): 8–14.

Warnick, Kate.

Papers   Kate Warnick Papers, Archives, Bridwell Library.

Weiss, Winifred T., and Charles S. Proctor.

1971   *Umphrey Lee: A Biography*. Nashville: Abingdon Press.

White, James F.

1966   *Architecture at SMU: 50 Years and Buildings*. Dallas: Southern Methodist University Press.

Who's Who in Methodism.

1952   Chicago: A. N. Marquis Company.

Who's Who in the Methodist Church.

1966   Nashville: Abingdon.

Wicker, Fenton, Jr., editor.

1954   "Student News." *Perkins School of Theology Journal* (Winter): 19–20.

Will, James E.

1982   "Ordination of Women." In *Women in New Worlds,* edited by Rosemary Skinner Keller, Louise L. Queen, and Hilah F. Thomas, 2:290–297. Nashville: Abingdon.

Williams, Cecil.

1980   *I'm Alive!: An Autobiography*. San Francisco: Harper & Row.

Wilson, Ann S.

1983   "A Portion of the History of Perkins School of Theology, SMU,
         with Particular Attention to 1945–1955: Years of Transition."
         M.L.A. thesis, Southern Methodist University.

Index

DATE DUE
